DAILY THOUGHTS ON HOLINESS

Compiled and Edited
by
Dr. Bruce Moyer

Pure Heart Publications

www.pureheartpublications.com

ISBN 978-0-9796756-1-4

Printed in the United States by Country Pines, Inc., Shoals, IN

INTRODUCTION

Daily Thoughts on Holiness began in the heart of Rev. David Weinert as a desire to provide his congregation with devotional materials that were truly consistent with the Biblical message of heart purity. Rev. Weinert published a quarterly booklet from 1987-1994, asking for friends in the Wesleyan-Holiness tradition to contribute their writings. That got me started writing devotionals, and I contributed several each year during that period.

Several years later, believing that much of the material would be appreciated by others, I asked for and received permission from Rev. Weinert for the publication rights to the devotionals, and since then I have tried to obtain permission from those whose contributions you find here.

Most of the contributors are not previously published. They are not "authors" in the professional sense of the word. Rather they are laypersons, missionaries, pastors, and church leaders who have a passion for the holiness message. Wanting their own style and "their heart" to come through, I have edited the contributions as little as possible. Some devotionals will be more pastoral, others like a story, and some like a short theology lesson – all reflecting their author. Some specific time references are changed, and longer devotionals are edited to fit on one page. In order to guard the integrity of each author's contribution, I have chosen to ignore some details of formatting.

The devotionals are ordered according to the main Scripture reading, except where a series appears, so the reader has something of a Genesis to Revelation devotional on holiness. There are a few that also appear out of sequence in order to place them near a special day (Christmas, New Year's, etc.)

I am deeply grateful for each one who has contributed to this work. Some of them are now with Jesus. I have known most of them personally. They were a blessing to me in past years, and I hope that now their writings will be a blessing to you, as they are to me. The final pages of this book contain a list of each, with an index to their contributions.

All of the writers are deeply committed to the Biblical truth that, subsequent to our conversion and entrance into the family of God, we must come to a place of full surrender in which God purifies our heart from the self-centeredness with which we're born, and fills us with the Holy Spirit.

It is entirely possible that a second volume will follow (*Daily thoughts on Victorious Christian Living*). After all, there were seven years in the original work. Those chosen for this volume are specifically related to the experience of heart cleansing. A second volume may include those that are focused more on the Christian life in general. Whether or not any individual contributor's work appears here is purely a matter of my choice, and not a reflection on their writing.

Pure Heart Publications is pleased to offer this compilation of devotionals to you with the hope that it will stir you to a deeper and fuller pursuit of God Himself.

Dr. Bruce Moyer

For The New Year
Jeremiah 6:16

There are a lot of things changing in this world around us. You and I can see it. Europe is coming together, Israel is seemingly going to make peace with its long time enemies. Truly old things are passing away. Cars, machines, and other things we hold dear are changing and in some cases becoming obsolete.

There are new "religions" coming out so often we can't keep up with them all. There are new thoughts and interpretations of Scripture we are to think on, thoughts that are pushing out the old truths that have been held as sacred and necessary to our spiritual lives.

And just to be honest with you, it all overwhelms me and scares me sometimes, because the thought comes to me, what am I going to do? The pressure to change my belief; the pressure to change for "fellowship sake;" the pressures of just serving God with compromise; and the list could go on.

But every year when I go through this thought process, my mind comes back, by the grace of God, to Jeremiah 6:16, "the old ways wherein is the good way, walk therein, and ye shall find rest for your souls."

Yes, it is another year. Yes, the pressures will come. Probably more and more people will be against us, but for the New Year we must determine to continue to preach, teach, promote, and live holiness "without which no man shall see the Lord."

Heaven and earth shall pass away, people will come and go, a few will find the way, but His word shall never pass away and praise God for the few!

Let us determine to magnify God and the Truth of holiness this year with all our hearts, with all our souls, with all our minds, and with all our strength, for Jesus' sake, for our sake and for the world's sake.

Rev. Rodger Moyer

What If?
2 Corinthians 1:8-11

A new year has begun. Millions of people take the new year as an occasion for renewed hope. They hope for better health, more wealth, peace and safety, success and stability. How will their hopes be realized? By the advances of medicine? By wiser investments in the stock market? By armies and governments? By education?

Paul's hope was for deliverance from a "deadly peril." It was a peril he faced because he preached Jesus Christ. How was he going to be delivered? By trusting in God and by his friends' prayers.

I know what I'm hoping for this new year. Success in holiness. Deliverance from giving up in the heat of the battle. Faith to keep going when not only does nothing good seem to be happening, but everything seems to be falling apart. It is then that I need to trust in God as never before. It is then that I need the prayers of my friends.

I have always known that trusting in God was the "secret victory." I have always known that "God answers prayer." But what if this year, more than any other year, I take seriously the help of my friends' prayers? Is it time to really draw close to each other and to ask for prayer help?

What are you hoping for this new year? How will it be met?

Rev. Ken Friesen

In Touch With Meaning
Genesis 3:1-8

"And they heard the sound of the Lord God walking in the garden in the cool of the day ..." Gen 3:8a.

This part of the verse has intrigued me for a long time, and more than that, it has had a kind of sad, haunting effect, in my heart, that here is something that man was made to have that put him in touch with meaning, but that now seems to elude him.

God used to converse with Adam and Eve, in the garden, "in the cool of the day" (lit. "the evening breeze"), and they felt the completeness of intimate, and intensely satisfying, fellowship.

Here lies exposed the reason for our being and the end of our longing. It speaks of something that was, and, instinctively, our hearts secretly long for it, as something that we are meant to have.

Here, in the quietness and stillness of a garden, God walked, talked, and had fellowship with man. There was no question but that man was inseparably linked to God and that anything apart from Him destroyed meaning. God's continued presence was essential to man's continued purpose.

We will not again, in this life, regain the Garden, but we can regain the God of the Garden, and, from the moment man fell, God pursued this end for him. God had designed man for intimate fellowship with Him and He made it possible that we might once again know that kind of fellowship, no matter our surroundings or circumstances.

But this comes only as we seek the holiness of the God who created us, rather than the happiness of the garden we try to create. Adam and Eve, as Lee Haines states, "By reaching for what they felt was a higher level of life ... lost the highest and plunged to the lowest." (*Wesleyan Commentary*) Ours is the privilege of reversing this, by the marvelous grace of God, and finding completeness of meaning again.

Dr. Hubert Harriman

7

You Will Be Like God
Genesis 3:4-7

When the serpent promised Eve that she would be like God if she ate the forbidden fruit, the implication was that God does not want us to be like Him. This flies in the face of God's revelation, however, for God <u>created</u> Adam and Eve in His likeness and image. This is what made man unique.

We get a hint as to <u>how</u> Eve wanted to be like God when we put together what the serpent told her ("knowing good and evil") and Eve's response ("the tree was desirable to make one wise"). Eve coveted after the knowledge and wisdom of God – and certainly the power that went along with it. The desire for self-sovereignty has been present ever since. There is no way, however, that we can get around the fact that we are creatures, not the Creator. Adam and Eve were less like God after eating the forbidden fruit than before. The craving for self-sovereignty made them less than they were – not more.

We cannot be God, but it is still God's intention that we be like Him. "Speak to all the congregation of the sons of Israel and say to them, 'You shall be holy, for I the LORD your God am holy.'" (Lev. 19:2, NASB) What a wonderful truth! God intends for us to be like Him – God intends for us to be holy! It is in holiness of heart and life that we once again bear the image of God.

The world is still running hard after knowledge, wisdom, and power in the quest for self-sovereignty, but God tells us that it is in holiness that we will be like Him. "O to be like Thee! O to be like Thee, Blessed Redeemer, pure as Thou art; Come in Thy sweetness, come in Thy fullness; Stamp Thine own image deep on my heart."

Rev. Glen Boring

Where Art Thou?
Genesis 3:7-10

Adam had sinned and God was searching him out. He had often heard God's voice before and he knew of no greater joy than the communion he had with Almighty God.

But now all had changed. Adam was no longer happy. He was no longer looking forward to communion with God. He was filled with fear and tried to hide himself from God.

The question of God to Adam, "where art thou?" was not a question of where Adam was physically. God knew exactly where Adam was hiding. The question was spiritual: "Where art thou Adam in relationship to me? Once you used to wait for me. Once you used to be excited about our communion. Once you loved me with all your heart. Why are you hiding?"

I think this is the history of every son of Adam since the awful day of sin. With sin in the heart, and sins in our lives, there is in every soul a tendency to hide from the all-seeing eye of God.

This is why some refuse to read their Bibles. Some will say it is because they have so much else to read, that it is not an interesting book, it is just a waste of time. But the real cause of man's neglect of God's Word is that the Bible brings us face to face with God, and the sinful heart hides from that.

This is why some don't like to get out to church. Some say their clothes are not good enough, they are too busy, they had a hard day, or the services are too dull and boring. But the real reason is the same, the songs, the prayers, the preaching all brings God near and makes men uncomfortable in their sin, so they hide from the presence of God.

Now this question comes to us, "Where art thou?" Are you reading your Bible and praying like you should, and are you attending all the services of your church, or are you hiding?

Rev. Rodger Moyer

It's Time To Dig A Well!
Genesis 21:22-34

Our society seems obsessed by the pursuit of many rights. The bottom line in each instance is: "I have the rights and I want someone to assure me that those rights will not be denied me."

This kind of determination is not consistent with Biblical models, the most familiar being our Lord's posture in the presence of His critics and His enemies. There is much to be said for the dynamic of silence in the face of challenge and criticism.

There is another approach that is equally dynamic and that is an act of meekness as taught in the scripture lesson for today.

In the disagreement that had arisen between Isaac and the herdsmen of Gerar there was no question but what Isaac's rights had been violated. For he was in the land under the shelter of a covenant that had been concluded between his father and Abimelech. Basically the agreement had two clauses: 1) No more treachery; the truth was to be told and 2) No more trickery; Abraham's wells were to be left untouched. And the agreement was to survive to following generations.

So when Isaac's wells were twice appropriated, what was his singular response in the face of such a flagrant violation of his rights? HE DUG ANOTHER WELL! (Genesis 26:32) And peace prevailed.

You can probably think of situations where you could have fostered peace within the family of God by simply digging another well – responding to tension or opposition by a generous act of submission and surrender.

There are probably some wells that need to be dug this very day – positive acts of surrender in your world that will foster peace and give integrity to our witness to heart holiness.

Dr. Merne Harris

Smelling Like A Priest
Exodus 30:22-38

In reading through the book of Exodus again, I have been struck with how much of the book is taken up with very detailed instructions concerning the tabernacle and its utensils, and the priest and his garments. In this particular passage, careful instruction is given regarding the composition and use of the anointing oil and incense. Both of them were to be used in the service of the tabernacle only, and both of them would have a fragrance that was unlike any other.

I enjoy the burning of leaves and other yard debris and come away from the fire with my clothes and even my hair permeated with the smell of the smoke. I come away from bowling permeated with the smell of cigarette smoke. It dawned on me that even a blind person could probably tell if he was in the presence of a priest. A priest would smell like a priest – there would be a particular fragrance to him because of the time that he spent before the Lord in the holy place. The fragrance of the holy anointing oil and the holy incense would cling to him.

The tabernacle is a thing of the past, but Peter tells us that we are "a chosen race, a royal priesthood, a holy nation, a people for God's own possession," that we may proclaim the excellencies of Him who has called us out of darkness into His marvelous light. (1 Peter 2:9, NASB) If we really are priests, we will "smell" like priests – the fragrance of holiness will permeate our lives. "But thanks be to God, who always leads us in His triumph in Christ, and manifests through us the sweet aroma of the knowledge of Him in every place. For we are a fragrance of Christ to God among those who are being saved and among those who are perishing; to the one an aroma from death to death, to the other an aroma from life to life. And who is adequate for these things?" (2 Corinthians 2:14-16, NASB)

Rev. Glen Boring

His Work – His Way
Exodus 31:1-11

I am interested in the fact that when Scripture first mentions someone being filled with the Spirit of God, it is not in reference to a priest, a prophet, a judge, or a king. The first one mentioned to be filled with the Spirit of God is Bezalel – an artist and craftsman. It is clear that God was the source of his artistic ability and craftsmanship and that this skill was to be used for God's purposes. The implication is that to do God's work in God's way, we must be filled with the Spirit of God.

Even though Bezalel was not a prophet or a priest, he was doing "religious work" in that he was making the things that would be used in the worship of God. It is all too easy for us to compartmentalize life into sacred and secular categories and to acknowledge that while being filled with the Spirit may be necessary for those engaged in sacred pursuits, I don't need to be filled with the Spirit to do my work my way, or to spend my money on what I want, or to use my time the way I please.

The prophet Zechariah looked forward to a day when there would no longer be the distinction between the sacred and the secular: "In that day there will be *inscribed* on the bells of the horses, 'HOLY TO THE LORD.' And the cooking pots in the LORD's house will be like the bowls before the altar. And every cooking pot in Jerusalem and in Judah will be holy to the LORD of hosts; and all who sacrifice will come and take of them and boil in them … ." (Zech. 14:20-21, NASB)

I need to realize that all of my work (not just "religious work") is to be His work, therefore I must be filled with His Spirit that I may do it His way and for His glory.

Rev. Glen Boring

Been Hitting Any Rocks Lately?
Exodus 33:11; Numbers 20:7-13

It is a sobering thought indeed to realize that a man with whom God was accustomed to speaking "as a man speaks to his friend" would one day speak to him hard words of rejection: "Because you did not believe me ... you shall not bring this assembly into the land which I have given them."

We are reading here of a spiritual giant – a man of obedience, courage, faithfulness and perseverance. But we are also reading of a man who, in an understandable moment of frustration ("Hear now, you rebels!") confused his associates, troubled his own spirit and displeased his God.

That says something important to those who customarily treat lightly manifestations which we label evidence of our "human nature." We need, I think, to be troubled about a testimony, which says, in effect, "I am saved and sanctified and any troubling behavior you may see in my life is simply my human nature coming through."

Let us be candid: Any conduct which baffles those who are watching our lives, brings a spirit of heaviness to our soul, and casts upon us the sense of God's disapproval is more than human nature – it is carnality and should be dealt with accordingly.

Further candor will also compel us to recognize that we have this treasure in a very earthen vessel which means there will be _inadvertent_ failures – these are not to be dumped into a convenient catch-all which we call our human nature but will be confronted responsibly through the powerful presence of the Holy Spirit who not only cleanses but also teaches and refines.

So, for whatever reason, we need no longer spend our energy kicking rocks. The abiding presence of the Holy Spirit is a better response to the rocks that confront us.

Dr. Merne Harris

The Indispensable One
Exodus 33:14-15

People are not indispensable. People come and go but God's work goes on. However in any genuine work of God, His Presence is indispensable.

More than anything else Moses wanted God's Presence. He would settle for nothing less. He had the pattern shown on the mount, that is the law and the design of the tabernacle. He had God's permission to go on. God had said, "Now go, lead the people to the place I spoke of and my angel will go before you." (Ex. 32:34) He had God's promise of victory over their enemies. (Ex. 33:2) But he had not the Presence, and therefore Moses refused to move unless God's Presence went with them. He said, "If Your Presence does not go with us, do not send us up from here." (Ex. 33:15)

Moses knew God's Presence to be a Delivering Presence. He had brought them out of Egyptian bondage. (Deut. 4:37-38) It was a Demanding Presence. God demanded that they acknowledge His Lordship and obey His leadership. (Ex. 20:3-4) It was also a Directing Presence (see Ex. 13:21-22). The Lord ordered their stops and starts. But above all it was a Distinguishing Presence. Moses said, "What else will distinguish me and your people from all the other people on the face of the earth?" (Ex. 33:16)

How true this is. It is not doctrine, not organization that separates and distinguishes God's people from others; it is His Presence. This is the mark, the seal, the stamp of authenticity – God's Presence and blessing among us.

Let us ask for it – claim it – and settle for nothing less.

Dr. Hollis Abbott

The Angry Mob
Numbers 13:30-33; 14:6-10; John 18: 39-40

We see in these scriptures the pictures of two angry mobs. The Old Testament mob is agreeing that Canaan is a great place and has many advantages but they refuse to go in because of the price to be paid. The New Testament mob is asking that Pilot release unto them Barabbas, a robber and insurrectionist, and to crucify Jesus, the Son of God. They chose sin and carnality rather than the Son of God and holiness. The Israelites chose the wilderness and went back to Egypt in their hearts, rather than forward to the Canaan Land experience flowing with milk and honey and God's blessing. That carnal spirit of mob rule still reigns in the hearts of the unsaved today.

A couple of years ago my wife and I had to change planes in St. Louis. After boarding for our flight to Portland and waiting on board for a couple of hours, the flight attendant announced that the flight had been cancelled and the airline would make other arrangements for us. Up to that time there had been much murmuring and complaining; but that was nothing compared to what was to follow. People that seemed to be kind, gracious, and well mannered, turned into crowd inciters and mob leaders. As the airline personnel were arranging accommodations and other flights they became the target for abusive language and personal insults. One individual even suggested hijacking an airplane to get to Portland. What a joy it was when my turn came at the ticket window to compliment the attendants for the fine work and controlled patience they were exhibiting under trying circumstances. The smile I received and the courtesy extended were reward enough.

Old or New Testament, or today; the need of man is the same. How sad that people still choose the wilderness of carnal desire over the joy and blessing of Canaan land experience.

Rev. David.Weinert

The Cost Of Kadesh Barnea
Numbers 14:20-45

The cost of the failure at Kadesh Barnea can only be measured at the Judgment bar of God. How many souls were finally lost, how much added suffering was endured, how much injury to faith to those who were weak, cannot be estimated accurately, but we can see that the cost was great.

There was an unnecessary delay of forty long years of wandering in that great and terrible wilderness, when all the time could have been spent in the luxurious surroundings of Canaan.

The rebellion of Korah would have been avoided which cost over 14,950 souls – to say nothing of the loss of all those 20 years and upward at the time of the turning back, who died in the wilderness during the 40 year period. Add to this the suffering of the innocent less than 20 years of age who were hindered from going into Canaan by the sins of their parents.

This is all carried out today in the life of anyone who refuses to enter into Canaan. They suffer – the children suffer – the friends suffer – the church suffers because the blessing of God in sanctifying power is withheld.

The church in the Book of Acts was a blessing to the world, and three thousand souls were added to the Lord on that first great Pentecostal outpouring of the Holy Spirit. It was the blessing of the sanctifying presence upon the leaders of the Methodist revival that made it such a blessing to the world.

It is the duty of each one of us to be filled with the Holy Spirit, to be a channel that is wide open so that the love of God can flow to the parched and thirsty land.

The greatest cost of all was the external loss of every soul who refused to go on to Canaan. God's Word is clear on this: "Follow peace with all men, and holiness, without which no man shall see the Lord."

Rev. M. Max Morgan

Dumber Than A Donkey
Numbers 22:31-35

Would it be safe to say that a prophet, Balaam, was dumber than a donkey? In this case, it might be said that fools rush in where donkeys fear to tread. Balaam's donkey knew better than to go forward in opposition to God, but Balaam was oblivious to the danger. Balaam, like so many others, chose to lash out at the very one that was there for his own well being.

To me, the awesome thing in this passage is the statement of the angel of the LORD to Balaam in vs. 32: "Behold, I have come out as an adversary, because your way was contrary to me." (NASB) What a terrible thing – to have God as an adversary! Balaam was a prophet, but because his way was contrary to God, God was his adversary. Jesus even looked at Peter and said, "Get behind Me, Satan; for you are not setting your mind on God's interests, but man's." (Mark 8:33, NASB)

It is all too easy for professing Christians (even clergy) to attribute every hindrance of their goals to the work of negative people or the devil – much as Balaam lashed out at his donkey. If a decisive blow has not been dealt carnality, however, the hindrances to our way could be life-saving. "For the mind set on the flesh is hostile toward God; but the mind set on the Spirit is life and peace, because the mind set on the flesh is hostile toward God; for it does not subject itself to the law of God, for it is not even able to do so; and those who are in the flesh cannot please God." (Romans 8:6-8)

I am dumber than a donkey if I persist in attempting to go forward if there is anything in my heart or life that is hostile toward God. It is foolish and deadly to have God for an adversary.

Rev. Glen Boring

Of Sores And Sin
Numbers 32:23b

Once, while cutting some lumber on a table saw, I failed to concentrate just for a moment and nearly lost my left thumb. After several stitches and weeks of healing, the scar remains but the thumb is fine. Not only did that experience teach me a new respect for saws, but I've noted some important comparisons with sin.

First, it all happened so quickly. Just one split second of not "keeping watch" was all it took. Scripture warns us often to "stay alert," "be on guard," "be diligent," for a very good reason.

As soon as I looked at my thumb I knew it needed immediate attention. I sure didn't look for a book on "the ABC's of thumb repair" or wait for a seminar to come along on table saw use and what to do if you maim yourself. I quickly drove to the emergency room and got immediate attention. When the Holy Spirit reveals disobedience in our lives – let's take care of it quickly. Waiting only compounds the problem.

I also knew I needed expert attention. I wasn't about to attend to it myself, and I certainly wasn't going to let one of the guys in the shop sew my thumb back together! I needed an expert in the field. How many times have we struggled with sin because we're trying to take care of it ourselves? God, and God alone, can deal with sin. There's nothing to do but go to Him and repent of it.

I went back to the shop with new alertness and a spirit of determination that I would never stick my thumb in that blade again. When we've succumbed to the lure of sin and then found grace and forgiveness, we need to keep in mind that there are some things we can't do, if we're going to continue to live in victory.

The wound has healed. Though I was miserable for a time (just try tying your shoes or a neck tie without using your left thumb!), there was healing. There is a complete remedy for sin too! There may be some remaining scars (as there are on my thumb) but we are enabled by God's grace to go on in victory.

Dr. Bruce Moyer

The Peril Of Kadesh Barnea
Deuteronomy 1

The children of Israel were poised on the southern border of the Promised Land, awaiting the report of the twelve spies, which presumably would show them the way to enter the land. Ten of the returning spies brought an evil report instigating an unbelieving refusal by the people to enter the land. The Lord's response was to sentence them to 40 years of wandering in the wilderness until all the rebels died.

The land of Canaan is an illustration of the life of heart holiness. The entering by faith illustrates the crisis work of entire sanctification, and the refusal to enter with the ensuing tragedy is a sobering warning to believers not to turn back as Israel did.

This warning to believers against turning back from the second work of grace is driven home by the name given to the place where Israel was encamped when they refused to enter the land. The name "Kadesh Barnea" is significant. "Kadesh" = to be clean, holy, consecrate; "Bar" = field or place; "nea" = to waver, stagger, wander, be a fugitive (*Strong's Concordance*). Kadesh Barnea was the place where Israel wavered at consecration, staggered at being clean, became a fugitive from holiness. The end of that wavering was death.

If we are not sanctified we face the peril of our own Kadesh Barnea, and many will waver. Saul staggered at the whole will of God concerning the Amalekites. The rich, young ruler backed up over money. Demas became a fugitive from God because he loved this present world. Peter wavered to save his own skin.

Usually we have one prominent place where the peril of Kadesh Barnea is most real. It may be money, reputation, lofty ambitions, self-will, unbelief, or any other issue. Regardless of the specific issue, Kadesh Barnea must be avoided at any cost lest we die in the wilderness. Rather, let us press on into the land and possess our inheritance by faith.

Rev. Dan Morgan

God At The Center
Deuteronomy 6:4-19

At one time people believed the earth was the center of the universe. It seemed that the sun and other heavenly bodies revolved around the earth.

Now we know differently. Beyond any question, the sun is the center of our galaxy and the earth revolves around it and spins on its own axis every 24 hours. This means order in the day-by-day sequence and in the seasons of the year. What a blessing!

Shift now into the spiritual realm. Instead of man being the center of his universe with everything revolving around him, we know that God is at the center. Not only are we to believe in Him, we are to love Him supremely and obey Him fully. The big "I" must learn that it is not the center. God moves into the center. As we revolve around Him and make every move out of reference to His will it will "go well with you."

Let's imagine for a moment that God gave "freewill" to the earth, just as He did to you and me. Suppose the earth decided "I am tired of obeying this law of God, with the sun always in the center. I will be at the center; I refuse to orbit any longer around the sun." Absolute chaos and destruction would follow.

Let us learn a lesson from the sun and earth. Since God has given us freedom of choice, let us say with all our hearts, "God will be at the center of my life – in everything." And not just from a sense of duty or fear, but out of love His laws will be my style – for God is at the center of my affections.

"Is there a thing beneath the sun that strives with thee
my heart to share? Ah, tear it thence and reign alone,
The Lord of every motion there: Then shall my heart from
earth be free; Then it hath found repose in Thee.

-- Charles Wesley

Dr. Gerald Dillon

God's Holy Plan For Bringing Up Our Children
Deuteronomy 6:5-9

We are probably most familiar with this passage as an instruction of our responsibilities to teach God's law to our children. That's true, but first we are commanded to "love the Lord with all our heart, and with all our soul and with all our might." God knows we cannot, and will not, instruct our children about something of which we know little or nothing. God's plan is to establish families, blessed with children instructed in the way of the Lord, by parents who first know Him and love Him perfectly.

Many parents today find themselves frustrated, fatigued, and failing with their children who manifest no interest in God, who are flirting with sin, and are soon caught up in a life of sin. As concerned parents they so want their children to love and serve God. Sadly, a closer examination often reveals parents whose first love was not God, and whose primary goal was not to live before their children a true example of holiness.

Are you living a life of holiness before your children, by having a daily family worship time . . . having your own personal devotions . . . being faithful at church . . . manifesting a selfless love to your partner . . . using opportunities to instruct your children in the right way to live, and doing it until it gets through? The father of John and Charles Wesley, asked his wife one time, "Why do you tell Charles a thing twenty times over?" "Because nineteen times won't do," replied the patient mother.

We can't hope for our children to live on a higher spiritual plane than they have seen us live. Before we run out of time, parents, pray with the psalmist, "Search me, O God, and know my heart. Try me, and know my thoughts: and see if there be any wicked way in me, and lead me in the way everlasting." We dare not allow anything to keep us from loving God perfectly, which is the only means by which we can teach our children truth.

Mrs. Sarah Harriman

Boundary Stones
Deuteronomy 19:14; Proverbs 22:28; 1 Timothy 4:16

A friend told me that a neighbor of his had brought a surveyor onto this friend's land without permission. The new survey stakes ended up cutting off a dozen feet of my friend's property. This caused problems, especially since fences which have been on property for fifty or more years, in some states, have precedence in boundary disputes.

Why would someone want to change boundary markers? A farmer might do it while plowing in order to increase his land. In my Uncle Wally's case, a neighbor's survey gave him the right to my uncle's well. Regardless of the reason, the result is gain for one, but loss to another.

As Christians, in our efforts to "reach our generation," or be "relevant for a new day," we can remove spiritual boundary markers that will bring not merely temporal, but eternal loss.

The Bible marks out the way to heaven, as well as the success on earth, with many boundary stones. As holiness people, zealous as anyone for the success of the gospel, we will be tempted to move the stones "only slightly" in order to "gain ground" with people. We do so at our peril and theirs.

What are some of these stones which should not be moved: repentance as a condition of salvation, instantaneous entire sanctification, the difference between temptation and sin, the difference between sin and humanity, the witness of the Spirit, growth in grace, and eternal punishment. There are more. Make your list. Check your preaching and teaching to see whether or not they are still in place where God put them.

Rev. Ken Friesen

Holiness – All Out Loyalty To God (1)
Deuteronomy 30:1-20

Deuteronomy 30 may have been Moses' last sermon to the people of Israel before they crossed over into Canaan. It is a clear call to holy living. He describes the life of holiness here in three ways which are set apart by the phrase, "with all your heart and with all your soul" (vs. 2, 6, 10). Today and the next two days we will meditate on and examine our lives in the light of this very practical definition of holy living.

In verse 2 holy living is seen to demand our total obedience to God. This demand is repeated in verse 16 ("keep His commands…") and in verse 20 ("listen to His voice"). In other words, we could say that holy living is characterized by our making God the focal point of our loyalty. It is interesting that in Psalm 78, where the carnal heart is illustrated by Israel's rebellion against God, disloyalty is listed as one of their main characteristics (vs. 8, 37, 57). Carnality is also described in Hosea 5:4 as "a spirit of prostitution" (that is, a spirit of unfaithfulness and disloyalty).

In entire sanctification God cleanses from our heart that spirit of disloyalty and replaces it with an intense desire and commitment to obey Him in all things. That means that not only do we obey in action, but that there is in the heart an attitude of "I want to obey God." The life of holiness is God reigning alone – God reigning supreme.

Holiness is all out loyalty to God! What "limits" have I placed on my obedience? On my loyalty? What things, or people, or activities share that loyalty that belongs only to Him?

Dr. Bruce Moyer

Holiness – All Out Love For God (2)
Deuteronomy 30:1-20

Yesterday we saw in verse 2 that holy living is characterized by obeying God "with all of our heart and with all of our soul." In verse 6 the description of holy living is further enhanced by the clear call to "<u>love</u> God with all our heart and soul" Just as God becomes the focal point of our obedience, He must become the focal point of our love.

This idea of all out love for God runs through all the Scriptures. It was the greatest command for ancient Israel (Deut. 6:5) and Jesus uses it (Matthew 22:37) to describe the greatest responsibility of the Christian church today. Holiness is, in practical terms, loving God above everything else. Life's most intimate relationships must take second place to our love for Him (Matthew 10:37). When we love Him like that, we begin to love all that pleases Him. Maturing Christians will quit asking about the rules (the "do's" and "don'ts") because they're caught up in enjoying the positive benefits of loving God "with all of their heart and all of their soul."

In verse 17 of our text, Moses explains in opposite terms the three main points of his sermon. The opposite of all out love for God id to be "drawn away to bow down to other gods and worship them." In other words, holy living (all out love for God) is characterized by a life without idols. An idol, according to one good definition, is "any substitution of the unreal for the real."

In entire sanctification God cleanses from the heart all the "substitutes" that we have enthroned and loved above him. Today, what is the supreme love of my life?

Dr. Bruce Moyer

Holiness – All Out Living For God (3)
Deuteronomy 30:1-20

In verse 10 we find the third part of this clear description of holy living, "Turn to the Lord your God with all your heart and with all your soul." This idea is repeated again in verse 16 ("to walk in His ways") and verse 20 ("hold fast to Him"). "Turning to God," conveys the idea of following after, cleaving to, or attaching oneself to something (or someone). Holy living can then be described as making Christ the focal point of all my living. It is seeking first (not second or third) the kingdom of God (Matthew 6:33).

In entire sanctification God frees us from attachment to this world and He alone becomes the center of our goals, ambitions, desires, plans, wants, and activities. He is the center of life itself! Holy living is being able to truthfully sing, "He is my everything, He is my all!"

At one time or another, most of us have learned by experience that we can't keep God at the center of our life, if we won't keep him at the center of every day. Holy living is a commitment to allowing God to be the focus of my living every day, now and forever. And, if I begin to sense a lack of desire for spiritual things, slow spiritual growth, and an attachment to other things in my life – it is time to stop and ask, "What am I living for?" "Who is at the center of my life?" "What drives me, controls me, governs me?" As long as I am holding to anything besides Jesus as the center of my life, I am not walking in holiness.

Dr. Bruce Moyer

The Challenge Is Ours
Joshua 1:1-9

"Every place that the sole of your foot shall tread upon, that I have given unto you…"

The original promise concerning this land is found in the words that God said to Abraham, "unto thy seed will I give this land." Now that "seed" stood within its borders ready to conquer Canaan. It was theirs for the taking. God could have cursed the inhabitants with disease, struck them dead, but He didn't choose to do it that way. He chose rather that His people be working, daring, trusting, and obedient people. They were not to hire help, but they themselves were to fight their own battles and win their own victories.

Many church people would be mighty men if they could hire someone else to do their duties and fulfill their responsibilities (the pastor for instance). Many would be glad to make great sacrifices if they could evade the way of the cross. The sad fact is, many do live this way. Too many church people are men and women of small vision, small interests, and small challenges. They say the same faithless prayers, they sit listlessly in their pew, follow the same old routines, and are never disturbed by their unproductive lives. They never invite a neighbor to church, never try any new areas of service, and never deal with anyone about their soul and they never see victory! How about you?

God brought Israel to the land and set it before them and challenged them to go in and possess it. God is challenging us! God has promised "the land" to His people, let's start conquering it, let us dare to go out in the name of God and win souls for Jesus' sake. Indeed the challenge is ours!

Rev. Rodger Moyer

Marks Of The Sanctified
Joshua 5:1-2, 8-15

Entire sanctification is designed to change us. There are some specific and identifiable evidences of that change. The primary characteristic of these marks of the sanctified is newness. We notice some new and clear differences about the Israelites immediately following the crossing of the Jordan, which is a wonderful type of the experience of entire sanctification.

First, there was a new authority about them. God was among them and His anointing was upon them and the people of the land couldn't stand before them. When we are "endued with power from on high," the result is a new authority about us. This authority is "new" in that it is in contrast with the instability, inconsistency and ineffectiveness that so often characterize the "double minded man."

With this new authority our preaching and witnessing are pungent. Our praying is fervent and effectual. Our walk is victorious though it is upstream against the strong current of a wicked age.

This is the kind of Christian God calls us to be and the world desperately needs to see. It is the kind Jesus prayed for, died for, and rose to make possible.

Rev. Dan Morgan

A Lesson From The Lawn
Joshua 14:6-15

This past summer I found myself so busy at one point that a number of little things that needed doing had been left undone. One of these things was mowing the lawn. Every time I walked up our sidewalk I would say to myself, "Boy, I've got to mow this lawn!" It finally reached the stage that it just had to be done. When I finally tackled this undesirable task, I decided that, since I was rushed, a "quickie mow" would do the job. That is, I walked as fast as I could, I skipped the hillsides, I left a patch (not seen from the street) in the backyard, and I certainly didn't trim with the weed whacker. At best it was a half-hearted effort. To passers-by, it looked mowed, but a closer inspection would reveal the truth.

That evening, as I pondered the activities of the day, I wondered how many Christians are living for God in the same way I mowed the lawn that day – half-hearted. To others who look on, everything appears to be all right, but upon Divine inspection the truth is revealed – some areas have not been fully yielded to God.

In today's Scripture reading we saw that is was said (vs. 8, 9, 14) of Caleb, "he followed the Lord wholeheartedly." (cf. Num. 14:24) Can that be said of me today? Or am I serving the Lord more like King Amaziah who "did what was right in the eyes of the Lord, but not wholeheartedly?" (2 Chron. 25:2) That kind of half-hearted commitment finally caught up with Amaziah and, in the end, it is said of him, he "turned away from following the Lord." (2 Chron. 25:27) That is always the result of half-hearted loyalty to God. Nothing less than absolute surrender and obedience will do.

So I find myself having learned a spiritual lesson from mowing the lawn. I wonder what great lessons are in store for me as I shovel snow this winter!

Dr. Bruce Moyer

God Looks On The Heart
Joshua 22:9-12; 15-34

In today's Scripture lesson, the two and one-half tribes whose territory lay on the East side of Jordan were released to go home after helping their brothers obtain their territory. As they neared the Jordan to cross over to their homes they began to look down the road to a time when they might be considered as outsiders to the Israelites. So they decided to build a big altar to remind them and their brothers of their unity as a nation. It was not an altar on which to burn offerings but an altar as a memorial. However, their building of this altar had a suspicious appearance to the other tribes and, therefore, appeared to be a wicked violation of the law. (Lev. 17:8,9; Deut. 12)

Phinehas, the high priest and the ten princes of the nine and one-half tribes jumped to a wrong conclusion and prepared to war against them before hearing the facts.

This seems to be a strong tendency of the carnal heart. According to 1 Cor. 13, perfect love keeps no record of wrongs, does not delight in evil but rejoices in the truth. It does NOT immediately suspect the motives of others – especially our brothers in the Lord. Rather than being ready to believe the worst of another, we ought to put the best light on it. Man judges on the outward appearance but God ALONE knows the heart. What appears to be wrong to us, may, in the heart of the other person, be an act of devotion – as in the case of the two and one-half tribes.

Jesus' words in Matt. 18:15 that tell us, "if our brother wrongs us, go and tell him his fault between you and him alone," are still the best advice. Rather than suspect someone's motives, let us clear the air for continued Christian fellowship.

Mrs. Clarice Moyer

Words From the Carnal Heart
Joshua 24:14-24

The way carnality is most often expressed is through its emphasis on the importance of self. You've probably noticed that the word sin has "I" in the middle of it.

In the days before Israel had a human king, "everyone did as he saw fit." (Judges 17:6) That was a clear violation of God's Word in Deut. 12:8. The spirit of the nation was – "I will do what I want. I will run my own life!" The carnal person is like that. He is characterized by an attitude of self-governing.

In Deut. 29:19 there is another phrase that is often expressed by the carnal person: "I will be safe, even though I persist in going my own way." The carnal person almost always believes that his way is the best and this is self-guidance.

The mighty Samson provides a third example for us in the demand he placed upon his parents: "Get her for me as my wife." (Judges 14:2-3) Samson's words represent the self-glorifying and self-seeking ways of the carnal mind. He failed to realize that marriage is for the purpose of giving one's self away.

Still another word that often flows from the carnal heart is illustrated in the life of the prodigal son and the insistent demand of his father, "Give me...." (Luke 15:12) This is the tragic nature of the carnal person – it is self-gratifying.

All of these attitudes are contrary to the nature of the sanctified Christian – which is self-giving and results in a life that is God-governed, God-guided, God-glorifying and God-gratifying!

Lord, is my life focused on self – or you?

Dr. Bruce Moyer

God's Garments
Judges 6:34; 1 Chronicles 12:18; 2 Chronicles 24:20

These passages introduce us to three men, Gideon, Amasai, and Zechariah of whom it is said, "the Spirit of the Lord came upon" them. This is said of many, many others in the Bible but there is something special about these three. Only in these three instances in all the Old Testament can the Hebrew be literally translated, "the Spirit of the Lord clothed Himself with" Gideon or Amasai or Zechariah. What blessed revelation of the relationship God wants to have with us, His servants.

God wills to clothe Himself with each of us. He is not too concerned with our social station or physical, intellectual or financial endowments. Gideon was a fearful farmer turned into a great deliverer. Amasai was a soldier with a message of encouragement to David. Zechariah was a priest who fearlessly pronounced God's judgment on Israel and was stoned for it. Yet they all had one thing in common and this is what God wants in us. They had the disposition of a garment. A garment:
-   conforms to the form of the wearer, undergoing whatever alterations are required.
-   goes where the wearer goes, bends and stretches according to the wishes of the wearer.
-   cannot stand on its own.
-   only fulfills its intended purpose when filled by its owner.

Regardless of our station or circumstances or abilities, may God help us to have the disposition of a garment, that the Spirit of the Lord can clothe Himself with each of us.

Rev. Dan Morgan

Second Thoughts
Ruth 1:1-19

The emotion of the moment had passed, and now the taxing journey to Bethlehem was before her. Ample time for Ruth to ask herself: "Did I do the right thing?" And that question would give rise to others: Will Naomi abandon me when we get to Bethlehem? Will I like it there? Can I really fit in as an outsider? Will I really be satisfied in my newly declared faith in God? Will I miss so very much my family and my country?

However hard the questions might press, there was one advantage Ruth had: she had made a rational choice based upon values that were important to her. And so we read, "she went until she came to Bethlehem." In the parlance of another day we would say, "Ruth had determined to go through."

In this day when we face so many challenges to commitment to full salvation, it is important that we do remember the past – that day when we made a volitional choice to go through with God because the Holy Spirit had put before us values meriting that choice. The prospect of a clean heart, the pleasure of daily victory, the promise of effective service – those values were appealing then and must remain so if we would persevere in our goal to live holy lives. It is when we begin to question the possibility or diminish the appeal of purity, victory and power that we falter in the journey.

In prospect Ruth probably found the road ahead daunting; in retrospect she must have thanked God again and again that she had persevered. And so do we, every day we live in the radiant reality of a holy life.

And by the way, whatever became of that other lady who did not pursue her first intention?

Dr. Merne Harris

The Steadfast Mind
Ruth 1:14-18

It has always blessed my heart in the way the Lord took time to include the story of Ruth in Scripture. Amidst all the stories of battles and kings, we have a story of love. We have an illustration of the love God desires from us (" Ruth clave" KJV).

And don't you just like the word "clave?" To say she held onto, or grabbed a hold of -- those phrases just don't say the same thing. "Ruth clave," and was steadfastly minded to go with God and His people. David put it this way, "Oh God my Heart is fixed!"

What is the testimony sinners need more than any other testimony on earth? To see Christians who are really Christians. People whose minds are steadfast, made-up, decided once-for-all to go with God no matter what, and who are not ashamed of truth and speak and live it freely.

There is too much religion today that is wishy-washy, neutral, insufficient, and indistinguishable from the world -- "Christians" whose thoughts and ways are more like the general population than like Christ.

We must be like Ruth who clave, who set her face steadfastly to go with God and His people, who would not turn aside, who would not go back, who would not even look back, but would glorify God in all she did.

The only way is through sanctifying grace when all reservations, all unhallowed regions of my heart and all sin is purged, and then filled with an all-out love, loyalty and faith in God.

Rev. Rodger Moyer

33

Empty Boxes
1 Samuel 4

Israel had gone out to fight against the Philistines, but had been badly defeated. The elders suggested, "Let us bring the ark of the Lord's covenant from Shiloh, so that it may go with us and save us from the hand of our enemies." The ark was brought from Shiloh. The men of Israel marched out to battle and again the enemy overwhelmed them and the ark was captured.

What happened? An examination of the story indicates that the confidence of Israel was in the ark of God, not in the God of the ark. They said concerning the ark, "That it may come among us, and save us." But when the pressure was on, the ark proved to be an empty box; God was not there. They had the symbol of the Presence, but not the Presence Himself. And in the hour of need the mere symbol was helpless to defend them.

In chapter 7 Samuel called the people to return to the Lord and to "serve Him only, and He will deliver you out of the hand of the Philistines." They obeyed and God gave them the victory.

Our "experience," if we trust in it, can become an empty box. Some have declared that if people would seek and find "this experience," meaning the experience of entire sanctification, it will keep them from backsliding. But it won't. No experience can keep us; it is the Giver of the experience who keeps us. An experience, which is not kept fresh through the constant indwelling of the Holy Spirit, is an empty box. It will let us down in the crisis hour. Our theology can become an empty box. It may be a beautifully developed structure, logically correct and Scripturally valid, yet, unless animated by the life of God, it will be cold, dry and lifeless.

Our talents may be excellent, our organization faultlessly developed, our plans well laid out but, apart from the presence and blessing of God, these are all empty boxes. More than anything else we need the presence and power of the Living God at work in us. Let us trust Him, for it is He who will give us the victory.

Dr. Hollis Abbott

Who Will Be King?
1 Samuel 8:1-9, 19-22

As a boy I enjoyed playing "King of the mountain." What constituted a "mountain" didn't matter much. It could be a mountain of dirt, hay bales, or an old stump. What mattered most was maintaining your position as "king." Or, if you were a challenger, knocking the "king" off the "mountain" and securing it as your own. For many people life has become their "mountain" and they want to control who will reign there.

In Samuel's day people rejected God as their king. They wanted to be like the other nations around them. In other words, they wanted a different king. What an awful trade! They rejected an all-powerful, all-wise, infinite King for a finite, usually unwise, powerless king who would tax and abuse them.

At the time of Jesus' birth the people rejected God as king because He didn't fulfill their expectations. John states, "He came to that which was His own, but His own did not receive Him." (John 1:11) In other words, they wanted a certain kind of king. They wanted a king who would deliver them from the Romans and the other trials of life. No babe in a manger fit that description.

Then came the crucifixion. Once again God was rejected as king because He had shown them their sin. In a nutshell, the people wanted no king. They wanted to rule themselves. They wanted a deliverer, but not a ruler.

Things haven't changed much, have they? People are still rejecting God's kingship (sovereignty) in their lives for the same reasons – they want a different king, or a certain kind of king, or no king at all. They foolishly trade Divine Kingship for some false, temporary sovereignty that never fulfills. According to God's Word, Jesus is King of kings and Lord of lords. Someday all will bow at His feet and recognize His sovereignty – either willingly or unwillingly. Which way will it be for you? Who is king of your "mountain" today?

Dr. Bruce Moyer

What Are You Seeing?
1 Samuel 16:7

Recently I attended a camp meeting, and at the close of the message when the altar call was given, young people filled the altar from end to end. Like others, I was glad for every move toward the Lord, but I couldn't help but wonder if we were really seeing what we seemed to be seeing.

The messenger of the hour had talked a great deal about commitment. Almost nothing had been said about having a clean heart and receiving the presence and power of the Holy Spirit. I couldn't help but think of what those youth were going to face as they returned to their homes and friends.

Peter made a very real and definite commitment: "Lord, even though I must die with you, I'll not deny you." The rest of the disciples said the same thing. But in a matter of a few hours, Peter had denied the Lord three times and the rest had left Him. The devil doesn't mind if we make that kind of commitment.

But there is another kind of commitment. Paul, writing to Timothy, says that he is "persuaded that He is able to keep that which I have COMMITTED unto Him against that day." (2 Tim. 1:12) Our Spanish Bible uses the word "deposito" (deposit). Paul didn't make a promise; he made a deposit of his all with God and took his hands off, leaving the Holy Spirit to take complete control. If we only make a promise kind of commitment, we are likely to end up with the problem pictured in Rom. 7:14-24 and Gal. 5:17. The flesh and the Spirit are contrary, the one to the other, so that ye "CANNOT DO" the things that ye would.

If you want real victory, first make a complete consecration, deposit your all, your possessions, your time, talents, desires, ambitions, all that you have and are with God. Then ask Him to send the Holy Spirit to cleanse your heart and fill you with His presence and power. "Faithful is He that calleth you, who also will do it."

Rev. Marshal Cavit

Carnality Revealed
1 Samuel 17:1-10

Life was a constant battle for Israel. The Philistines pestered them all through Saul's and David's reigns. The difference was that David did something about it.

Goliath gives us a picture of the carnal mind that is at enmity with God and is not subject to the law of God, neither can it be (Romans 8:7). Goliath's name comes from the root meaning exile or stranger. Isn't that true of the sinful nature? It is an intruder. It is something that has invaded our hearts as a stranger. It is an exile that has been accepted into our territory.

But this giant rebel must be conquered because he defies the God we love. Sin is a stranger to the soul and God wants to conquer it.

Like Goliath, carnality will intimidate. It looks like an unconquerable foe. And when allowed to intimidate and control, it causes God's people to be powerless.

It never ceases to amaze me to see carnality reveal itself in children. These little three-foot pip-squeaks have Goliath in their hearts that will tell a six-foot tall parent a defiant "NO" when asked to do something.

What will God's people do with Goliath, that stranger within? Will we allow him to continue to intimidate and defy, or will we believe God to give us victory?

Rev. John Moyer

Death To Amalek
1 Samuel 31:1-5; 2 Samuel 1:1-10

In the scripture for today we notice right away that there are conflicting accounts of the death of Saul. One account tells us that Saul took a sword and fell on it. The other tells us that an Amalekite stood over him and killed him at his request. Which one is the true account of what happened?

Commentators are in agreement that the Amalekite wanting to find favor with David, fabricated the story. He probably found Saul dead on the battlefield, took his crown and bracelet and brought them to David with his story of how he was asked by Saul himself to stand over him and kill him.

Whichever account is correct is probably not of vital importance to our salvation. What is of importance is that the Amalekite should have never have been there. In 1 Samuel 15:3 Saul was given the instructions to "attack Amalek, and utterly destroy all that they have, and do not spare them. But kill both man and woman, infant and nursing child, ox and sheep, camel and donkey." If Saul had fulfilled these instructions from God there should not have been an Amalekite present to try to take credit for his death.

We have also received instructions from God. 2 Corinthians 7:1 tells us that we are to "cleanse ourselves from all filthiness of the flesh and spirit ..." All outward sin, filthiness of the spirit or carnality, must be cleansed from our lives. No part must be allowed to remain. If we do allow any to remain, it will still be there at our physical death and just like the Amalekite did with Saul, will try to take credit for our death. But worse yet, whatever has been allowed to remain will keep us from entering heaven. Have all the Amalekites been destroyed from your life?

Brad Weinert

Vessels Of Bright Brass
1 Kings 7:45

This morning I polished doorknobs – **tarnished** brass doorknobs – 14 of them. I spent half an hour on the first one with comet, steel wool, and pressure. And how it shines! It reflects! It's beautiful!

Strange. We've lived in this house for 33 years, and, until today, I had not noticed how **tarnished** and **dull** the knobs were. My negligence startled me. As I worked (with brass polish on the others), I thought about how God "filled Bezaeel with the Spirit of God ... to work in gold ... silver ... and in brass" (Ex. 31:3); how Jesus revealed Himself to Ezekiel, Daniel, and John as One whose arms and feet "sparkled like the color of burnished bronze ... like polished, fine brass."

For the temple which Solomon was to build, David "prepared ... brass in abundance without weight" (1 Chron. 22:3), and Hiram made "vessels of bright brass" for the "house of the Lord." (1 Ki. 7:45) How did the Levites keep all that brass polished?

What about my spiritual house? Can **tarnish** build on Christians – sanctified Christians? Might it happen almost unobserved – little by little – until we are startled by the lack of luster? Spiritual loss always begins in a wrong attitude. **Tarnish** can be anything that dulls our relationship with Christ – attitudes, suspicion, bitterness, criticism, actions, or words.

Someone said of Tersteegen of Holland, "O how the image of the Lord Jesus shone through him!" Paul wrote that as we behold "as in a mirror the glory of the Lord, He transforms us into His image ... by His Spirit." (2 Cor. 3:18)

Holy Spirit, whatever it takes of beholding, or scouring, of time – remove any tarnish on my relationship with YOU or with others. Polish my spirit until, like my doorknob, it radiates with brightness – the reflection of Your holiness!

Mrs. Alice Fisher

He Didn't Practice What He Preached
1 Kings 8:22-23; 1 Kings 11:5-10

Solomon – one of the most tragic figures in Biblical literature. He had a great inheritance from his father David. He was richly endowed with talents and abilities. He was known far and wide for his wisdom. He had a great beginning, but a sad ending.

He prayed beautifully, but didn't live according to the ideas expressed in his prayer. Read 1 Kings 8:22-53 and note the emphasis on repentance. There is no record that Solomon repented of his sin. Even Manasseh, wicked as he was, repented (2 Chron. 33:12-13) but not Solomon.

He built magnificently (see 1 Kings 6:37-7:12). The temple – God's house – was beautiful, but his own house took almost twice as long to build and was much bigger. What does that say to us? Who came first?

He taught wisely. The book of Proverbs is testimony to that. But, he didn't practice what he preached. Proverbs 4:23 says, "Keep your heart with all diligence; for from it flow the springs of life." But the record shows that Solomon's heart was turned after other gods.

He planned carefully and traded profitably. See 1 Kings 9:20-27. As a result he prospered unbelievably. The gold that came to Solomon amounted to over 25 tons per year. (2 Chron. 9:13-21)

But he compromised tragically and backslid horribly. (1 Kings 11:5-10) He married women who were pagans and not only allowed them to worship their own gods but joined in that worship. God warned Solomon (1 Kings 9:4-9), but he did not heed the warning.

There are two basic lessons here: heart relationship is more important than head knowledge, and human achievement can never take the place of personal godliness.

Dr. Hollis Abbott

Do Not Let One Of Them Escape
1 Kings 18:20-40

The contest between Elijah and the prophets of Baal is one of my favorite stories in the Bible. Elijah prayed a short, to-the- point prayer in asking for the fire of God to fall and consume the sacrifice. The reason Elijah was able to give a short prayer in public was undoubtedly because he had spent much time in secret prayer. This is an important lesson for us to learn concerning our own prayer life. If we want there to be power in our public prayers we better be spending much time in secret prayer.

Another important lesson for us can be found in verse 40 when Elijah said to the men of Israel, "Seize the prophets of Baal; do not let one of them escape." There's no doubt that when the men of Israel began killing the prophets of Baal that many of the prophets tried to hide in order to avoid death.

When one is seeking to be sanctified God will begin to show the seeker certain things in his life that must die. Pride is always a big one and a difficult one to put to death, but it must be done. Envy, jealously, bitterness, carnal ambitions, and many other things must also be put to death. Not one should be allowed to escape.

Just as I'm sure that prophets of Baal tried to hide from the Israelite swords, Satan will also try to hide some of these manifestations of carnality from the deathblow. If the seeker is not careful, some of those manifestations will avoid detection and death.

It we are to heed the words of Elijah and not let one of them escape we must pray the words found in Psalm 139:23. "Search me, O God, and know my heart." If we allow God to search our heart, He will reveal the location of those prophets who are hiding. He will reveal what manifestations of carnality are still lurking around so the death blow can be delivered, so we "do not let one of them escape."

Brad Weinert

41

Has The Fire Fallen?
1 Kings 18:30-39

It seems almost unbelievable that Elijah, standing alone when there were 450 prophets on the other side, had faith to trust God to prove Himself. All agreed that the god who answered by fire should be known as the true God. Being a great number, and Elijah on the other side alone, they must have had great confidence that the multitude was right, and they would be confirmed. The prophets of Baal built up their altar, killed their sacrifice, and had everything in order; set to have a beautiful convincing service. They cried to their gods, but there was no answer. Elijah even dared to make sport of them. "Cry a little louder. Maybe your god is out for a walk, or maybe asleep." Nothing happened.

Then Elijah "repaired the altar of the Lord that was broken down." He put everything in order and even made it difficult for fire to do its work by putting 12 barrels of water on it. As he called on the Lord it was with the purpose that "it be known this day that Thou art God in Israel, and that I am Thy servant, and that I have done all these things at Thy word." He only asked that God be glorified. God did not fail. "The eyes of the Lord run to and fro throughout the whole earth, to show Himself strong on behalf of them whose heart is perfect toward Him." This was a perfect consecration on the part of Elijah, and a perfect consuming of the sacrifice on the part of God.

Did you ever imagine what would have happened if the fire had not descended? They would have said, "The crowd is right. We'll follow them." This is happening today to a great degree. Many churches put on a wonderful program, but there is no fire. Be sure the consecration is complete and consuming fire has fallen, even if you find yourself among the few.

Rev. Marshal Cavit

Leprosy Of The Heart
2 Kings 5:1-14

It is a well-known fact that the disease of leprosy is used throughout Scripture as a type of sin. Its detection and the deliverance from it also serve as special illustrations for the spiritual life of man. In our Scripture for today we have a picture of what carnality is like. We have space to point out just a few comparisons.

In the first verse we read this striking phrase, "He was a valiant soldier, <u>but he had leprosy</u>." God has many valiant soldiers – but they are afflicted yet by "leprosy" (that is, carnality). In fact, most people are not aware of this affliction until they have joined the Lord's army and become one of His.

The reaction of Israel's king (v. 7) to the demand that Naaman be healed of his leprosy shows us that no human means could avail for this dreaded disease. There is only one cure for the sin problem, and it is a divine cleansing!

Naaman's first response to the remedy (vs. 10-12) is also typical. It seemed ridiculous and he rejected it. Isn't that the reaction of so many today? "What? I must die, so that I might live?" The remedy was not accomplished by the spectacular, but it brought humility, and then victory.

Finally, vs. 13-14 clearly point out that Naaman's healing came only by obedience and faith. That was, and is, the only way to victory!

Dr. Bruce Moyer

Majesty! Worship His Majesty! (1)
1 Chronicles 16:29; Psalm 29:2; 96:9

On my drive down I-84 toward Portland, Oregon I came to a sign reading, "Entering the National Columbia River Gorge Scenic Area." I had already been reveling in the glorious natural beauty around me. I was now thrilled to realize that others share the same sentiments of awe and wonder that I did. They even cared enough to own it for the entire nation and call attention to all passersby to take notice of these grand splendors of creation. After passing through about 90 miles of it, another sign informed me that I was now leaving the Scenic Area. I was sorry to be leaving it!

My inclination, through the whole 90 miles, had been to be on my knees in worship to the ONE Who had envisioned all of this glorious magnitude, then brought it into reality by His great, beauty-loving power. Obviously, it was important for me to keep most of my mental and visual attention on the road, and my body and limbs alert and active in guiding my car. Yet I couldn't be unaware of the awesomeness of driving along side of a moving mass of vast water on the one side, and breathtaking walls of massive pillars and immense formations of stone on the other. Enjoying all the sensations of admiration and joy which came to my heart through my eyes could only impress me with a deepening adoration for the CREATOR of it all. Inwardly I was singing:

"Majesty. Worship His Majesty.
Unto Jesus be all glory, honor and praise.
Majesty. Worship His Majesty.
Jesus who died, now glorified, King of all kings."
(Jack Hayford)

And I was reminded that He is <u>worthy</u> to receive glory and honor and power; for He has created all things, and for His pleasure (and ours) they are and were created. (Rev. 4:11, KJV)

Miss Jeanne Saeger

Majesty! Worship His Majesty! (2)
1 Chronicles 16:29; Psalm 29:2; 96:9

Oh, worship the Lord in the beauty of holiness. (KJV)
Worship the Lord in the splendor of His holiness. (NIV)

I am enriched in my understanding of these words as I note the Webster definitions of "beauty" and "splendor."

Beauty: An assemblage of perfections through which an object is rendered pleasing; any quality that delights the eye, ear, or mind. Splendor: Brilliancy; resplendence; magnificence; pomp; glory; grandeur; eminence. These are true of God's holiness.

In observing the grandeurs of the National Columbia River Gorge Scenic Area, I was inspired to worship their Creator. Yet the beauty of His holiness is greater than what He created.

I asked myself, "What is it to worship Him in His holiness?" First, there is His inherent holiness – that highest and whitest point of purity and light which is His character. Nothing is more beautiful the uncompromising justice of His absolute sinlessness. We can but worship Him Whom we see reflected in His majestic handiwork and hear extolled in the song of the morning birds.

Secondly, we worship Him in His beautiful, splendid holiness which is imparted to us when we open our whole heart to Him for His cleansing, His possession, and His control. That holiness in us responds to His expression of holiness in His creation. We think, "It is our wonderful, almighty, beauty-loving, omniscient God, Father, Savior, Lord, Gentle Friend and Shepherd, Who has made all of this."

"Majesty. Worship His Majesty.
So exalt, lift up on high the name of Jesus.
Magnify, come glorify Christ Jesus the KING."
(Jack Hayford)

Miss Jeanne Saeger

Battle Plans
2 Chronicles 20:14-30

There is a New Testament truth that shines through this passage as we see Biblical faith at work. Faith is: 1) a conviction of God's truth or will, 2) a correct action upon it, and 3) a trust that God will bring to pass His will. Faith is not a one thing in the past deal. It is a continuous action and it requires our participation (note Hebrews 11). By faith Noah didn't sit on his hands – he built. By faith Abraham didn't visualize a great nation – he obeyed.

The people of Judah exercised faith in the time of King Jehoshaphat, and there was a four-fold plan of action. First, was that God sent relief to His people, by sending His Spirit. (v. 14) When our agonized soul is before His throne, the Holy Spirit comes. Oh what a blessing!

With the Holy Spirit's coming we can then have release (vs. 15-17), for God takes over. There is no need to continue worrying over our problems for He now has them. This is possibly the hardest part, because we do not yet see victory, but God calls on us to have reliance upon Him for that victory. This calls for both our trust and obedience. (vs. 18-22)

Finally, we see our rest. (v. 30) Our rest can only come after victory and it comes from Him who gave the victory.

While these four "R's" can apply to any Christian's battles, there is strong analogy to entering "that rest" found in Hebrews 4:9-11. If we are to have that rest, we too must first have the Holy Spirit. That purifying flame of Pentecost must cleanse us of that bent towards sinning, but that can only happen as we release our hold on all that is ours – our future, our health, our family, our problems, our anger – and in faith rely upon God to do this gracious work.

"Let us therefore be diligent to enter that rest." (Hebrews 4:11, NKJV)

Rev. Roger Schoenborn

"… Many … Not Sanctified" (1)
2 Chronicles 30:17a

"There were many in the congregation that were not sanctified." While these Israelites were unsanctified in a ceremonial sense, this description is true in a moral sense in all too many of our holiness churches. Unfortunately this is often a large group. While they have in common the fact that they are unsanctified, they are not all alike. There are widely different reasons for their unsanctified state and in God's attitude toward them.

There are those who are "babes in Christ." These are the newly converted whom we trust are walking in the light but who do not yet have light on the deeper issue of the carnal mind and their need of a second crisis experience cleansing their hearts from all sin. These people enjoy the favor of God, their names are in God's Book and, should they die, they will go to heaven.

Another group we could call "Toddlers." They are beyond "babes" but still relatively new to the faith. They have received some light and are seeking entire sanctification, or have sought and think they have obtained, but have not, for the need is "deeper down and further back" than they yet realize. They lack a clear witness from God and their own changed hearts that the work has been done. As long as they walk in the light, they are in God's favor and will soon get through to a solid experience of heart purity. They too are bound for heaven.

Then there are those who are "still" carnal. They have known of their need for some time, but are lethargic about seeking a clean heart or, if they do seek, it seems that they lack the "I will not be denied" earnestness. These people are entering a danger zone where they will soon backslide if they don't get in earnest. Sometimes, long-time inhabitants of this group find that they need to be reclaimed because they have cooled off to the point of loss.

Rev. Dan Morgan

"… Many … Not Sanctified" (2)
2 Chronicles 30:17a

We always find some "Pharisees" who are staunch supporters and professors of the message of holiness but are hard, harsh, brittle, intolerant, unloving, legalistic, etc. Their "bunker" is well fortified with faithful attendance, good works, heavy giving and a generous dose of spiritual pride; therefore they rarely admit to any need. Some may maintain a grim, joyless, stiff Christianity (if there is such a thing), but many are "wells without water …" and their lot at Judgment is not to be envied.

There are usually some secret skeptics in the congregation too. These privately feel that "too much is made of sanctification," "the crisis is emphasized too much," and similar sentiments. They defend their unsanctified state by denying the existence of a second work of grace and/or by finding fault with those who profess sanctification. With some exceptions, these have gone against substantial light and are fallen from grace.

No doubt these categories do not exhaust the list and some people straddle the line rather than fitting neatly into some group. Nevertheless, the point remains that if we have adequate light on the need for entire sanctification and are not hungering after it, we are either in danger of loss or have already suffered loss of life from our soul. This may sound extreme to some but the alternative is to suggest that Jesus came all the way from heaven and endured the cross to provide for us a non-essential work. Properly qualified, the title of W.B. Godbey's little book is true; it is either "Holiness or Hell." If we take seriously the scripture, "Follow peace with all men and holiness without which no man shall see the Lord," we should be alarmed if we find ourselves in any but the first two of these above-mentioned groups. We can perish from the pews of a good holiness church. We would do well to heed the words of Joshua's reproof, "How long are ye slack to go to possess the land which the Lord God of your fathers hath given you?"

Rev. Dan Morgan

I Love You With All My Heart
Deut. 6:4

Valentines is a time for showing love. Shortly after Christmas, stores will put out their Valentine items. Many cards will be purchased and exchanged, gifts of candy will be given or sent to a loved one, and hearts will be in abundance everywhere. It is a time to say to that special someone that we really love him or her, and it is with all of our heart.

Our Christian culture has been influenced by the Jewish culture in this area. We perceive the heart to be the center of our personality and the organ of affection. For the Jewish person the heart was the seat of emotions, intellect and will. The term heart in Scripture is almost never used to refer to the physical organ but its common usage is in the figurative sense.

Not all cultures consider the heart the center of the personality. The Greek culture placed it in the intestines. Paul in Philemon 7 writes, "For we have great joy and consolation in thy love, because the <u>bowels</u> of the saints are refreshed by thee, brother."

Some cultures considered the kidneys (KJV, "reins") the center of affection. Marilyn Laszlo of Wycliffe Bible Translators tells of the Sepik Iwam people who consider the throat the center of affection and consequently invite Jesus into their throats. I don't know how they tell a lover of their deep feeling of affection.

The last time we were in Africa I learned that the Maasai and the Barundi would still call a child, particularly a daughter or granddaughter, "My intestines."

I assume this Valentines most of us, as we tell our lover of our love will assure him/her that it comes from the heart, another organ wouldn't quite communicate our feelings. The lover of our souls likewise wants our whole-hearted devotion. He wants to be the supreme affection of our lives.

Dr. Donald Hohensee

God's Sanctified
Job 1:1; 2:3

The character of Job is the character of all sanctified men. We are living in a day when the results of God's work of sanctification has been so misunderstood, and so misrepresented that people today are claiming God's sanctifying work without the corresponding character. Job's character was right and so must be ours. Job's character was:

1. PERFECT & UPRIGHT: Job was an upright man because he had a perfect heart. The word upright tells us that he was "straight and correct" in his morality. He treated people right. He treated God right because He was perfect in heart. Friend, if you don't truly love God with all your heart, and your neighbor as yourself, you are yet lacking sanctifying grace.

2. FEARED GOD: There was in Job, and IS in every truly sanctified soul, a continual reverence for God and His will and Word. People who do not wish and inwardly desire with all their heart to pray, read God's Word, worship Him at every opportunity, are yet lacking true sanctifying grace.

3. ESCHEWED EVIL: Job avoided all evil. A clear witness to sanctifying grace IS following the command of God's Word to "abstain from all appearance of evil." Whether at work or at home, we must avoid it. If you watch things on T.V. that are anti-holiness, it is because there is yet something in your heart that would rather watch it than avoid it. It is called carnality, and you are yet lacking the character God truly gives.

Friends, "God has not called us unto uncleanness, but unto holiness." Be perfect and upright, fear God, and eschew evil! It is only possible as a result of true sanctifying grace. A true experience works; don't let anyone convince you otherwise!

Rev. Rodger Moyer

Fruit In Season
Psalm 1

A good many years ago I listened to Dr. Paul Rees comment briefly on the words found in verse 3, "bringeth forth his fruit in his season." I have never forgotten his comments. It is true EXERCISE unto godliness to "bear fruit in season." Jesus said, "Herein is my Father glorified, that ye bear much fruit; so shall ye be my disciples." But fruit out of season is not in evidence.

The world has great joy at times. They have a measure of peace and rest. At times they walk in righteousness and show forth a measure of meekness, gentleness, and goodness. If we bear these fruits only when the world does, God is not glorified in them. When the world cannot do it, that is in season for us, and this is exercise unto godliness. This can only be when the Holy Spirit is in control. The natural man will act the same as the world.

The lives of many religious people look beautiful when they are in church, in the pulpit, teaching a Sunday School class, leading in prayer, or singing hymns, but even sinners can look good under such circumstances. Everything is favorable. When pressure is on to try the very inner spirit and depths of the heart, then what shows up? Is it godliness? When your enemy shows up, can you love him? When others despitefully use you, do you pray for them? Can you still do good to those who hate you? It is real exercise to do so.

Only with the Holy Spirit in control can one come out victorious, and sometimes only through agonizing prayer. But this is in season. It is power to show forth the beauty of godliness. It will honor the Father, and the world will become hungry to know this life of love.

Rev. Marshal Cavit

Good Food And Talking To Myself
Psalm 1

The second verse of the first Psalm talks about both good food and the often-ridiculed idea of talking to oneself. The first phrase clearly states that the righteous person's delight is in the law of the Lord. A careful study of the word "delight" indicates that it includes the idea of savoring. It means to relish; to take joy or pleasure in something. My mind immediately went to good food. Tasting it is the best part. The real connoisseur will handle it carefully, breathe in the aroma as he brings it to his mouth, and then chew it slowly, allowing the taste buds to soak up every ounce of flavor. Is this my manner of handling the Word of the Lord? Or, do I rush through it, oblivious to the many delightful and body strengthening morsels to be found there?

The second phrase of Psalm 1:2 uses a different picture to convey a similar truth. Here the righteous are seen as those who "meditate" on God's Word day and night. I used to assume that meditation was simply allowing my mind to slip into neutral so God could reveal to me whatever He wanted to about a particular passage of Scripture. I later discovered that the word "meditate" is more active than passive. It actually includes something of the idea of talking to oneself. As I study the Word I should be asking, "What does this mean?" "How can I apply this to my life?" "Have I been practicing (or avoiding) this?" As I "talk to myself" in this way, the Holy Spirit enters the conversation and helps me find the answers!

It's interesting to me that the Psalmist uses the word "law" in this verse. The law includes both "do's" and "don'ts." Am I able to delight in both? And, by the way, when was the last time you talked to yourself?

Dr. Bruce Moyer

Take The Time To Be Holy
Psalm 1

It never ceases to amaze me how the Lord comes and speaks to my heart in some of the most unlikely situations. The following thoughts came to me as I sat steaming in the sauna at the YMCA. It was a cold January morning and I was contemplating the new year ahead of me. I recalled what a glorious experience it was when I had finally yielded to the convictions of the Holy Spirit and gave myself up in utter consecration. God responded by cleansing my heart of all sin. That was several years ago. Since then it has been just as glorious to walk with Him on a daily basis – and that was the thought that overwhelmed me as I sat in the sauna that morning. The words of Longstaff's hymn ran through my mind and I meditated on the practical exhortations (there are nearly a dozen of them) that I'd sung so many times before. Maybe they will be helpful to you today.

"Take time to be holy. Speak oft with thy Lord;
Abide in Him always, And feed on His Word.
Make friends with God's children; Help those who are weak,
Forgetting in nothing His blessing to seek.

Take time to be holy. The world rushes on;
Spend much time in secret with Jesus alone.
By looking to Jesus, Like Him thou shalt be;
Thy friends in thy conduct His likeness shall see.

Take time to be holy. Let Him be thy Guide;
And run not before Him, Whatever betide.
In joy or in sorrow, Still follow thy Lord,
And, looking to Jesus, Still trust in His Word."

Dr. Bruce Moyer

Shopping And Holiness
Psalm 1

I know you're already asking what Psalm 1, shopping, and holiness all have in common. The first verse of the Psalm is the connection. It speaks of walking, standing and sitting. Quite often (or so it seems to me) I accompany my wife to a mall to do a little shopping. I usually try to find a parking spot close to the tool department at Sears. On some occasions, somewhere near the table saws, I get by with, "Go ahead, I'll catch up in a few minutes." However, I am sometimes coaxed to tag along down those long corridors of almost-too-good-to-be-true bargains. It starts with walking, just harmless "window shopping." It soon progresses (or should I say, comes to a halt?) to standing, as Ruth stops to look, compare prices, colors, etc. I've patiently learned to maintain the "standing" position for about 5 minutes now, and then I look for a place to sit and begin to calculate my forthcoming losses.

There is something of this same progression in the spiritual realm for those who are not careful to say a resounding "no" to the very appearance of evil. The downward progression starts with walking. That is, just simply becoming familiar or acquainted with someone or something – like harmless "window shopping." The righteous are to avoid, as much as possible, even casual acquaintance with the counsel (advice, thoughts, ideas) of the wicked. This counsel may come through a variety of channels, including television, radio, literature, friends, etc.

The danger of window-shopping, as we saw, is that we tend to stop and look. We assume the standing position. Association begins to take place. Counsel, advice and ideas soon become a "path" – a way of travel, a way of life. It is not long then until sitting becomes the desired position. Ideas and counsel that became a way of life are now assimilated and one finds the "seat of mockers" a place of comfort and rest. The lessons of shopping are easily applied – walk not, stand not, sit not.

Dr. Bruce Moyer

Rejoice With Trembling
Psalm 2:10-12; Luke 10:20

We often stand in greatest peril when we are most successful. I have the words underlined in my Bible: "Rejoice with trembling." When Jesus sent His disciples out, giving them power to do miracles, He cautioned them, "Rejoice not that the spirits are subject unto you, but rather rejoice, because your names are written in heaven." When Paul speaks of "forgetting those things which are behind, and reaching forth unto those things which are before," I wonder if he was not thinking as much of his successes as of his failures. We like to forget our failures, but boast of our successes. In this we stand in danger of losing God's blessing. At times God may withhold the blessing He would like to give, because He knows that we will fail to give Him the glory He deserves. You may remember that He told Gideon, "The people that are with thee are too many for me to give the Midianites into their hands, lest Israel vaunt themselves against me, saying, mine own hand hath saved me." (Judges 7:2)

Then there are times that God will let us go ahead in our self-confidence and utterly fail, to let us know that we are not sufficient in our own strength, but that we need to trust in Him. First of all, we need His direction. Jeremiah 10:23 gives us a wonderful word that we need to remember. "O Lord, I know that the way of a man is not in himself: it is not in man that walketh to direct his steps." Then we need His strength to do His bidding. "Cursed be the man that trusteth in man, and maketh flesh his arm, and whose heart departeth from the Lord." (Jeremiah 17:5)

In Psalm 107 we read that God let the people go their own way until they came to their wits end, and only then did they cry unto the Lord for help. Each time He says, "Oh that men would praise the Lord for His goodness, and for His wonderful works to the children of men." Thanks and praise should be His.

Rev. Marshal Cavit

The Good Life
Psalm 4

In a recent re-reading of the Psalms, I noticed a question in this fourth Psalm that had not caught my attention before. It appears in the sixth verse: "Many are asking, 'Who can show us any good?'" The point of David's immediate situation was that there are no other gods who can show mercy and grace to man like God does. However, as I pondered the question further, it began to sound like the question of hungry hearts today. "Are there any moral people left?" "Who can I trust?" "To whom can we look as a model for righteous living in the 20th century?" "Who can show us any good?" This is one of the reasons we preach, teach and live holiness! The world needs to see it. It is the one great hope for our society.

In the last three verses of the Psalm we see the characteristics of those who would show us good.

1) They are experiencing the presence of God. "Let the light of your face shine upon us, O Lord." (v. 6)
2) They are experiencing His provision of a heart full of joy. "You have filled my heart with greater joy." (v. 7)
3) They are experiencing God's peace, even in the face of adversity (v. 1). "I will lie down and sleep in peace. (v. 8a)
4) They are living under His protection both spiritually and physically. "For you alone, O Lord, make me dwell in safety." (v.8b)

That sounds a lot like the sanctified person who is walking and growing in holiness. And that's the answer to the question, "Who can show us any good?"

Dr. Bruce Moyer

What Can The Righteous Do?
Psalm 11

In these days when the very foundations of human life are being attacked, where truth and justice are no longer respected, where honesty, honor, ethics, and integrity are held lightly, if at all, "What can the righteous do?"

This question must be faced squarely and successful within and without the ranks of even our "holiness churches." We are living in a day of the ever-present question mark, where traditions are flouted, and biblical demands for holy living are explained away. Somehow in this setting, faith and reason must be allies, not adversaries!

What can the righteous do? Well, they can go on enjoying the sanctifying power of the Holy Spirit in spite of opposition. Believers can go on so rooted and grounded they are not shaken by the sneer of cold liberalism; warming their corner of the world and brightening the corner where they are. *There is no visible argument against holy living!* An experience that transforms lives and brings the whiteness of purity to a dirty, unclean world is its own best testimony and witness.

Then, holiness people must protect and preserve their experience on the solid foundation. They have found that the Solid Rock will not move! Whether attacked by cold-hearted liberalism or spiritual extremes. They have learned that heart holiness is not to be argued but accepted, not to be fought but to be found, not to be considered lightly but to be lived!

What can the righteous do? They can go right on believing, proclaiming, and living scriptural holiness!

Rev. Gene Moyer

Holiness: God's Perfecting Work
Psalm 19

For the first half of my life I lived primarily in the states of Oregon and Washington. I loved the beauty of nature around me – streams, woods, mountains, and the beaches of the vast Pacific Ocean. Although the four seasons (drizzle, showers, rain, and downpours) were not clearly distinguishable, I loved it. The last half of my life has been lived primarily in the Upper Midwest where the ice goes off the lakes about July and returns about September – but I've learned to enjoy God's beautiful creation here as well.

The Psalmist was awestruck too as he considered God's handiwork. In the first six verses of Psalm 19 he expresses again and again how God's perfection is seen in nature.

In the next five verses (7-11) he points out how God's perfection is seen through His Word. It is "perfect" – that is, it is complete. There are neither superfluous parts nor are there any omissions. It is "trustworthy" – certain, sure, and definite. It is "right" – always. It is the prefect revelation of His will for me, and what it teaches me is always right. It is "pure." It is "sure" and "righteous." God's Word is everything that He is!

Finally, after stating that God's perfection is so clearly expressed in both nature and in His Word, the Psalmist's prayer is that God's perfection would be seen in him (verses 12-14). Here is a beautiful statement of what holiness is: "To be kept from willful sins" (v. 13) and that both the words we express as well as our innermost thoughts would be that which pleases Him.

God's perfection will be seen in nature, and through His Word. Will it be seen in me?

Dr. Bruce Moyer

Clean Hands and a Pure Heart
Psalm 24

My wife and I spent four years serving as missionaries in the country of Bolivia, South America. One of the things we missed most was the availability of good, pure drinking water. Even the water from our tap had to be boiled for twenty minutes before it was safe to drink. There were a few occasions when we were served water that was not boiled and those were usually followed by a trip to the doctor and a round of antibiotics. For the most part, there just wasn't any pure water to be found.

The Psalmist describes (Psalm 24:3-4) the person who will make it to heaven as one "who has clean hands and a pure heart." He is speaking about bringing both what we do (our outward actions) and what we are (in our innermost being) into accord with the Divine will. The person who is "pure in heart" is sometimes about as hard to find as a pure drinking water in Bolivia. In fact, we hear from many pulpits and classrooms across our land, that such purity is not possible in this life. After all, we are human. As I study God's Word, however, I learn the truth. Jesus also stated that the pure in heart shall see God. (Matt. 5:8) The Apostle Paul was inspired to write that our goal is to allow love to flow freely from a pure heart. (1 Tim. 1:5) He went on to admonish the young preacher Timothy to keep himself pure. (1 Tim. 5:22) The Scriptures teach us that Jesus dies on the cross to purify us from sin (Heb. 1:3; Titus 2:14). We have a personal testimony that, in fact, God does purify the hearts of those who will yield fully to Him. (Acts 15:9) And, the truth is, He will still do it today! (1 John 1:9) The next time you drink a glass of cool, pure water, think about the promise of Psalm 24:3-4.

Dr. Bruce Moyer

Who? What? Why? How? When?
Psalm 24

"Who shall ascend into the fill of the Lord? Or who shall stand in His Holy place?" (Psalm 24:3) Can there be any question more important than this? Our eternal destiny rides on the answer. Since it is God's Word that asks the question, it must be God's Word that provides the answer.

What is the answer? Here it is, "He that hath clean hands and a pure heart ..." (Ps. 24:4) And note it is a twofold answer – clean hands – a symbol of a clean life by "the washing of regeneration" (Titus 3:5), and a pure heart – a sure evidence of personal, private, and positive purity as wrought by the Holy Spirit. Purity within -- purity in the inward temple, the holy of holies of the human psyche. Hallelujah!

Clean hands and a pure heart! Why are they necessary? The answer is nearby and it is very plain: only such people "shall ascend into the hill of the Lord," only such people "shall stand in His holy place." (vs.3-4) This makes it an essential demand. Whatever else we may or may not have, this is the minimum requirement! If heaven is eternally holy then holiness of heart and life is everlasting necessary! Amen! So be it!

How is this twofold condition to be expressed? By not lifting up our souls unto vanity (pride) or swearing deceitfully (greed). (v.4) This is but a sample, a reminder, that true holiness is more than an essential demand for our eternal destiny. Of necessity, and altogether logically, there must be an experiential deliverance that is evidenced by the ethical dimension or we are deluded and misled.

When? The answer is now! "Clean hands and pure hearts are needed now! And they may be experienced now! And what we are now will determine where we shall be then. That is what Psalm 24: 3-4 are saying to us.

Dr. Eldon Fuhrman

The Beauty Of Holiness
Psalm 29

Here are four Biblical texts that are alike in one phrase. 1 Chronicles 16:29 says, "... worship the Lord in the beauty of holiness." Psalm 29:2 echoes it "... worship the Lord in the beauty of holiness." Psalm 96:9 adds an exclamation, "O worship the Lord in the beauty of holiness." And in 2 Chronicles 20:21 King Jehoshaphat appointed "singers unto the Lord ... that should praise the beauty of holiness, as they went out before the army." Of course the phrase common to these four texts is "The Beauty of Holiness."

In its very nature sin is ugly. It creates scowls, frowns, sneers and looks of hatred. It brands the body and scars the spirit of man. It contaminates the conscience, mutilates the mind, and sours the soul. Nothing is more ugly than sin unless it is the author of sin, the devil.

In total contrast to the sordidness of sin is the Beauty of Holiness. But what can be done for the souls who have been scared by sin? Can humanity be restored to the likeness of God? Can we share the beauty of the Lord? That is exactly what He is calling us to do! "O worship the Lord in the beauty of holiness!"

Yes, we are ugly with sin until transformed. But, "There is a fountain filled with blood, drawn from Immanuel's veins. And sinners plunged beneath that flood lose all their guilty stains!" No longer hide the scars and stains. Bring them to Jesus, Who at Calvary provided the perfect remedy. Your soul can be beautiful again, and that beauty will shine through the vessel of clay.

Albert Orsborn expresses it well in his prayer-poem:
"Let the beauty of Jesus be seen in me,
All His wonderful passion and purity,
Oh, Thou Spirit divine, all my nature refine,
'Till the beauty of Jesus be seen in me."

Dr. Wilfred Fisher

Where Are the Boundaries?
Psalm 32:8

"Papa, where are the boundaries?" This was our five-year-old grandson's first question when we arrived at our vacation cottage nestled among tall pines at Sunriver, Oregon. He was really asking, "How far – on which roads and paths – may I ride my bike?" We grandparents were both amused and touched by the obviously wholesome father-child relationship. "Where are the boundaries?"

Children and young people need and appreciate definite guidelines. It gives them a feeling of security and of belonging.

A sovereign God set boundaries in Eden: "of every tree of the garden you may freely eat; but of the tree of the knowledge of good and evil you shall not eat." (Gen.2:16-17) At Sinai He gave specific directions for worship, for holy living, for right human relationships.

After Saul's conversion on the road to Damascas, Saul sought divine counsel: "Lord, what do you want me to do?" (Acts 9:6) David prayed, "Teach me Your way, O Lord … lead me in a plain path." (Psalm 27:11)

And he promises to guide us continually! What a privilege!

I, too, need to ask, "Father, what are the boundaries of your will for me,
- in my work?
- in prayer?
- in giving?
- in reading?
- in recreation?
- in everything?"

Instruct me! Teach me! For your will is my delight!

Mrs. Alice Fisher

Sing A New Song
Psalm 33:3; 32:1-11

We are familiar with the Psalmist's exhortation that we should "sing a new song." But what will be its subject? "Songs of deliverance" we are told in Ps. 32:7.

And like most songs we sing there are several verses. The first verse has to do with our deliverance from our transgressions – a deliverance that <u>must</u> come. (Ps. 31:1, 5) We say "must" because, like David, there can be no peaceful relationship with God until our transgressions are confronted and confessed. But what a song issues forth when we can "remember when my burdens rolled away!"

Then there is that verse which describes our deliverance from our iniquities – a deliverance that <u>can</u> come. (Ps. 32:2, 5) For despite the teaching of troubled theologians or the fears of frustrated Christians, there is deliverance from the carnal nature. And when that deliverance comes it is with conviction we sing, "The Comforter has come!"

The final verse of this new song had to do with our deliverance from the tyrannies of life – a deliverance which <u>will</u> come. (Ps. 32:6-11) Our greatest opportunities to witness come as we face those issues of life that are so defeating to the unsanctified Christian. So we can expect "floods of great waters," "trouble," times of indecision and sorrows. But we can also expect to sing the song of deliverance in those contexts of reality for it is the lot of the righteous to "be glad … rejoice … shout for joy."

What a beautiful, new song that comes from the liberated heart of the sanctified!

And let's sing ALL the verses of this song.

Dr. Merne Harris

Not Tracing butTrusting!
Psalm 37:1-11 (Exodus 23:20)

From my dormitory room at the Missionary Training Institute, Nyack, N.Y., I could see the moonlight shimmering on the Hudson River. Far from family and home in Minnesota, I needed re-assurance. Was I really called to be a missionary? Why couldn't I, like my peers, say with certainty that I had "the call," some even specifying India, China or Japan? The icy fingers of fear gripped my heart. In early youth I had made a total commitment to the Lord and I felt certain that to this point the Lord had clearly led me. But what about my tomorrows? I wanted above everything else, to be a missionary.

That night with the future still veiled He assured me that He would "keep me in the way," and would "bring" me into the places which He even then was preparing for me.

Through the years He has truly "kept me in the way"-whether in times of crisis, decision-making, near fatal illness and critical surgery, financial stress or overwhelming responsibility. As He has led from one phase of life to the next, it has been truly rewarding to find that all along He is preparing me for the place(s) He has prepared for me.

Yes, eventually He led to the mission field, not according to my timetable, but His. And the most precious lesson has been this: first of all, I must be what He wants me to be--cleansed and filled with His Holy Spirit. Then, and only then, am I ready to do His bidding, at home or abroad. Joseph H. Gilmore voices my testimony:

"He leadeth me, O blessed thought!
O words with heavenly comfort fraught!
What-e're I do, Where-e're I be,
Still 'tis God's hand that leadeth me."

Mrs. Susan (Schultz) Rose

Holiness: A Thirst For God
Psalm 42:1-2; 143:6

It was the find of a lifetime! My wife and I had been serving as missionaries in Bolivia for a couple of years. It was long enough to really begin craving for some of the delicacies of America ... you know, Big Macs, onion rings, pizza, Betty Crocker cake mixes, and Cheerios! Well there it was on the highest shelf in the back of a small hole-in-the-wall "store" in the market place ... the dustiest, most faded box of cheerios I'd ever seen in my life. But after having lived so long without them, the box sure looked bright to me, and it seemed like a bargain (being 6,000 miles from home) for only $5.00. It's hard to explain the great disappointment I experienced when I got the box home, opened it, and discovered that it contained as many weevils as it did cheerios (no, I didn't eat them anyway!).

I've discovered that holy living is a lot like that craving I had for those cheerios. The psalmist describes it as a "thirst for God." The carnal heart desires God too, but not enough to want to be cleansed from the sinful nature, if that's the price (and indeed it is). Holiness wants Jesus more than anything in life, no matter what the cost. He is the fountain of living water. (Jer. 2:13) He is the spring and source of everlasting life. (Rev. 22:1)

Jesus promised, (Matt 5:6) "Blessed are those who hunger and thirst for righteousness, for they will be filled." Though He keeps filling me up, I continue to crave more of Him!

Thought: The water I gave my plants last week was not sufficient for this week.

Dr. Bruce Moyer

The Holy Life Is Fragrant
Psalm 45

"The fragrance of your garments is like the fragrance of Lebanon," "Your God has anointed you with the oil of gladness…All your garments are scented with myrrh and aloes and cassia." (SS 4:11; Psalm 45:8, NKJV)

God gave special directions to Moses for making the hold anointing oil. He was to take quality spices-myrrh; calamus and cassia-and make "a holy anointing oil…compounded according to the art of the perfumer." (Ex. 30:25, NKJV) With this fragrant oil, the priest's were anointed for holy service; the tabernacle and furnishings for holy worship.

The Hebrews believed that the anointing affected transference of the holiness and virtue of Deity and the impartation of a special endowment of the Spirit of the Lord to the anointed one. And indeed, at Pentecost, this is exactly what happened. The waiting ones were filled with the Holy Spirit and spoke "as the Spirit gave them utterance." (Acts2:4) As Christians today are endued with power from on high, their lives become fragrant with right attitudes, godly living, sacrificial love and holy joy.

Someone said, "God's saints are fragrant without knowing it because they keep company with the great Perfumer." One who works in a perfume factory need not announce where he spends his time. People took knowledge of the disciples "that they had been with Jesus." (Acts 4:13) When Mary anointed Jesus "with very costly oil," the house "was filled with the fragrance" of her poured-out love.

A converted drunkard prayed earnestly for the pastor and people as he cleaned and dusted the sanctuary. His minister said, "He perfumes the church with power."

Psalm 92 encourages all of us: "I shall be anointed with fresh oil…"to bring forth fruit," to be "fresh and flourishing," even in old age! (Psalm 92:10, 14) Hallelujah!

Mrs. Wilfred Fisher

A Cry For Holiness
Psalm 51:10

We have probably all heard many messages from this passage of Scripture and that is good for there are many clear and unchanging truths taught in it.

But the thing that always stirs my own heart about David is that he didn't mess around when he dealt with God. David sinned against an Almighty God. He knew he had, God knew he had, and so he doesn't hide anything nor play any games with his repentance.

Likewise David doesn't mess around with his need of a pure heart. Now this may sound simple, but he prays for a clean heart. He doesn't complain about how hard it is to live right - so Lord help me to do better. He doesn't pray for a better testimony, or for a better family life.

No, David is clear and David is definite, he wants a clean heart and a renewed spirit. I think in these last days we are losing the clear definite cries for holiness that need to be prayed. More and more we are having people come to our altars to feel better about themselves, but not to get saved or sanctified. They pray about family, better prayer lives, for about everything but what they really need, to be clean, to be sanctified.

Let us seek God for the real need of the human heart and life, that is, "holiness without which no man shall see the Lord." God still sanctifies, praise His name! David, in another Psalm said, "when I cried to the Lord, he heard me." Let us cry for holiness, it is our only hope, it is our only deliverance.

Rev. Rodger Moyer

Down In The Valley (1)
Psalm 84:1-12 (vs. 6-7)

The Valley of Baca means valley of weeping. This valley is mentioned in the midst of a pilgrim psalm, which was used as faithful Jews approached the city of Jerusalem to go worship in the Temple to seek the presence of God.

The hope of the pilgrim was centered in the dwelling place of God. And the hope of Christians is in the heavenly home with God. But to get there we have to go through the valley of weeping – perhaps the death of a loved one, the announcement of cancer, the loss of a good job.

It's comforting to know that we will not dwell in the valley of weeping; we're just passing through it. The pain and sorrow we feel there will not last forever. "Weeping may remain for a night, but rejoicing comes in the morning." (Psalm 30:5)

As pilgrims pass through the valley, it says in verse 6 that they make it a spring. Water was a precious commodity in that land. The tears in our valley of weeping can be springs of God's comfort to others. They can be a refreshing spring for others on their pilgrimage into the presence of God.

We do not know how we will even get through today, sometimes, but God has promised that our strength will equal our days. (Deuteronomy 33:25)

God gives strength today, tomorrow and the next day. We go from strength to strength until we reach our heavenly home and appear before God. To be a doorkeeper (10) in the presence of the Lord is infinitely to be preferred to all the world has to offer. One day in the place of God's presence will be worth more than a thousand days anywhere else. To be the humblest servant in the Temple will be better than a permanent place where wickedness abounds. It's not the beauty of the place that attracts the pilgrim, but the beauty of the Person (11) who will withhold no good thing from those who walk uprightly

Rev. John Moyer

Down In The Valley (2)
Psalm 23:4

If you have ever driven through a mountain valley you will soon realize that dawn comes late and evening comes early. If you want to see you must look up. Many of the valleys we pass through in this life are filled with shadows. In order to see light we must look up.

The valley of the shadow of death is a <u>walk</u> for the believer. It's a steady advance of the soul that knows its road, knows its end, resolves to follow the path, feels safe and secure, and is calm and composed. The believer who is in this valley is not running in alarm, nor is standing still as though he would go no further, he just keeps pace.

And notice the believer knows he is going "<u>through</u>" the valley. We do not live there, because the Good Shepard is leading us through.

Notice also that it is a "<u>shadow.</u>" Death in its substance has been removed and only its shadow remains for the believer. Someone has said that when there is a shadow there must be a light somewhere. Death stands by the road of the path we are traveling, but the light of heaven is shining on us and throws a shadow across our path. But it is only a shadow, and a shadow cannot stop a person in their walk. The shadow of a dog cannot bite, nor can the shadow of death destroy.

Because of this truth, we need not fear evil. It doesn't tell us anywhere in this verse that there will be no evil, but it says not to fear it. We don't even have to fear the last enemy, death, because it is a conquered foe.

The paths of righteousness do not protect us from the valley, but it is the Lord who leads us through those times of shadows. It is the Lord's presence alone that can give us complete comfort and security in the valley of shadows.

Rev. John Moyer

Down In The Valley (3)
2 Chronicles 20:12, 20-26

When Jehoshaphat was king of Judah, a huge army came against him. In a public prayer the king acknowledged their helplessness against the enemy (6). Then God spoke through His prophet and told them the battle was not theirs but His (15). The men of Judah were to take their positions, stand firm, and see the deliverance of the Lord. The next morning as they went out to battle, Jehoshaphat assigned men at the head of the army "to sing to the Lord and the praise Him for the splendor of His holiness" (21).

What a way to go to battle, not with weapons, but with singers praising God. And when they came to the place for battle, they saw nothing but dead bodies. It took them three days to gather up all the loot.

On the forth day they assembled in the Valley of Berachah, where they praised the Lord (26).

Praise is taking the Lord at His word, though the external situation remains unchanged. We see this throughout the Scriptures. Paul and Silas in the Philippian jail is an example.

Praise is not an indicator of our feeling or an impulse to our circumstances; it is a commitment of our will.

Believers are not exempt from circumstances and fears, but they have a God to whom they may take their fears. And when we do that, He uses them as vehicles of spiritual comfort and praise.

Rev. John Moyer

Down In The Valley (4)
Deuteronomy 1:21-25

The Valley of Eshcol was the valley of Unbelief. The Israelites found it a fertile land where one cluster of grapes was so large that it took two men to carry it on a pole.

But there were giants in the land. Even though God had promised the Children of Israel this land, they refused to go in and possess it. They were afraid, and because of their unbelief, God let them wander in the wilderness for 40 years.

Have you ever been in the valley of Eshcol, where you have seen the provision of the Lord, but you still do not believe? You miss God's blessings that are surrounding you, because you will not take God at His Word.

The enormity of their failure in turning back from the Promised Land, in spite of the undoubted and confessed attractiveness of that Land, is an unbelievable lesson in unbelief. There are those who remain outside the promised blessing of God through entire sanctification and never enter in. They listen to the Gospel and they see the attractiveness of the new life, they even taste, so to speak, the grapes of Eshcol, and savor the blessings of God's sanctifying grace through hearing the Word; they stand on the threshold and yet turn back and turn away.

The Israelites swept aside the great prospect that stretched before them, that for which they had been called out of Egypt and bondage. They weighed the blessings of life against the doubtful attractions of the Egypt that was still in their hearts, and they missed the blessing of God.

Too often we only see the problems, and then use them as an excuse to stay right where we are. Our Heavenly Father asks us to trust Him today. He is faithful; His promises are sure. He does all things well, and He cannot fail.

The Valley of Eshcol is before us. Let's trust Him!

Rev. John Moyer

Down In The Valley (5)
1 Kings 20:26-28

A prophet came to Ahab, King of Israel, and told him what the Lord said, "Do you see this vast army? I will give it into your hand today, and then you will know that I am the Lord" (13). And God gave Israel the victory.

The prophet told Ahab to get ready, because the next Spring the King of Aram would attack again. And sure enough, next Spring, the Arameans went up to fight God's people. Israel marched out to meet them. Israel looked like a flock of goats, while the Armeans covered the countryside (27).

God spoke again to Israel with these encouraging words, "Because the Syrians have said 'the Lord is God of the hills, but He is not God of the valleys,' therefore I will deliver all this great multitude into your hand, and you shall know that I am the Lord." (28)

Sometimes we may feel that the problems and circumstances we face are like a vast army covering the countryside. We may win one battle, but the next Spring a bigger battle comes. We see how small and weak we are compared to the forces against us, but our God is all-powerful. There is no valley too deep or mountain too high, but that He is there. His love and His might have no limits. We can trust Him and know that He is God. He is the God of the hills and the God of the valleys. Wherever you are at in your spiritual journey, He is there, whether on the hills of joy and prosperity or the valleys of trouble and adversity.

Rev. John Moyer

Down In The Valley (6)
Joshua 10:6-14

Where did Joshua find the courage to ask God to make the sun and moon stand still?

It goes back to the promise and encouragement he received when Moses said, "Do not be afraid, do not be discouraged" (Deut. 31:7-8). And then the Lord Himself spoke to Joshua these words, "Be strong and courageous ... I Myself will be with you."

Then when Joshua was on the brink of crossing the Jordan with Israel into Canaan, God again said, "Be strong and courageous. Do not be terrified; do not be discouraged, for the Lord your God will be with you wherever you go." (Josh. 1:19)

Joshua became a mighty man of God because he was careful to obey the Word of God. In fact, God's Word was not to depart from his mouth, and he was to meditate on it day and night, and do everything written in it. (1:7-8)

If we know God's Word, meditate on it, and do what God is telling us to do, then when we find ourselves in the Valley of Aijalon, we too can call out to God for the impossible, knowing that He will listen. When we are on God's side we have supernatural resources. We are not limited to only that which makes sense in the terms of this world. We are in a relationship with the God who can go beyond the natural for the glory of His Name and for the victory of His saints.

God's supernatural resources are available to us when we are on His side, even in the valley of battle.

Rev. John Moyer

Down In The Valley (7)
Hosea 2:14-23; Isaiah 65:10; Luke 3:5

The valley of Achor is the valley of the trouble. Joshua had led Israel in the great victory at Jericho, but at Ai they met with humiliation and the agony of defeat, because of Achan's sin. Sin had to be removed before God could bless. It was in the Valley of Achor that Achan was stoned to death.

We may find ourselves in the Valley of Achor, because of sin in our lives. If so, we need to confess it to God (1 John 1:9 and James 5:13-15).

In Isaiah 65:10 we find the Valley of Achor becoming a resting place for those who seek God. In Hosea we see it becoming a door of hope.

Life has its valleys, dark, shadowy places of haunting memories of failure and remorse. These valleys often block our vision for the future and close us in on the past.

Hosea teaches us that we can sing a song of hope in these valleys. Two valleys are mentioned – Achor and Jezreel – both filled with anguishing memories of Israel's past failures and disobedience. God excavates the memories of these valleys to show them His forgiveness. Christ has become our Door of hope (John 10:9-10). If we have drifted into old patterns of resisting God, the door of repentance and renewal is open. We don't have to stay in the Valley of Achor with its memories of failure – of mistakes, poor judgments, mishaps, taking on too much, goofs, or sins. Whatever our failure, self-condemnation or self-justification is not the way out of this valley. The only way out is God's forgiveness and responding to His love.

In Luke 3:5 we see that we will one day have no more valleys, when we see our Blessed Lord Jesus in all His glory. Until then, let's walk by faith, be aware of all our weaknesses and depend on our Guide, Who is with us even to the end of the age.

Rev. John Moyer

An Undivided Heart
Psalm 86:11

David is praying for a devotion to God that has been cleansed from double mindedness. Only then will he be able to walk in God's way consistently and fear God's "name" (His holy character) with both reverence and affection.

He is praying for a work of divine power to be wrought within him. "Give me." He pleads. He knows he cannot create an undivided heart within himself; it must be a gift of grace.

There is no question as to the supernatural nature of heart holiness. We can surrender, consecrate, and trust, but only the Holy Spirit can change the very foundations of our nature.

People ask, "Do you believe in eradication?" My answer is: "If you mean, does God eradicate my natural instincts and propensities, both physical and mental, in such a way that these faculties can no longer be avenues of temptation, thus making sin impossible, my answer is no. I do not believe in that kind of eradication."

"Further, if you mean the annihilation of my selfhood, with its nature self-awareness and instincts of self-preservation, again I must answer no."

"But if you mean the cleansing of my inner motives and springs of action from that lurking reluctance to embrace the full lordship of Christ in every detail and in all its personal ramifications, then I gladly say yes, I do believe in eradication. I believe I can be purged from that carnal mindedness which is 'enmity' against God (Romans 8:7). Nothing less than this will give us the inward foundation for happy service and growing maturity."

Dr. Richard S. Taylor

Preferring And Pursuing Godly Company
Psalm 101 (verse 6)

The old adage is true, "Birds of a feather flock together." Nothing could be more true for the perfect in heart! A person who loves God with a perfect heart wants to be with the people of God. After all, a key characteristic of the Church is the pronounced love in and for the brotherhood.

I recall a situation in my own life when I was away from God and as lost as I could be, yet, as the son of a pastor, I was required to attend the worship services, for which I thank God. As I attended those services, I found that one man in particular simply grated against my carnal nerves. He simply glowed with the presence of the Holy Spirit, and his testimonies were like sharp piercing arrows to my heart. I avoided him like the plague, for I was not comfortable in his presence. However, after I was converted and later sanctified wholly, my heart actually sought this man out for fellowship and conversation. I wanted to be with one of like heart and mind.

David's oath is that he will seek out the faithful of the land so that he may associate with those who have a right heart. The holy of heart was his crowd. So it is and will be for all who have a clean heart. Do you love to be with the people of God? Do you eagerly search for opportunities to fellowship with those whose hearts are perfect towards God? If you have a clean heart, you will prefer and pursue godly company. You will find this association with fellow believers to be a grace which God supplies to help you on your way. Dwell with the faithful of the land!

Rev. Jonathan Morgan

Heart Inclination
Psalm 119:33-40

David, the man after God's own heart, knew how to pray. He spent little time on the inconsequential. He concentrated on the vital. Hear his request: "Incline my heart unto Thy testimonies, and not to covetousness." Psalm 119:36

Rivers flow the way the land is inclined. Lives go the way the heart is inclined. That is why Proverbs 4:23 exhorts, "Keep thy heart with all diligence; for out of it are the issues of life." And that is why God in 1 Samuel 16:7 declares, "man looketh on the outward appearance, but the Lord looketh on the heart."

Heart inclination determines conduct. Conduct determines character. Character determines destiny. What then could be more important than heart inclination?

But how can a wrong inborn inner inclination be corrected? Man cannot do it for himself, but he can come to God in prayer. The psalmist had the problem of covetousness; so he prayed, "Incline my heart ... not to covetousness." Thank God the evil inclinations can be destroyed! "Incline my heart to Thy testimonies ..." God's testimonies, the very Word of God, can be written in our hearts.

When every valley (our lack of right desire) is exalted and every mountain (the piled up desire for evil) is brought low then the heart is inclined in a new direction. We surrender our covetousness to possess His testimonies. What a marvelous exchange!

Dr. Wilfred Fisher

Strength Through Quietness
Psalm 131:1-3; Isaiah 30:15

As Dr. Dobson and his guest were speaking of religious ecstasy as addictive behavior, I was reminded of an incident in my life. When living in Salem, Oregon, a favorite noontime practice was jogging in a primitive downtown park. The seasonal sights, smells and quiet sounds of the woods were obvious and refreshing. It was easy to become absorbed in a quiet time of meditation with the Lord.

A gift given in love quickly interrupted my times of quietness. I fast learned that my new Walkman radio was an intrusion – even when it played gospel music. It distracted from that time when I "composed and quieted my soul." (Psalm 13:2a)

While a student in seminary one of the professors said more than once that we become like the God we love and serve. God is holy. Following the experience of entire sanctification we must cultivate the ideal of holy living. This new "strength" is processed in "quietness and trust." (Isaiah 30:15) As we quietly focus upon the Lord and His holiness in reference to our daily experiences, we more and more discover our souls are like a weaned child within us. (Psalm 131:2b)

In an insecure society full of droning noises we must have times of quietness. Even as times of soothing quietness between spouses and friends can be powerful builders of rapport and cohesiveness, so much more our times of quietness with God. What a privilege to have times when we compose and quiet our souls.

Dr. John Sills

Examine Me!
Psalm 139

My boyhood was not unlike that of other children, and I don't think things have changed too much over the years. You will probably recall, as I can, making sure that you were out of voice range after accomplishing some feat (either accidentally or purposefully) that did not meet with your parents' approval. Sometimes, even though I was within hearing range, my ears just didn't function properly – or I was already absorbed in another great venture and my dad's voice would go unanswered. I suppose it could be compared to the "hearing loss" that Adam and Eve suffered in Eden.

In verses 23-24 of Psalm 139 we find quite a different picture. Here is a man actually inviting God to examine him thoroughly, within and without. It is highlighted by the four verbs: <u>search</u> (my heart), <u>test</u> (my thoughts), <u>see</u> (my ways), and <u>lead</u> (me).

I read this Psalm again this morning and saw something I had never noticed before. In verses 1-5 the Psalmist declares that all of this has already been done. God has searched and known him (v. 1); He perceives his thoughts (v. 2); He is familiar with all his ways (v. 3); and He leads him along (v. 5). What we have then in verses 23-24 is the prayer of a man who has already submitted to God and found Him to always be just. He has also found that God's way is always best, and though he has yielded himself to God's scrutiny before, he wants to continue in that relationship as long as he lives. Because he has obeyed he has no fear of appearing before his Father. Oh yes, new things may come to light, but that is just what he desires. Can I honestly pray Psalm 139:23-24 today?

Dr. Bruce Moyer

Being Known of God
Psalm 139

God in His omniscience knows not only all about the universe as a whole but all about you and me. What folly it is to try to hide anything from Him. The only one we fool is ourself.

The most intelligent thing that we can do for ourselves is to know ourselves as God knows us, and then let Him make the necessary adjustments.

I remember when I was seeking to be entirely sanctified. After I had asked God to search me and let me know my heart as He saw it, some of the things He showed me hidden there (such as self-pity, jealousy, etc.) I, at first, denied. "That can't be true!" I cried – but then the Holy Spirit would remind me of instances where I had felt those sinful attitudes even though I had often suppressed them. What was there to do but to agree with God that those sins did exist and ask for the blood of Jesus to purge them.

That same heart attitude, to know oneself as God knows us, is essential to our continued victorious walk with Him. Anytime we try to excuse ourselves or to cover over anything the Holy Spirit is trying to point out to us, we draw a veil between our soul and the Savior. How much better to open our heart completely and be absolutely honest with God and ourselves – "nothing between my soul and my Savior."

Personally, I'm glad my heavenly Father knows every nook and cranny of my heart and knows how to keep me clean.

Mrs. Clarice Moyer

Satisfied
Psalm 145:16-17

The greatness of the holy works of God is never ceasing. God is so good to us. One of the great and wonderful aspects of experiencing holiness of heart is that it satisfies like nothing else in this world can. The truth is we will never be satisfied without holiness of heart and life.

We can look at the world and see the emptiness of life that so many are experiencing. They have a natural hungering in their souls to be satisfied. The devil tells them "I have the answer" and offers them pleasures, sex, games, drugs, or winning lots of money in the lottery.

But only God can satisfy the hungering of the soul. Until a man knows God in His fullness, until the very chambers of the heart have been cleansed of all carnality, until you are so submitted to God that this world indeed grows strangely dim in the light of His glory and grace, a man cannot be satisfied.

We all know the testimony of the song "All my lifelong I had panted for a draught from some cool spring, that I hoped would quench the burning, of the thirst I felt within. Hallelujah! I have found Him!"

One of the greatest things about holiness is that God opens His hand and satisfies the desires of the soul! "Hallelujah, I have found Him whom my soul so long has craved, Jesus satisfied my longings, thro' His blood I now am saved!" And sanctified!

Rev. Rodger Moyer

Doing The Appropriate Thing!
Psalm 147

Have you praised the Lord <u>today</u>? One student found in the Bible more exhortations to praise the Lord than to pray to Him. Christian experience confirms that <u>praise</u> begets <u>prayer</u>, even though for many, prayer does not always generate praise.

The psalms are loaded with commands to praise, especially the last five – 146 through 150. One basic reason why praising the Lord should be a dominant spiritual practice is found here in Psalm 147:1, as well as in Psalm 33:1 – "it is fitting" for the upright in heart to do this (NIV). In the light of all that the Lord is in Himself, and all that He does for us, it is our most appropriate response, to praise Him!

One day a Christian lady came to the late Joseph H. Smith, and exclaimed: "Oh, Brother Smith, my heart is so full of praises to the Lord!" With a smile the saintly minister replied: "Sister, that is not the place for your praises, for the Psalmist said, 'His praise shall continually be in my mouth.'" (Ps. 34:1)

Who should be more given to praising the Lord than the purified in heart? For they can truly say, "Bless the Lord, O my soul; and <u>all</u> that is within me, bless His holy name." (Ps. 103:1) The norm for New Testament Christians is found in Heb. 13:15, "By Him (Christ Jesus) let us offer the sacrifice of praise to God continually, that is, the fruit of our lips giving thanks to His name."

Heart-felt praise will change our <u>attitudes</u> in the midst of life – situations we cannot change. It displaces grumbling or complaining, and lifts the soul to those higher <u>altitudes</u> where we sit together with Christ Jesus in heavenly places (Eph. 2:6). And praise creates an <u>atmosphere</u> about our lives, which has within it the aroma of the heavenly world (2 Cor. 2:14-15).

Dr. Delbert Rose

The Day God Left Me Breathless
Proverbs 3:6

I was preparing to leave for a meeting one evening when I began to feel troubled about attending it. It wasn't a feeling you could explain, just sort of an uncomfortable "heaviness." The problem was, I had agreed to go to this meeting at the special invitation of a friend, and I felt I should keep my word.

For about an hour I juggled my thoughts around trying to decide what I should do. Where were these feelings coming from? Was this the voice of the Holy Spirit or was another influence at work here? I have learned that impressions must be considered with great caution. It came down to a simple prayer: "Father, I don't know what to do here, but I have promised to attend this meeting. I don't think it would be right to disappoint a friend because of a 'feeling,' but my heart wants only what You want. If I shouldn't be at that meeting, I am willing to be stopped by any means necessary. Please, block my way if that is your perfect will."

I had agreed to drive to the meeting but when my friend showed up several minutes later, he insisted on driving. I relented, and we had gone less than a mile when his car began having problems. For the next ten country miles, I repeated my prayer. We were just one mile from our destination, when the car finally died and rolled to a stop next to a pay phone. Merciful Father! I had my answer and, breathlessly, rejoiced.

When our hearts are pure, it is easy to spot blatantly sinful choices and reject them. However, the real test often comes when we are faced with choices that are neither questionable nor clearly sinful. What does God want then? He wants our completely surrendered wills. What peace belongs to His fully surrendered and cleansed children. They accept every form of His guidance, leading and correction gladly and with eagerness.

Mr. Kerry Kistler

Dead Flies and a Little Folly
Ecclesiastes 10:1

For those of us who believe in and claim holiness of heart, it is our holy obligation that we live above reproach on the three major testimonies of our lives:

OUR CONDUCT Peter wrote, "but like the Holy One who called you, be holy yourselves also in all your behavior." (1 Peter 1:15, NASB) A man who claims to be a Christian but misconducts himself, is a discredit to the purpose and power of God. Jesus said, "Let your light so shine before men, that they may see your good works and glorify your Father who is in heaven." The Apostle Paul states, "For we are His workmanship, created in Christ Jesus unto good works, which God hath before ordained that we should walk in them." (Eph. 2:10) A holy conduct has a beautiful fragrance about it.

OUR CONVERSATION Whereas our conduct relates more to our actions, our conversation relates more to our attitudes. Jesus said, "Out of the abundance of the heart the mouth speaketh." The tongue is an outlet for the contents of the heart. Many professing sanctification of heart have caused their lives to send forth a stinking savour just by a few dead flies in their conversation: a nasty word, a needless word, a negative word, or a noxious (harmful, injurious, destructive) word.

OUR CONSCIENCE Friends, there may be times when we are criticized unjustly, but here is one area of our lives that we must be above reproach in, and that is to ourselves. "To yourself be true." The Apostle Paul's greatest strength was a pure conscience. When he stood before the council that was trying him, he was able to say, "Men and brethren, I have lived in all good conscience before God until this day." (Acts 23:1) Oh the power of a good conscience. To know that our motives and attitudes have been pure before God, this is strength.

Dr. Hubert Harriman

Watch Out For The Foxes
Solomon 2:14-17

It had been a shattering discovery. For weeks the owner of a flourishing vineyard had watched his vines come alive with their blossom-promises and then the early stages of the grapes in formation. It looked as though it would be a good harvest; his days were full of promise and anticipation.

But then came the terrible discovery: the dreaded little foxes, subtle and devastating, had invaded the vineyard. Gone were the vines and with them the tender grapes, harbingers of a harvest that was not to be.

It is no irreverence to present the Father as a vinedresser eagerly awaiting the fruit of His Presence in the heart of the sanctified. Nor is it unrealistic to believe He is often disappointed because of the work of the little foxes in our lives.

There is complacency, that dangerous feeling of such total satisfaction that we come to believe there is no more God's grace could do for our satiated souls. Or competition, the instrusion of so many legitimate but time-demanding enterprises that there is little time left to heed the admonition of the hymn "Take time to be holy ..." And there is compromise, that bargaining tool of the devil which would challenge our loyalties, confuse our purposes and blunt our witness.

It might be a good idea to check the vineyard – there is little fruit on barren, broken, brittle branches.

PRAYER: Dear Lord, let the fruit of Thy Holy Spirit grow in abundance and maturity in the garden of my heart – even today. Amen.

Dr. Merne Harris

Vision
Isaiah 6:1-8

Vision! Passion! Action! These three factors were present on the Day of Pentecost (Acts 1, 2); they were involved in sending Barnabas and Saul on the first missionary tour (Acts 13); they burned in the heart and mind of John Wesley when he set out to spread Scriptural holiness throughout the world.

"Where there is no vision, the people perish..." (Prov. 29:18) For the lack of vision, new Christian projects are not undertaken, new thrusts of evangelism are not made, and new conquests for Christ are not achieved. But with vision, when combined with passion, new realities of Christian enterprise are born.

The source of Christian vision is the heart of God, which is made known to us in the written Word of God. Thus it is that devout and prayerful reading of the Holy Scripture provides the Holy Spirit with special opportunity to make known to us the Father's purposes for reaching the lost, for discipling believers, for setting up training centers for the ministry of today and tomorrow.

It follows, then, that the scope of our vision ought to be as great, as far-reaching, as all-inclusive, as world-wide, as that of God Himself. We cannot "think small" if we share the divine vision. If we think in lesser dimensions we are sure to grieve the heart of God and disqualify ourselves for our greatest usefulness.

The secret of Christian vision is especially in the grace of heart purity. The "pure in heart" (Matt. 5:8) share His sentiments, sense His concerns, see the possibilities of fulfillment through the power of the Holy Spirit. They know that being Christ's witness is a mandate, not a matter of option. Hence the response of the holy heart is to be that of Isaiah: "Here am I; send me."

Dr. Eldon Fuhrman

Holiness Is A Work Of Heart
Isaiah 29:13-16

A few years ago, one of the most talked about news items was the frequent use of "lip syncing" by many of the popular singers. They were only mouthing the words to their songs as their audiences enjoyed highly sophisticated recordings. Their hearts weren't really in it, but most of the time no one knew the difference. It really became an issue though when one group was given a very prestigious award and it was later discovered that the singers had never even made the recordings. They were declared to be frauds.

Our text for today reveals that this sort of thing has been going on ever since the Garden of Eden. The Lord declares in Isaiah 29:13, *"These people ... honor me with their lips, but their hearts are far from me."* That statement is too often the case for those who have not yet experienced entire sanctification. They honor God with their talk, but not with their walk. There is something within (carnality) which continues to cause them to do things which are inconsistent with their testimony. Many times they even have everyone else convinced and nobody seems to know the difference, but there remains something in the heart that is far from God.

Jesus used this passage in Matthew 15:7-8 and coupled it with the term "hypocrites" as He spoke of the Pharisees.

Jeremiah (31:33) records God's promise that the new covenant would be written on the hearts of people – there is a remedy!

Are my lips expressing the true nature of my heart ... or am I only "lip syncing?"

Dr. Bruce Moyer

The Way of Holiness
Isaiah 35

Someone has said that it is easier to be an obstetrician than a pediatrician. This is true in the realm of holiness, also. It is often easier to work evangelistically to get people into an experience of holiness than to work pastorally to help people live the life of holiness. Isaiah teaches that holiness is a **way**. John puts emphasis on the **walk** and **abiding** in holiness. (1 John 1:7; 2:6)

It is significant to note how Paul, that great expositor of the experience of holiness, actually wrote more about the life of holiness. I have often quoted 1 Thes. 4:3 urging the necessity of the experience of holiness, but the context (v. 3-12) describes what holiness is all about. It is about **possessing** or keeping our vessel in sanctification. In other words, the **way of holiness** is important, to remain morally pure, both man and wife, hating the lust of the world, avoid cheating and deceitfulness at all costs. He goes on to teach that the way of holiness has a lot to do with getting along together, finding ways to be quiet in our soul, tending to our own affairs, doing an honest day's work and being reputable and conscientious in our dealing with unbelievers.

Paul's own testimony (1Thess. 2:1-10) is a tremendous example of how he **walked** the way of holiness, exhorting us to likewise **walk** worthy of God (v.12). Thus we conclude that this way is a way of boldness (v.2), honesty, purity and guilelessness (v.3), truthfulness (v.4), noncoveteousness (v.5), humility and helpfulness (v.6), gentleness (v.7), affection, compassion and love (v.8), hard work, prayer and concern (v.9), and a holy, just and unblameable behavior (v.10).

No wonder Paul could say in Rom. 6:18, "Being made free from sin, ye became the servants in righteousness" (holiness). Friends, let us walk worthy.

Rev. Harold Harriman

The Holy Highway
Isaiah 35:8-10

A highway serves only one purpose: to provide a route by which we can get from one location to another. Our road maps outline a multitude of different highways leading in many directions, but this is a different kind of highway, the "Highway of Holiness," leading to a different destination.

This holy highway is a <u>toll road</u> whose construction cost (the blood of our Savior), can never be repaid. It also costs the believer to travel this way. It costs complete consecration to God of our will, way, ambitions, hopes, desires, and life itself. But the rewarding travel and eternal destination more than compensate for the initial price.

Isaiah described the way as a <u>pure way</u>. The unclean shall not pass over it. Only those with "clean hands and a pure heart" are allowed. This is Divine requirement.

The way is <u>simple</u> for those who have simple faith and love God with all their hearts, minds, souls, and strength, and their neighbors as themselves. We have an accurate and Divine Road Map.

The way is <u>sure</u>. We shall not err - make a mistake therein. We need not stray because we have a Divine Guide.

The way is <u>safe</u>. Travel has its dangers with "lions and ravenous beasts" lurking everywhere, but these shall not be on the Holy Highway. We have Divine Protection.

The way is <u>exclusive</u>. Only the Redeemed shall walk there. We have a Divine Savior.

The way is <u>victorious</u>. Verse 10 paints the picture of victorious soldiers returning from battle. The way may have been long and travel difficult, but now there is singing, everlasting joy, and gladness. Sorrow and sighing are gone. We have a Divine Conqueror to receive us into our Divine Destination. Praise His Name!

Mrs. Leona Morgan

Dig Deep Or Dry Up
Isaiah 37:31

The sun seemed boiling hot. The southwest wind felt like a blast furnace. The earth was almost as hard as pavement. There had been no rain for weeks. The crops were nearly dead. Not much greenery could be seen. But there was one exception. In the midst of all the drought and death the alfalfa field continued to be a dark green – and even grow a bit. What was the secret? Why did the alfalfa remain alive and grow when all the other crops were brown and dead?

The answer: the long deep root system of the alfalfa went down into the soil, perhaps as much as twelve feet, into the cool and moist subterranean depths to continue to draw moisture and sustenance.

The spiritual application is obvious. If we are to remain alive and grow and be fruitful we are going to have to "launch out into the deep," or, to preserve our analogy, to dig deep lest we dry up and die. We must "dig deep" in repentance and faith, in consecration and sanctification, in daily devotions and obedience, in constant submission and service if we are to find hidden streams of refreshing from the hand of the Lord.

We have no alternative: It is dig deep or dry up! But, praise God, we seek no alternative, for we have found security, strength, sustenance and stimulus for continued life and growth in that wonderful stream of salvation that never runs dry. And to dig deep prepares us to dwell deep and to keep us alive and fresh in an otherwise dry season.

Dr. Eldon Fuhrman

Racehorse or Workhorse
Isaiah 40:31

Some people are like racehorses; some are like workhorses. Racehorses are high-strung, quick starters, independent, competitive, temperamental, and easily spooked. Workhorses are strong, plodders, slow starters, and long endurance team workers with a "steady-as-she-goes" temperament. We "racehorses" should take a lesson from the workhorses.

We live in Amish country where teams of workhorses are a common as well as beautiful sight. I've watched them. When they are harnessed to plow, they plow - heads down in a rhythmic bob, in step with their teammate. When left standing while the farmer tends to other things, they stand there, waiting their next command. They can work all day -- pulling the plow, standing, waiting . . . pulling the plow, standing, waiting . . ..

By observing these beautiful creatures, I ("a racehorse") have learned some valuable spiritual lessons. We needn't jump at the start and tear off at the first impression we get, and in so doing waste time and energy, leaving us feeling frustrated and downcast. We needn't run all the time, but rather walk, heads down in a rhythmic bob with our Team Mate. We needn't panic when we feel we've been left alone a while by our Master, but simply stand and wait patiently for His next word of direction. We needn't gallop through life alone, but walk with God, Who has promised to never leave us nor forsake us.

Mrs. Sarah Harriman

Hephzibah
Isaiah 62:1-5

Hephzibah – now that name may be beautiful to your ears, but I must admit that it never crossed my mind when it came time to name our daughters (and I have a sneaking suspicion that both they and my wife are grateful). I am glad, though, that the translators of the New American Standard Bible chose to put that name in the margin and put the meaning in the text. Hephzibah – "My delight is in her."

I live in a religious culture that spends an inordinate amount of time and energy debating "styles" of worship and types of music. Everything around us seems to be market driven, so we take polls to determine whether people prefer organ or drums, hymnals or overhead projectors – and the majority rules. It seldom seems to occur to people that worship is not intended to be pleasing to the world, but that it is to be a delight to God.

While I believe that there are important issues that are often ignored in discussions about music in the church, I am convinced that music is not at the heart of worship – obedience is. Samuel indicates to Saul that obedience superseded what was thought to be the heart of worship in his day. "And Samuel said, 'Has the LORD as much delight in burnt offerings and sacrifices as in obeying the voice of the LORD? Behold, to obey is better than sacrifice, and to heed than the fat of rams.'" (1 Samuel 15:22, NASB) God told Israel, "Take away from Me the noise of your songs; I will not even listen to the sound of your harps. But let justice roll down like waters and righteousness like an ever-flowing stream." (Amos 5:23-24, NASB)

Organ and drums can both be offensive to God. What He delights in is obedience, justice, and righteousness – holiness of heart and life. Hephzibah – We may not have used that name for our daughters, but I would be happy to have Jesus use that name for me.

Rev. Glen Boring

Beulah
Isaiah 62:1-5

There are many who could give sad testimony to the fact that it is better to be single than to wish you were. Christians, however, whether single or married, male or female, by God's grace have the joy of making up the bride of Christ.

God said through Isaiah that there was coming a day when Jerusalem would no longer be called "Forsaken" or "Desolate," but rather "My delight is in her" (Hephzibah) and "Married" (Beulah). The picture is one that grows on me as I reflect upon it.

We often sing and testify of our delight in the Lord. How could we do otherwise? When we were dead, He made us alive. When we are in sorrow, His presence provides comfort and peace. With Paul, we can experience abundance or privation with grace and victory through Him. We, too find that in the perplexing difficulties of life, His grace is sufficient. How could we not be delighted in Him? He has faithfully supplied all of our needs.

What captures my attention with amazement and wonder is that God uses nuptial terms to describe His delight in us! I will never forget the night I saw my bride coming down the aisle. There were many people crowded into the church, but she had dressed herself to please me, and words could not describe my delight.

What a wondrous joy to realize that whether married or single, male or female, as Christians we are the bride of Christ and He delights in us and rejoices over us! Just think of it – we can bring delight to the God who made us! Could not Peter's admonition to wives be applied to those of us who make up the bride of Christ? "And let not your adornment be merely external – braiding the hair, and wearing gold jewelry, or putting on dresses; but let it be the hidden person of the heart, with the imperishable quality of a gentle and quiet spirit, which is precious in the sight of God." (1 Peter 3:3-4, NASB)

Rev. Glen Boring

Thou Art the Potter
Isa. 64:8; 24:16; 45:9; Rom. 8:29; 9:21

"Have Thine own way, Lord! Have Thine own way!
Thou art the Potter; I am the clay.
Mold me and make me after Thy will
While I am waiting; yielded and still.

Have Thine own way, Lord! Have Thine own way!
Hold o'er my being absolute sway.
Fill with Thy Spirit til all shall see
Christ only, always, living in me!"

Adelaide Pollard

These words so beautifully express the longing of the sanctified heart. It is often good and wise to remind ourselves that all God is permitting to come our way is aimed at conforming us more perfectly into the image of His Son.

If a lump of clay had feelings, it surely would not enjoy the process by which it is rounded and smoothed and molded until it is a useful vessel. Neither is the molding process for us always a pleasant experience but if we can keep in mind that what God is trying to do in us and through us, that goal sanctifies the painful process. How important it is that the clay remain pliable in the potter's hands! If it should become hardened or brittle in the process, the goal can no longer be achieved.

You may be going through some bitter or trying experience just now. Why not just bow your heart before the Potter and ask Him to use the trial to make you more like Jesus. Ask Him to remove the rough edges, the excess clay, and to shape you into a vessel "meet for the Master's use."

Mrs. Clarice Moyer

Let's Keep On Track
Jeremiah 6:16

One of the things I've learned in my Christian walk is that there is nothing more lifeless and hopeless than a church or a Christian without the Holy Ghost in His fullness.

We live in a day when churches are better, but people in general are not. I really believe the main reason is because people want a different and easier way to true holiness. In fact I read not too long ago about how a bunch of people were gathering together to see the face of Jesus on a tortilla shell, on a door, and on a water tower. Yes, people are always looking for something different than what they really need, and what they need is the "old path."

We need to continue to preach the awfulness of sin. The horrors of hell, the glory of heaven and eternal life, until the conviction of God seizes every heart and people weep their way to a place of prayer and are truly born again.

We need to preach salvation so great that when people experience it they will never forget that sacred place where they met God, and you can hardly keep them away from the church!

We need to keep preaching the power of God to come and sanctify every heart, the beauty of perfect love, until the entire church becomes so hungry for the fullness that they once again weep their way to the place of prayer, consecrate all, look up through their tears in simple faith and trust and receive the Holy Ghost in His fullness and cleansing into their hearts.

If we keep on the "old paths" our churches will march through this old world in victory and the old devil will fear and tremble, the angels of heaven will rejoice, and God's people will shout glory be to God forever!

Friends, it's the old path that leads to rest for our souls, let us keep on track.

Rev. Rodger Moyer

The Heart Of The Problem
Jeremiah 17:1-14

Before God can heal our land He must heal our hearts, because the heart of the problem is the problem of the heart. We are born into this world with a sin-prone heart.

Notice the **impact of sin.** (vs. 1-6. Judah's sin was deeply engraved on their heart. Sin was Judah's settled disposition. It was her affection, her habit of mind, and her direction. Sin was engraved upon their hearts and it affected every area of their lives, as it still does today.

Then Jeremiah describes **the infection of sin.** (vs. 9-11) Judah's trouble can be traced to the heart; the inner disposition of the people. There is something desperately wrong in man. And who can know it? That's why the Lord is constantly searching the heart and trying the reins. By our selves we cannot even know the problem of the heart, so God shows us by giving to man according to his ways and according to the fruit of his doings. The heart is so deceitful that it prompts a person to evil by promising joy and reward, but then leaves the soul empty. It has deceived many to believing that forms of religion are the reality of Christ in the heart, and that pleasure comes from temporal things instead from the eternal things of God.

Thank God! There is the **invitation to healing.** (vs. 12-14) There is a sanctuary (v.12) not just for worship but also for refuge, safety, and healing from the deceitful heart. God is the only One who can heal this heart. And if God does the work, we know it will be done thoroughly and right. Only he can renew us in righteousness and true holiness all the days of our life. He can restore the inward inclination of the heart toward holy living, which had been lost when Adam and Eve sinned, and fill us full of the Holy Ghost.

Rev. John Moyer

A Craftsman At Work
Jeremiah 18:1-10

Even as I write this morning I can hear the sounds of the craftsman at work. Sue is in her "candle room" just down the hall from my study. Right now she is pounding vigorously on blocks of wax that just arrived from the supplier. After awhile the broken wax will be put into kettles to be reduced to liquid. Several molds will receive the melted wax and in a few hours will return to what she calls "star" candles. From the same substance, pulled from identical molds, there is little to distinguish one from the other.

But then the important processes begin. The look-alike candles are dipped into various colors of wax and are then cut, carved, twisted and shaped – each in a different manner for each to serve its own distinctive purpose. The one being made today will end up as a unity candle at the wedding of a special person. So what was once plain and rather uninteresting has become strikingly unique.

But that's not all! After the candle has been dipped in a sort of shellac to give it a final sheen it is carefully inspected. And that is a rigorous inspection – I have seen more than one candle go back to the bin to start all over again – even though it looked great to me. If and when the candle is approved, a label is affixed to the bottom, which reads, "Crafted by Sue." It is, I can assure you, a special candle that bears that label.

There is another process going on as I write. The Holy Spirit is in His "workshop" doing what needs to be done to prepare me for the purpose He has for my life. And I welcome that process despite the sharpness of the discipline, the mystery of His plans, the losses that come along the way. For I want so much to bear that label, "Crafted by the Holy Spirit." (Romans 12:1-2)

Let us today submit ourselves to His design for us rather than to the design of others or our own selves.

Dr. Merne Harris

"…I Sat Where They Sat…"
Ezekiel 3:1; 2 Cor. 1:3-6

It was my father's funeral. I had just graduated from high school filled with dreams and plans for my future, but now my world had fallen apart. It seems my plans were devastated. Instead of bright hope, I was inundated with grief and sorrow at the loss of my father. As the congregation of friends and neighbors attending the service were ushered from the church, a classmate put her hand on my shoulder as she passed me. Only a touch, but what encouragement and strength passed from her touch to me. I remembered that she, too, had lost her father a few months before. She understood! She had "sat" where I was now sitting.

The use of this phrase from Ezekiel in a contemporary sense means simply to "…make an identification of (oneself) with someone else; to put oneself in another's place so as to understand and share the other's thoughts, feelings, problems, etc." (Webster) St. Paul further explains the value of this identification with others in 2 Corinthians 1:3-6.

As Christians we sometimes question some of the difficulties and dark days, which make up our circumstances of life. "Why?" is a question we ask ourselves, (and sometimes, God) as though being a Christian should make us immune from any and all of life's sorrows. But our loving God not only permits our testings, He knows that we become stronger as we exercise our faith and trust in Him. When we come through difficulties victoriously we can then "touch" a fellow-sufferer. We have "sat where they sat."

Mrs. Leona Morgan

A Man God Can Use
Ezekiel 22:30

God used Martin Luther to proclaim the doctrine of justification by faith. John Wesley proclaimed the doctrine of entire sanctification. William Carey, David Livingston, Hudson Taylor and a host of others have been used of God to carry the Gospel to the people of the world. God is looking for those He can use today. Who are they?

God uses men of purity. Jesus called the twelve and used them but indicated He could not use them as He desired. Thus He said, "Tarry ... until ye be endued with power from on high." Peter testifies that at Pentecost he received a pure heart. Afterward he was greatly used of God.

God uses men of purpose. Daniel "Purposed in his heart not to defile himself." (Daniel 1:8) He maintained that purpose and God greatly used him to influence men and nations. God uses men that are totally surrendered to His.

God uses men of prayer. E.M. Bounds said, "Not until we prevail with God will we prevail with men." Samuel Logan Brengle said, "There is no substitute for waiting upon God. If a man fails at this point ... he may soon fail at every point." All greatly used servants of God have been men and women of prayer. Nothing develops and empowers Christians like daily prayer. Nothing increases wisdom like prayer. Nothing is as dangerous to the kingdom of darkness as prayer. Nothing brings blessing to churches, equips missionaries or ministers more than prayer.

God uses men of passion. These have an intense ardent love for Christ, the will of God, the Word of God and the souls of lost people. Their hearts burn with love for Christ. They forsake all for Him. They are moved as Christ was moved for the multitudes that know not Christ as Savior and Lord.

Will you be the one the God can use?

Rev. J. Eldon Neihof

"And The Heathen Shall Know …"
Ezekiel 36:16-23

God, in His great concern for this wicked world, has always worked through people. Even as sin came upon the whole world through Adam, even so restoration comes and will come through people – God's people. E.M. Bounds was right when he said "God's method is to work through men. Men are looking for better methods, God is looking for better men." When God "in the fullness of time" was ready to reveal what He was really like, He didn't send a proposition, He sent forth a Person, even Jesus who said, "If you have seen me, you have seen the Father."

In every age when sin has had its way and God's great name has been forgotten and profaned, God has declared exactly how it can be reversed. So in the time of Ezekiel during the great captivity He gave us a precious truth that is both fitting and practical for every age. He summed it all up in the twenty third verse of the thirty sixth chapter of Ezekiel when He said, "And I will sanctify my great name, which was profaned among the heathen, which ye have profaned in the midst of them; and the heathen shall know that I am the Lord, said the Lord God, when I shall be sanctified in you before their eyes."

Some make the verse entirely prophetical for a later day and especially for the nation of Israel, but this truth that is relevant to every generation is so plain that only a bigot or a blind man could miss it. The truth hardly needs commentary because it is so evident and "New Testament" in its method and its solution.

We see that man is both the problem: "which ye have profaned …" as well as the solution: "the heathen shall know … when I shall be sanctified in you before their eyes."

God's method is still people – people like you and me who have allowed and are allowing the Lord to work His great sanctifying work in our hearts. "Then the heathen shall know …."

Dr. Delmer Ransdell

Called to Perfect and Follow Holiness
Amos 7:8; 1 Thess. 4:7; 2 Cor. 7:1; Heb. 12:14

For the believer sanctification should be a passion, not a pastime! We are called unto holiness. We are to perfect holiness in the fear of God. We are to follow after holiness, without which no one shall see the Lord.

There is a real sense, indeed, in which the entire New Testament was written to motivate Christians to do the will of God – even their sanctification. (1 Thess. 4:3)

In the Gospels we have our Model, our Example, the Lord Jesus Christ. He was holy, harmless, undefiled (Heb. 7:26). In Him the fruit of the Spirit was brought to perfection.

In the Epistles we find there are instructions, promises, encouragements, and warnings, all designed to promote in us a desire for holiness of life.

In the Acts of the Apostles, by the power of the enabling Holy Spirit, we are given pictures of men and women working in God's highway of holiness. We see the pitfalls and the problems that will arise as we press on in the royal road.

In a word, the New Testament is our handbook on holiness. In it we shall find God's explanation of what sanctification is all about. In it we shall discover how holiness relates to personal, family and church life. Ignorance with regard to God's requirements and our responsibilities in the matter of holiness is not bliss! God has given us His Word in order that we may read and apply its truths. Friend, His Word is not a dictionary to be consulted once in a while, but a map to guide us into holy territory.

Regardless of our theology of holiness, we must translate our understanding of the Biblical teaching on this subject into terms of life and character and action! What does it profit a man if he claims the most correct theory, and fails to manifest holiness of life?

Rev. Gene Moyer

Sustaining The Spirit's Flow (1)
Zechariah 4

The Jews had returned from Babylonian exile and promptly set out to rebuild the temple. An altar was temporarily set up along with the foundation for the temple. But the work soon stopped because they saw the smallness of their group and the vastness of the project, along with the opposition from some enemies. The Lord is here trying to stir up the people to press on with the project, telling them that it's not by their might or power but by His Spirit that the work will be done. A symbolic vision was given to Zechariah, which encourages us in the Spirit-filled life.

Our Source

The source of oil to the lamp stand is two olive trees, which represent Joshua the priest and Zerubbabel the prince. They represent our Source in Jesus Christ – Jesus our Priest and King. He will supply the oil of the Holy Spirit to the Church. Our light will never go out as long as the channels are open to receive from Him the oil that keeps us burning. Paul said in 2 Cor. 3:5, "Our sufficiency is of God." Years ago Nellie Reagan, the President's mother, wrote in his Bible: "A thought for today: You can be too big for God to use but you can't be too small." We are all earthen vessels but we can all be filled with the oil of the Spirit that keeps our lamps burning bright. All Christian living flows from God, and returns to Him. A person that is not depending on our Source can be identified by their attitudes and actions. Pride, arrogance, indifference to others, and contempt for the weak all become smoke that dims the glass so our light cannot shine. But the confident-in-Christ are self-denying, patient toward the weak, meek, and willing to be least, lowest, or last. They willingly trim their wicks so their light can be seen.

Remember our Source!

Rev. John Moyer

Sustaining The Spirit's Flow (2)
Zechariah 4

Our Sustenance

The crisis and the process of the Spirit-filled life are both important. We need to have the oil of the Spirit flow to us and light our flame in the crisis. Dr. Dennis Applebee shared in the *Call to Prayer* about the plague in London in 1666. Carts roamed the streets and the drivers continuously called out "Bring your dead." There seemed no end to the plague until after a year, an unsuspecting woman left some sticks too near her baking oven and the great fire of London began. That great fire took 13,000 buildings, but it ended the plague. That's what the baptism with fire will do to the plague of carnality, but what about after the crisis?

The Bible tells us to be led of the Spirit and to walk in the Spirit. The wick can only stay aflame while in the supply of oil. The tendency of fire is to go out, that's why we need to keep the channels open. In *Pilgrim's Progress*, Bunyan illustrates this when Christian enters the house of Interpreter. Christian saw a fire burning with Satan continually pouring water onto the flames. Christian asked how the fire could keep burning. Interpreter then took him behind the back of the fireplace and showed him Jesus continually pouring oil into the flames. Did not Paul tell us (Eph. 5:18), "be being filled with the Spirit" (literal translation)?

How about it? Are we up to date in our walk with the Spirit? Are we in the oil that will never run dry?

"Give me oil in my lamp, keep me burning,
    Give me oil in my lamp, I pray,
Give me oil in my lamp, keep me burning,
    Keep me burning 'til the break of day."

Rev. John Moyer

Sustaining The Spirit's Flow (3)
Zechariah 4

<u>Our Supply</u>

The supply of oil in this vision of Zechariah is endless, because of the vastness of the Source. The flow of oil comes down to the lamp through golden pipes, which represent the channels of God's grace. The channels must be pure (gold) so that the oil can flow freely. Wiley defines means of grace as "divinely appointed channels through which influences of the Holy Spirit are communicated to the souls of men." Those influences are private and corporate worship, prayer, private and family devotions, preaching, and the sacraments. John Wesley urged people to observe all means of grace until faith came, then to use those same means to maintain and grow in grace. While in Mississippi a few years ago, cold weather brought the threat of freezing water pipes. Spigots were turned on slightly to keep the water flowing because moving water won't freeze as easily. Those who had trouble with water pipes bursting were the ones who did not let the water flow freely and their pipes froze. If the spiritual flow to our souls is shut off we are in danger of freezing up and losing our effectiveness for God.

Our lights will go out if the supply of oil is stopped to us who are dependent on it to be lights in this world. Paul said, "Quench not the Spirit." Building the Kingdom is not a work we can do. We must have the Spirit flowing through us. In times when the Spirit has been poured out, wealth, numbers and influence were given to the Church. But when the supply has been shut off by neglect of the means of grace, the Church tried to continue to do the Lord's work without the Spirit. Without the Spirit all efforts and material equipment fail. With Him, even the weakest are powerful, like the disciples. "The power that compels comes from the Spirit that indwells."

Rev. John Moyer

The Proof of a Sanctified Heart
Matthew 3:10-12; Galatians 5:22-23

There are two things that are essential to an inward and an outward witness of entire sanctification: fire and fruit.

THE EFFECTS OF FIRE ... There has been a renewed emphasis upon the Holy Spirit in our day, and in a rush to be in on what is in, either because of pressure or pride, many claims are being made to the presence and power of the Holy Spirit. As a result, never has such disrepute been brought upon One whose very name and person is "Holy."

John the Baptist said of Jesus, "He shall baptize you with the Holy Ghost and fire." Where there is fire, there is the effect of fire. Fire speaks of His cleansing and His empowering. Our affection is pure, our attitudes are pure, our motives are pure, our witness is pure, because our hearts have been made pure.

This work removes all sham, and fills the heart with truth. This man doesn't need emotionalism, sensationalism, or any other kind of ism, to prove that he has been sanctified wholly. His own heart speaks it for him, even in quietness and in confidence. This is quickly evident to others, for he has the effects of holy fire on him.

THE EVIDENCE OF FRUIT ... The truth about life in the Spirit is that "where the Spirit of the Lord is, there is fruit." Paul wrote, "But the fruit of the Spirit is love, joy, peace, longsuffering, gentleness, goodness, faith, meekness, temperance."

Wesley writes, "Let none ever presume to rest in any supposed testimony of the Spirit which is separate from the fruit of it." And "Let none rest in any supposed fruit of the Spirit without the witness." (*Works*, 5:133 As individuals see evidence of this fruit, they cannot gainsay our testimony. This is our greatest witness to the work and presence of the Holy Spirit: holy fire and holy fruit.

Dr. Hubert Harriman

A Desire For Holiness
Matthew 5:6

Many souls are not experiencing the great work of sanctifying grace because they don't desire it with all their heart.

Mr. Booth said: "God never gave this gift to any human soul who had not come to the point that they would sell all they had to get it."

R.A. Torrey said: "No man ever got this blessing who thought he could get along without it."

Amanda Smith testified: "When I was convicted for holiness I was in a clearly justified state. I had no doubt about my acceptance with God. When I was convicted it was a conviction of guilt; now it was a conviction of want. As a hart panteth after the water brook, so my soul panted after God, the Living God."

God says: "Blessed are they which do hunger and thirst after righteousness, for they shall be filled."

Again Mrs. Booth: "I think it is the most important question that can possibly occupy the mind of man, how much like God can we be? How near to God can we come on earth preparatory to living with Him forever in Heaven?"

The Bible tells us that the disciples tarried ten days, for ten days they hungered and thirsted for righteousness. And, at the end of those ten days, they were filled! They had a desire for holiness.

Friends, until in your soul you sense the importance, the great need for holiness, until it is the desire of your soul, you will never have it.

BUT, if you "hunger and thirst after righteousness," you "shall be filled."

Rev. Rodger Moyer

The Kind Of Religion God Wants Us To Have
Matthew 5:1-12 (verse 8)

The beatitudes are not being handed out randomly as a token of God's generosity. They are, in fact, given to demonstrate the kind of religion God wants us to have.

A HEART RELIGION ... This is not a religion of the head. This is not a religion of the hands. This is not a religion of habit. This is a heart religion: the seat of attention, affection, and ambition. We will never do anything fully, or properly, unless our heart is in it. We are able to discern when someone isn't doing his job right, by stating, "his heart isn't in it." We know that the heart affects performance. That's why God commanded, "Thou shalt love the Lord thy God **with all thine heart**." This cannot be a half-hearted religion. It must be all or nothing.

A HOLY RELIGION ... Blessed are the **pure** in heart. The word "pure" is *katharoi* in Greek. It means to be without admixture, to be clean. This purity is not just outward, it is inward: in the heart. We echo John Wesley's sentiments. "But how little has this purity of the heart been regarded by the false teachers of all ages. They have taught men barely to abstain from such outward impurities as God hath forbidden by name: but they did not strike at the heart . . .."

A HAPPY RELIGION ... John Wesley translates the word "Blessed" as "happy." "Happy are the pure in heart." Because of man's cheap pursuit of happiness, we may shy away from this translation, but, in fact, it is quite accurate. This is a happiness not contingent on outward circumstances, but on an inward state. It is not the goal of our seeking, but the result of our seeking. The goal of our seeking is inward holiness, but the result is certainly inward happiness: happy, "for they shall see God." That's certainly cause for happiness! Friends, we ought to enjoy the blessing of the second blessing!

Dr. Hubert Harriman

Purity of Heart: Essential and Available
Matthew 5:8

Certainly purity of heart isn't essential for everything, but clearly stated in our text, it is essential if one would see God.

The implication is irrefutable: only the pure in heart will see God. Therefore, we should want to know what Jesus means.

The word "pure" means unmixed; without alloy. Alloy is an impairing alien element. In that Jesus has referred to the "pure in heart," we know that this has to do with purity in the inward man, the very seat of one's affections, attitudes, and will.

Of course if one's priority is not God, then this statement by Jesus has no effect. It doesn't startle the heart. But, when God is our priority then purity will be our purpose.

Just from the fact that Jesus stated, "Blessed are the pure in heart." We are assured that there can be such a heart. The mighty implication is that this is available to any man.

This what the heart of every believer desires with intense desire, but our distress is that we keep having things rise up from within our heart that reveal impurity. We no sooner become a Christian than we learn that there is a fountain in our heart that, by its very nature, is sinful. And, since purity of heart means to be without admixture, or without alloy, then what can cleanse us of this deep impairing alien element?

There is a key testimony in relation to this, given by Peter in Acts 15:8-9, "And God which knoweth the hearts ... put no difference between us and them, purifying their hearts by faith." Concerning this, Purkiser says, "the enduring importance of Peter's testimony lies in his clear identification of the effort of Pentecost as purifying or cleansing the hearts of those 'upon' whom the Holy Spirit comes." (*Exploring Christian Holiness*, I:240)

Dr. Hubert Harriman

The Potency Of Purity
Matthew 5:8

Purity and power -- these have long been regarded as the twin benefits of the Pentecostal baptism with the Holy Spirit. (Luke 29:49; Acts 15:8-9) But the longer one understands the nature of heart purity and its attendant consequences, the more one is convinced that purity is power! Power to purify the heart, power to unify the body of Christ, power to qualify for Christian service.

The power of purity is the power of contrast. What a filthy age is this! And for people to be pure in heart, in thought, in motives, in affections, in words and deeds, well, the contrast is convicting to the impure. If proof is needed, practice purity when a story or joke is told. If they are off color, and one doesn't laugh when they are told, the one telling them gets a message loud and clear. Purity is the power of contrast! Amen!

It is also the power of concentration. "Purity of heart is to will one thing." So said the Danish philosopher Soren Kierkegaard. Heart purity is the power of the undivided mind. (James 1:8, 4:8) It is the power of the unclouded eye. (Matt. 5:8, 6:22, 23) It is the power of the unfettered spirit. (Gal. 5:1ff) It is the power of the unashamed hope. (1 Peter 3:15) Purity is the power of concentration! Hallelujah!

It is also the power of consistency. No, the pure heart and holy life are not automatic or reflexive. Yes, some who have once known the beatitude of purity have fallen, some even making shipwreck of the faith. But it need not be, indeed, it should not be. Given the fulfilled work of purging from the law of sin and of death (Romans 7:21-23) there comes a fullness of life and peace (Romans 8:5-7) that makes for stability and serenity, both of which are components of consistency.

So, let's hold our heads high and continue to bear witness to God's gracious and powerful work of heart cleansing, by faith, here and now. Amen.

Dr. Eldon Fuhrman

Happiness And Holiness
Matthew 5:8; 1 Peter 1:15; Hebrews 12:14

The secret of happiness is hidden from a world that seeks it in sense experiences, sensual pleasures, physical and mental stimuli. Sadly, even Christians are tempted to confuse the upbeat feeling they get from certain kinds of music, ritual, preaching, or free expression with genuine happiness.

Jesus said that happiness is found in seeing God in our hearts now and in heaven later, and that the requirement for this is a clean heart.

Happiness and holiness go together like fire and heat; you can't have one without the other. An unholy happiness and an unhappy holiness are both unknown in God's kingdom. Still, many in the church continue a pursuit of happiness while rejecting holiness. Likewise, others continue thinking they are holy, all the time looking as though they are sucking on lemons.

Wisdom lies not in seeking holiness alone, or happiness alone, but in following the words of Jesus. Seek God as your highest happiness and a clean heart where He can live; then you will be always happy in the vision of Him.

Rev. Ken Friesen

Holiness Affects The Nitty-Gritty of Life
Matthew 5:13-16

While preparing for a trip to Africa, I began thinking about my previous visit to Kenya. "Holy Living" was the theme of the class sessions held during revival meeting. As the Lord led, I tried to help people see how holiness relates to their everyday lives. We especially looked at certain cultural practices in the light of scripture, praying they would begin to view these issues from a Biblical perspective. (Holiness is very practical!)

"Restitution" generated a great deal of discussion. God's Word says to make restitution. The people I was working among in Kenya are a very forgiving people and expect others to forgive them. Seldom is restitution made or required. However, since all sin is against God, I can't waive anyone's need to pay back. It is God with whom we are dealing and His Word is clear.

There was much reflection going on when we talked about persons being sacred because God created them. To look down on someone because of his tribe or color is to bring charges against God. (Tribalism is still strong over much of Africa.) A newly saved person may drag some of these feelings along with him for a while, but when our hearts have been cleansed and we've been walking with the Lord a number of years, we begin to see people as Jesus sees them since holiness by definition is being brought into conformity to the image of Christ. His love for them is poured through us.

We looked at subjects such as bribery, handling church money, church attendance, tithing, growth in grace, husband/wife relationships, paying our debts and returning borrowed items. God did some deep work relative to these issues. For you see, holy living will be reflected in all these areas of the African's daily life. Come to think if it, that will be true for us too!

Rev. Nevin Williams

Shaving A Dead Man
Matthew 5:43-48, Romans 12:19-21

My friend, Earl, now walking the streets of Glory, shared with me that a young man, working his way through college, he, for a time, worked in a mortuary. One of his less thrilling jobs was to shave the dead men. It seems that beards don't know enough to stop growing just because we die! They keep right on for several hours, or at least they did back in those days. One day he slipped and cut the fellow quite badly. But you know something? That fellow did not get angry, he didn't say any bad words, and he didn't try to hit Earl. He just kept on smiling, and had no evil reaction!

This is what really frustrates the Devil, and drives him crazy! When he runs into a person who is so truly sanctified that he is dead and will not have carnal reactions, even though, humanly speaking, he would be justified in getting angry. This does not mean that sanctified people no longer have normal human feelings. I think that, in fact, they may be even more deeply hurt because of a tender Spirit-filled heart. But with the carnal reaction gone, that inner hurt will cry out with Steven, "Lord, lay not this sin to their charge." (Acts 7:60)

This can come only following a genuine "Death at the altar" experience that makes it possible for us to "die daily" as we run into those who cut, and bruise, and hurt us. No one in their right mind says this is easy, but (hallelujah!) it is real, and Calvary makes it possible.

Rev. John Kunkle

Holiness In The Lord's Prayer
Matthew 6:5-15

In a recent re-reading of the Lord's Prayer, I was struck by the various phrases and their relationship to holy living. Let me suggest a few.

In v. 9, "hallowed be your name" bears directly on my daily walk. His name is sanctified by my living in a Christ like manner.

The phrase, "your kingdom come" (v. 10), means that I want God to reign supreme in my life. It also means that "my kingship" must cease! Which naturally leads to the rest of v. 10, "your will be done!" That is the cry of every sanctified heart. When God cleanses the heart from all carnal rebellion, we want His will to be carried out just as swiftly and completely as it is in the heavenly realms.

In v. 11 an attitude of complete dependence on God is reflected.

In v. 12 we are reminded of the necessity of a clean heart by the phrase, "Forgive … as we have forgiven." The "root of bitterness" in the unsanctified heart puts one in danger of missing out on God's forgiveness (see vs. 14-15)!

This great prayer ends on a note of victory in v. 13. The cleansed heart will never cease to be tempted, but there is greater power than ever before to be an overcomer!

Dr. Bruce Moyer

The Will Of God
Matthew 6:9-13; Ephesians 5:15-17

When we pray the Lord's Prayer, the only way to avoid hypocrisy in saying "Thy kingdom come" is to say "Thy will be done" – <u>in me</u>.

Unconditional surrender to the total will of God underlies all personal holiness.

I cannot know what the will of the Lord is until I accept in advance His will no matter what it is. You mean, just blindly, sort of like a blind date? I mean, more than that. It's more like a blind date which includes a promise of marriage on the spot.

You see, we don't ask God to give us a trial sample of His will to see how we like it. God doesn't wheedle us into "surrender" by an advertisement, "Examine in your own home for ten days; if not entirely satisfied return without obligation." If God had to show us His will in advance so we would know whether or not we liked it, we would be ruling, not God. We would still be king, and God our Lackey.

Suppose we didn't like it? In that case we would say, "No, thanks, that's not my cup of tea." And go right on being a rebel. Or, suppose we like it, and exclaimed, "That sounds exciting! When do we begin?" We would still be in the saddle, with the Lord our free transportation to where we wanted to go. This is not doing the will of God; it is doing the will of self.

So a deliberate acceptance of the total will of God, now, in advance, unseen and unknown, without hidden strings, is the only way we will ever know God's will for us. This, of course, is an act of faith. It is putting absolute trust in the character and wisdom of God.

Dr. Richard S. Taylor

Godly Treasure Hunting
Matthew 6:19-24

When our now grown daughters were pre-schoolers, a favorite event was the annual community Easter egg hunt. How they enjoyed scrambling for hidden treasures. The Bible in today's lesson speaks of a treasure hunt for God's people. Its importance is illustrated by a pointed story.

A teenager was calling upon her godly grandfather, now confined to a nursing home. She visited him often. In the same nursing home was a lifelong friend of her grandpa – a non-believer. Gradually, she discerned the tremendous difference in how these two men faced each day, their illnesses, the approaching time of earthly departure.

One day she ventured to ask her grandpa's friend why he was always so sad, when her grandpa was always so hopeful. Having been witnessed to about God's grace many, many times, he knew the answer. His reply was clear, "Well dear, your grandpa is about to receive his treasure. I am about to leave mine."

The sanctified heart knows where the treasure is to be buried. And when the treasure is in the right place, the focus of this life is surely put in proper perspective.

Enjoy treasure hunting today!

Dr. John Sills

Getting Our Priorities Straight
Matthew 6:25-33

God has powerful ways of bringing truth to our attention. When we were preparing to return to Africa for a third term of service, our barrels and crates were shipped six months before our departure. All the things we thought we had to have for the next four years plus many things given to us by others were in the shipment. To make a long story short, in four years only two crates showed up in Burundi; one with tires for our truck, which we desperately needed, the other with equipment for welding which we needed for building projects. The other things we thought we just had to have really weren't needed at all.

Jesus says in verse 33 that when we seek first the Kingdom of God and His righteousness, all the truly needed things will be added unto us. How prone we are to reverse that order. We feel we must look out for ourselves, provide for all our needs and even make a place for our desires, after which we fit the Kingdom of God into the leftover corners of our lives.

Now Jesus doesn't expect us to lean back with our hand out and our eyes towards heaven doing nothing. God has given us certain abilities and common sense to work and provide. But He is warning us about the tendency to put our material concerns ahead of our relationship with Him. Our trust is to be in Him, not the things of this world and our ability to provide them.

The Holy Spirit, residing in a clean heart, is able to help us keep the priorities straight. And it takes the Holy Spirit to do it because even if I do it by self-discipline, pride sets in.

As I keep everything surrendered to the Lord, He really does take care of all my needs. We have the problem of sorting out needs from wants. The Spirit has no such problem. We are more valuable than all the rest of creation for which He so marvelously cares. Yes, I can trust Him with the everyday concerns of living.

Rev. Nevin Williams

Of Specks And Planks
Matthew 7: 1-6

In fellowships that exist to proclaim, "the end of the commandment is love from a pure heart," it is distressing to so often encounter a judgmental, condemning, critical spirit. This is the unholy spirit Jesus cautions us to avoid like the plague! He speaks of two problems to be found among God's people.

The problem of the specks. A speck in the eye is an annoyance. It isn't a big thing but it is bothersome. And it needs to be dealt with or it will cause a bigger problem. We all have specks; of immaturity, of infirmity, of disadvantaged opportunity, of personality, and of peculiarity. Any Christian who deems himself to be "speck-less" ought to consult with his brethren!

The problem of the plank. Here is the greater problem Jesus is confronting. This plank or "saw log" is that which is in the eye of the one manifesting a judgmental, condemning, critical spirit toward his brother. This prideful, unloving, unmerciful, self-exalting spirit is nothing other than pure, boiled, concentrated carnality! It is the exact opposite of love from a pure heart. It is quick to throw out to the dogs and the swine those who, in the estimate of God, are "holy" and valuable as "pearls." The old saying "what goes around, comes around" has never been truer; those who continue to throw their brethren to the dogs and swine will some day get torn to pieces by the very same devourers!

Jesus prescribes the remedy for both the specks and the plank: remove it! Abandon efforts to educate it, discipline it, refine it or suppress it. Remove it! Only God's sanctifying work in the heart, cleansing the devilish spirit away and filling it with the love and Spirit of Christ can remove the plank! Then the believer can be of use to his brother in his struggle with his speck.

Rev. Chris Neilson

A Tree Is Known By Its Fruit
Matthew 7:13-23

Some time ago I heard a noted denominational speaker challenge a congregation to "live their religion." I think I know what he meant. He wanted people to truly live a life that was an example of what they professed to believe. That is a very different thing. Most people who attend church profess to be following Christ and obeying His teaching, but their lifestyle is not convincing. Isaiah made a statement about the people of his day; Christ repeated it about the people of His day; and the very same is evident today: "This people draw near me with their mouth, and with their lips do honor me, but have removed their heart far from me." This truth was evident from their lifestyle and actions.

Across our land on Sunday morning our churches are pretty well filled, but on Sunday night, if they have a service at all, there will be less than half of the morning attendance. If they have a mid-week prayer meeting there will be only a handful. This is far from the "hungering and thirsting after righteousness" that God promises to bless and satisfy. Something else has taken first place – something that will satisfy the flesh. Jesus made it very clear that the material needs for our life would be supplied if we keep in first place "the Kingdom of God and His righteousness." To have His Kingdom established in our hearts, all that is carnal and at enmity against Him must be cleansed away.

When our hearts are in harmony with God's perfect will, our actions will verify it. We will "worship the Lord in Spirit and in truth" and "in the beauty of holiness." David said, "As the hart panteth after the water brooks, so panteth my soul after thee, O God. My soul thirsteth for God, for the living God." Some may fail for lack of knowledge, but for most it is failure to have a clean heart, filled with the Holy Spirit.

Rev. Marshal Cavit

After The Crisis
"Learn of me."
Matthew 11:23-30; Ephesians 4:1-2

Have you enrolled in the school of the Master Teacher? You have responded to His invitation: "Come … and I will give you rest." You can sing: "Now rest, my long divided heart; fixed on this blissful center, rest." Thus you have begun a great adventure with God. Now follows the life-long process of learning how to maintain this relationship.

Hear His invitation. "Take my yoke … learn of me!" The Lord of all creation offers to be your partner and teacher – not by telling you of His great works, but by showing you what He is: "For I am meek and lowly of heart." In sanctifying grace He has imparted His nature to you. Now He desires to teach you how to manifest His Spirit of meekness and humility, resisting temptations to harbor resentment, pride, etc.

At every turn of the road He is there to teach those who seek Him. Are you facing difficult, life-changing decisions? Are you over-anxious about the unknown tomorrows, tempted to resent seeming injustices, baffled by fellow Christians' inconsistencies? Are you tempted to be destructively critical? Do you have problems with relationships?

Do not allow these testings to overwhelm you. Take time to sit at Jesus' feet, as Mary did (Luke 10:39), feed on His word and learn of Him. How much grief could be spared, how much conflict resolved, if every true believer would heed His invitation to learn of Him, facing with meekness and humility each day's demands!

Dear Lord, keep me in the grace of teachableness – edifying fellow Christians and effectively witnessing to the lost. Amen.

Mrs. Susan (Schultz) Rose

Who's Running The Show?
Matthew 12:25-26

Ruth and I served as missionaries in Bolivia for four years. During those four years we saw at least four changes of government. We never knew for sure who was "running the show." No one was to be trusted. A president's "faithful" military leader might be the one who overthrew him the next day. This, of course, led to a great deal of instability and turmoil. Laws passed by one government might be reversed by a new one the next week. Government simply was not trustworthy. In fact, it was difficult to find anyone who trusted anyone.

In Mathew 12 we find Jesus addressing the problem of "a divided house." It's the same old "Who's running the show?" syndrome. James repeats the same idea when he says that a double-minded man is "unstable in all he does." (James 1:8)

The carnal heart is a divided heart and is, therefore, unstable. It can't be trusted. At times it is quite content to let God "run the show." But moments will come when it must simply have its own way. The result is spiritual instability and that always results in a lack of trust. God simply cannot trust the carnal Christian to be dependable. For that reason He has designed a remedy. The double-minded man is to seek God for a pure heart. (James 4:8) It is the only remedy, and it is the only method for establishing stability and trust.

"Lord, make me clean, and make me one - a stable, trustworthy servant, which you can use!"

Dr. Bruce Moyer

Hey, What's That On Your Lips?
Matthew 12:33-37

"Hey, what's that on your lips?" That's a pretty embarrassing question to hear, isn't it? Immediately the napkin comes out and you start cleaning. It reminds me of one of my favorite childhood pictures. I was about two or three years old. Mom had made spaghetti for dinner. There I was, in my high chair, spaghetti (especially the sauce) everywhere but in my mouth. No one needed to ask what I had been doing, it was rather obvious!

In today's passage Jesus also addresses the question about what's on our lips. What we say becomes an important matter when we realize that we will be judged for the words we have spoken. That is why James says we should be "slow to speak." (James 1:19) He also goes on to say, as Jesus does in Matthew 12, that holiness is vital to the matter of controlling what graces our lips. "For out of the overflow of the heart the mouth speaks." (Matt. 12:34; compare James 3:1-2)

This is one of the things that makes Christian holiness so practical. What's in our heart will be expressed on our lips. And, just as with the spaghetti, no one will have to ask what's there, it will become rather obvious. Sanctified discernment will help us to be "slow to speak." Even in moments of human frailty, when something is spoken that is better left unsaid, the cleansed heart will immediately follow the leading of the Spirit to correct the matter.

Prayer: "May the words of my mouth and the
meditation of my heart be pleasing in your sight,
O Lord, my Rock and my Redeemer." (Psalm 19:14)

Dr. Bruce Moyer

The Loaves And Fishes
Matthew 14:13-21

In our scripture we read of a very distressing situation, a wearied multitude, numbering well above five thousand, that had followed Jesus all day long; and a perplexed, slightly disturbed band of disciples who wished Jesus would dismiss the meeting so the people could go into the villages and get something to eat.

But, instead of complying with their wishes He simply told them to "give them something to eat." What an astounding reply! The truth is they had nothing whatsoever, and only one small lad had five loaves and two fishes. Yet, by the power of Christ, this became the means through which Jesus fed the hungry multitude – and filled 12 baskets full, one for each of the impatient disciples.

So often Christ takes the small things in life and uses it to bless the multitudes. Paul saw this and wrote, "God chose the foolish things of the world to shame the wise; God chose the lowly things of this world and the despised things – and the things that are not – to nullify the things that are; so that no one may boast before Him." (1 Cor. 2:27-29)

When God wanted a leader He went to the backside of the desert and chose a sheepherder to deliver His people from bondage of the Egyptian nation. When God chose a king over Israel He refused the expected ones, and went out into the fields to find a boy named David whose heart was perfect toward Him. When God selected foundation stones upon which to build His church, He walked along the Sea of Galilee and chose fisherman. When God started the modern missionary movement He went to the shoe cobbler's workbench and tapped William Carey on the shoulder.

One could go on and on with the recounting of how amazing God works. But, the great and wonderful truth is that when any life is wholly put in His wonderful hands, He takes it, breaks it, blesses it, and distributes it to the hungry world. He uses the yielded life!

Dr. Gerald Dillon

Renouncing Ungodliness
Matthew 16:21-28

In almost all protestant denominations we are asked to take certain vows as we unite with the church. One of these vows has to do with our manner of life in following Christ.

In my church it reads as follows: "Do you promise to renounce all ungodliness, to follow Christ, to diligently make use of the means of grace and sincerely seek the advancement of the Kingdom of God?" Let us note what we are promising.

"To renounce all ungodliness." Everything that man does or that which is within him that is contrary to God's will can be safely determined as ungodliness. In our salvation through Jesus Christ, there has taken place a change in many of the things we do, so that we are now living for Him. Scripture indicates that there is within man, "a bent to sinning." ("Love Divine" by Charles Wesley)

So, as we promise "to renounce all ungodliness," it would include seeking the fullness of God through Jesus Christ by cleansing and infilling with the Holy Spirit. For that carnal nature within us is contrary to God's will for us and must and can be eradicated through the provision made by Jesus Christ on Calvary. In promising to "renounce all ungodliness" we are saying that we will seek and pray for the death (Crucifixion) of carnal self, the cleansing of the heart and the infilling of the Holy Spirit.

When this is done, "to follow Christ" can more easily be done for we are totally His. (Matt. 16:24) "Making diligent use of the means of grace" now becomes a delight (Bible reading, prayer, church attendance, etc.). The advancement of the Kingdom will take place for with the Psalmist we can say, "I delight to do Thy will, O God!"

Rev. David Weinert

What Will A Man Give?
Matthew 16: 21-28

One day it occurred to me what Jesus asked in v. 26, "What shall a man give in exchange for his soul?" Give? Yes, that is exactly what Jesus asked!

The Devil is good at reminding us how much we have to "give up" to be a Christian. Yet, when one considers it, we have to give up everything when we leave this world. Paul wrote, "For we brought nothing into this world, and it is certain we can carry nothing out." (1 Tim. 6:7) Since this is true, the real question is when and to whom will we give? If we wait until death, when our earthly existence is no more, there is no virtue in that! All will do that with or without God. Also, people give a lot to be happy -- for pleasures, for the "good things of life." Tragically, this giving to self is also in vain.

Jesus' instruction to his disciples applies to us today. "If any man will come after me, let him deny (give) himself, and take up his cross, and follow me." Verse 25 reinforces this thought, "For whosoever will lose his life for my sake shall find it."

Only if you and I "give" ourselves, and allow the "Old Man" to be put to death on our personal cross, can we ever follow Christ in this life or into eternity.

Isn't it interesting? We all must give! Only those who recognize and gladly give ALL to Him NOW in this life receive God and His blessings both here and in eternity!

Rev. Stephen Burkhart

Christ's Minimum Requirements
Matthew 16:24-26

What are the "minimum requirements of Christ?"

1. "Let him deny himself". Sounds kind of simple doesn't it? But are you living it? It means I'm always putting God's will above my own. It means truly putting Christ first; He is truly Ruler and King of my life. It means that, if there is a conflict between His will and my will, His will wins out. Now it doesn't sound so simple does it?

Who wins in your life? Are you denying yourself? Is God first when the easy chair and TV come in conflict with the Wednesday night prayer service, or the revival meeting? What about when family or friends want you to do something besides go to church on Sunday? You're not meeting the minimum requirement of Christ if God is not first.

2. "You must take up YOUR cross." Back in Jesus' day if you went to the cross you weren't expected to come back. It was an instrument of death. Jesus died on it, Peter died on it, and we must take up our cross and die on it.

This cross isn't "a cross" of sickness, bearing pain, putting up with sinful people, or going through tough times. It is death to carnality, the old man within the soul! Paul said "I am crucified with Christ, nevertheless I live, yet not I, but Christ liveth in me." Friends there has to be a crucifixion before there can be a glorious resurrection.

3. "Follow me." You've denied yourself, you've taken up your cross and died to all that is sinful in your soul, now you must continue to walk with Jesus. Down the road things will come up that will test you. Friends will come, family will come, but you have to continue to mind God. If you don't you will lose your soul!

These are "Christ's Minimum Requirements," not options or extras. Thank God He has provided grace sufficient to experience all this and more!

Rev. Rodger Moyer

Deficiency In The Midst Of Abundance!
Matthew 19:16-22

When compared with most people of the world the majority of Americans are clearly rich people. We are rich financially, with gadgets, electronics, appliances, etc. But we have also been rich in another way – the Gospel, especially those of us that have been raised attending church regularly.

This young man in our text parallels too closely to many today! To look on this man outwardly, there are few preachers that wouldn't consider him a real asset to their congregation. He kept all of the laws that Jesus originally mentioned (vs. 18-19), but not being satisfied in his soul he still asked, "What lack I yet?"

Jesus faithfully told him the solution just as He will do today, v. 21, "If thou wilt be perfect, go and sell that thou hast, and give to the poor, and thou shalt have treasure in heaven: and come and follow me."

How many in our churches today are rich? They maybe work as S.S. teacher, or trustee, or song leader, etc. hearing the truths of the Gospel preached service after service but yet are not perfected in holiness. Christ's answer has not changed. It's still true today "Go and sell that thou hast …" Consecrate your "all," allow the Holy Spirit to cleanse you and "all these things shall be added unto you." Our "possessions" are not worth our opportunity of being cleansed from carnality and being filled with His Spirit. It's not worth missing His blessing and discipleship each and every day of our lives. But finally, "riches" are not worth missing heaven eternally, forever separated from Christ's splendor and glory! Don't be "deficient" when you can have Christ's "abundance!"

Rev. Stephen Burkhart

Are You Unemployed?
Matthew 20:1-16

We hear a lot these days about unemployment. I live in a town that has much of it and it's really a sad situation. People are out of work, businesses are closing, families are out on the streets, and it's appalling! But when we turn to the church world, the unemployment situation is even more appalling!

If we go to the average church we find only a few who actively participate in its work. Most are idle. A few do all the work. A few do all the giving. A few bear all the responsibilities. A few carry the burden of prayer, calling, and witnessing. And few attend all services during revivals. It's appalling!

Now it is easy to see why unemployment exists in society, not enough work. But that doesn't help us to account for the unemployment in the church; there is plenty to be done. Christ said, "The harvest truly is great."

Never-dying souls about us are heading to hell forever! "Why stand ye here all the day idle?" What about on your street, at your job, and in your school? Are you one of the many who are idle?

There is no lack of work! There is no lack in God's grace and power to give us strength and courage to do the task! There is no lack of knowledge about the dying soul! What then is the lack?

There is only one way we can account for this lack of love, concern and the abundant disinterest and idleness; there are many within our churches who yet need to be converted themselves! Friend, are you unemployed? Are you idle? If so you need to renew through repentance and faith your relationship with the Lord. Will you do it today?

Rev. Rodger Moyer

Proof-Texting The Christian
Matthew 22:34-40; John 14:23

Occasionally some people attempt to Biblically document a pet theory or idea by one or more "proof-texts." Fortunately, the genuine needs no such search for a Biblical base; it flows throughout the Scripture. Biblical documentation for a valid holiness life-style is easily found.

When asked the identity of the most important commandment of all, Jesus summarized the whole law of God. He said that, if a person professed to be completely and unquestionable committed to God … one with a holy heart, it would be evidenced by an all-embracing love appropriately directed toward God, others, and self.

But how easily one may testify to loving God! Who knows? How can love be measured? Where or what is the proof? Jesus did not simply state: "Here's the proof – just love God with all your heart, soul, and mind." He gave us the "proof-texts!" John carefully stated that love for God is proved by obedience

And to further clarify what it means to fulfill that all-important, number one commandment, John wrote that we can know we love God when that love is transformed into actions that meet the legitimate needs of others. (1 John 2:3-5; 5:2-3; 3:16-18)

In other words, holiness is evidenced by obedience! Holiness of heart and life is loving God with the entirety of one's being, and that love is proved when we obey God's commandments. And to obey God's commandments is to act to meet the legitimate needs of one's self and each Biblically significant neighbor. For God's commands are His enablings. He will never assign a responsibility – love-in-action – apart from showing us how and when to do it, and will add to that the enabling wisdom and strength to fulfill His command! By this the validity of one's holiness meets the test of the Biblical "proof-texts!"

Dr. Robert Morris

Who Are You?
Matthew 23:23-28

Just the other day I was picking up a few items in our local Wal-Mart store. As I stood looking at a display, a man nearby kindly said, "Hi, how ya doin'?" I had no idea who he was but I responded, "Fine, thanks." Then apparently after he had taken a second look, he said, "Sorry, you're not who I thought you were." We parted ways, probably with both of us a bit embarrassed. On the way home from the store I reflected on the incident and the question began to take on spiritual significance. In the passage we read for today, Jesus had some tough words of warning for the Pharisees because they weren't who they pretended to be – they were hypocrites. What they were on the inside didn't match up to what they pretended to be on the outside.

One of the key words for "holiness" in the New Testament carries the root idea of sincerity. It means that, when an item is examined in the sunlight, it is found to be clean. It is transparent and is seen to be clear all the way through. Paul's prayer for the Philippians was that they would be pure (without hypocrisy) until Jesus returned. (Phil. 1:10) He could testify to the Corinthians that he had conducted himself among them in holiness and sincerity (purity without hypocrisy, 2 Cor. 1:12).

How sad to see people who have known the saving and sanctifying grace of God but have failed to keep that relationship up-to-date. Hypocrisy begins to take over and, sooner or later, someone will end up saying, "Sorry, you're not who I thought you were!"

So ... who are you?

"Oh to be like Thee! Oh to be like Thee!
Blessed Redeemer, Pure as Thou art!"

Dr. Bruce Moyer

Holiness Gone Sour
Matthew 23:23-33

Many years ago I took some correspondence Bible courses from Vennard College that were written by Dr. Harry Jessop. In the course on the Gospels he compared the Scribes to the modernists of today who deny the miracles of God's Word. Then he went on to compare the Pharisees to the holiness movement of today "gone sour." This is food for thought to us who profess holiness of heart and lives.

Let us examine exactly what Jesus was seeing in the Pharisees that brought His most scathing remarks.

First, they were careful to obey God's call to tithing but neglected to care for the needy – even their own parents. They paid their tithes but apparently did not give the love offerings.

Second, they cleansed the outside by forsaking bad habits but their hearts were full of "greed and self-indulgence" (NIV).

Third, He says that their outward appearance was clean and white but inside they were dead. The life they once knew was gone. What a warning! They had the form of religion but denied the power thereof.

Perhaps the message for us of the modern day holiness movement is that we make sure our hearts are clean and pure and then the outside demonstration will manifest that purity. (v. 26) Notice in verse 23, He says we should practice the tithing and the clean life but we should be sure this is coming from a heart filled with love, justice, mercy, and faithfulness. Lord, help us not to become Pharisees!

Mrs. Clarice Moyer

If I Had My 'Druthers'
Matthew 26:36-46

I'm too young to know where the phrase "If I had my 'druthers'" originated. In fact, I don't know that I've even heard anyone use it in daily conversation. Wondering if "druthers" is even a word, I went to the dictionary – one of those big, unabridged editions with over 2,000 notebook-size pages that weighs about ten pounds. I could hardly believe it, but there was "druthers" about halfway down the third column on page 438! It is defined as an alteration of "would rather" meaning "one's own way, choice, or preference."

I don't suppose that the word "druthers" had been invented yet in Jesus' day – but the concept was. And it seems likely to me that had "druthers" existed back then, Matthew 26:39 might read something like: "If I had my 'druthers,' Father, I'd do it another way – nevertheless, I'll gladly do it your way." You see, when God sanctifies us, He does not remove our ability to desire and decide. Even Jesus – holy, perfect, and sinless as He was – because He was human, could desire an easier way. And, He did not hesitate to express this to the Heavenly Father. The important thing is that Jesus did not argue with the Father, and that when it came to the point of decision – He obeyed, willingly.

That is what God does for us in sanctification. Although we may still see an easier way – that is, we may have our "druthers," and we might even express that to God in intimate prayer – when it comes to the point of decision, we have already committed ourselves to glad obedience and He has cleansed from our hearts the spirit of choosing our "druthers" over His perfect will and way. Glory!

Dr. Bruce Moyer

Go! Wait!
Matthew 28:18-28; Acts 1:4-8; Acts 13:1-3

It began for the disciples on the mountain in Galilee. Jesus said, "Go!" He would say it to His people again in many places in various ways. He said, "Go" to Paul and Barnabas, to Paul and Silas, to Timothy, and to thousands more. He always wants us to "go" into the world and preach, teach, heal, comfort, confront, or whatever is needed to build His church and to extend His kingdom.

"GO," however, is only one of His commands. After He told the disciples to go, He told them to "wait." That's the way it always was. That's the way it always is. Read the book of Acts, and you will see.

Going must always be preceded by waiting, for the waiting means power to go. That was the meaning of Pentecost for the disciples. They were powerless to go in the way Jesus intended. They needed to wait first for the purifying, power-giving presence of the Holy Spirit.

In waiting, our motives are sifted: "Why do I want to go?" Our message is clarified: "What shall I say?" Our spirit is strengthened: "You shall receive power." Waiting always means that the going will be successful.

In any going, begin by waiting. You will go in the power of the Spirit.

Rev. Ken Friesen

All These Evils Come From Inside
Mark 7:14-23

Again, as part of my "once-a-year" gardening venture, I tackled that small plot of ground we can call a "garden." Sometimes, I think of it as a "ranch" when I'm good and tired with muscles aching and hands cramping. Anyway, it was just a year ago I tackled the same job and spent umpteen hours (minutes) getting ready for our new seeds. This meant the weeds - with their roots – had to come out. What a mess! What a job! But, I knew that if I left the roots in, they would come up pronto. In fact, I even wrote a devotional about "roots and all."

Now, a year later, I find the roots are back! Evidently, my job wasn't thorough last year. So, this spring they all start growing at once. Do you see any similarity between my garden and our lives? Evidently, Jesus did.

Jesus said, "For from within, out of the heart of man proceed" a whole bunch of "weeds", sins, or whatever, and they "defile" the life. The writer of Hebrews admonishes us (Hebrews 12:15) to "see to it that … no bitter root grows up to cause trouble." He mentions other roots that can spring into life and cause trouble – sexual immorality, covetousness that lives for the moment, and numerous other weeds are mentioned.

Life springs from the heart – the innermost sanctuary of our souls! If life is to be clean, pure, and wholesome, the heart must be cleansed and kept pure. Thank God for His great provision of grace whereby the heart can have the weeds removed. The last vestiges of the carnal mind ("enmity against God," Romans 8:7) must be removed.

So, let us "keep the heart with all diligence for out of it are the issues of life." (Proverbs 7:23) "Blessed are the pure in heart for God has poured out His love into their hearts by the Holy Spirit whom He has given us." Praise the Lord.

Dr. Gerald Dillon

A Snakebite and an Instant Cure
Mark 9:43-48

A German man, who had moved to Bolivia many years ago, settled out in the jungle area, not far from where we later lived. In those days there were no automobiles, planes or medical attention. One day while chopping wood, as he reached for a nearby limb, he was instantly bitten on the end of his index finger by an extremely poisonous snake. Like a flash this man put his finger on the chopping block, and cut it off with his axe, as close to his hand as possible. He knew his drastic need demanded a drastic solution. There was no doctor, no way to get to a doctor, and no anti-venom, closer than 150 miles away. It was harsh treatment, but it saved his life. What a man!

This is the only way our sin problem can be taken care of. On the cross Jesus provided instant forgiveness, and instant cleansing too. Some think we have to struggle on and on in our own strength until we get ourselves "good enough" to be saved or sanctified. It does not work, and never will. I am reminded of the man who wanted to cut a puppy dog's tail off. He couldn't bring himself to just cut the whole thing off at once. He said, "Why that would be terrible, to cut the whole thing off at one blow. I'll just cut off about an inch each day." The problem was that after the second day he never could catch the pup again to cut off another inch!

Jesus wants to set us free at once. The Philippian Jailor cried out, "Sirs, what must I do to be saved?" And they said unto him, "Believe on the Lord Jesus Christ, and thou shalt be saved, and thy house." (Acts 16:30-31) No inch at a time deal, but God's instant work of grace met the need!

Rev. John Kunkle

Christian Ambition (1)
Mark 10:35-41

Is ambition a vice or a virtue? Is it good or bad? Is it to be cultivated or rejected?

Ambition is usually defined as, "An eager desire for the attainment of honor, fame, wealth, prestige or power." An ambitious man is thought of as one who goes all out to get what he wants and what he wants is generally some form of advancement.

An athlete wants to win an Olympic Gold Medal and the fame that goes with it. Consequently everything in life bends to the achievement of that goal. A businessman is ambitious for success, to make money. He devotes his time and energy to building his business. That takes first place in his life. A politician wants the prestige and power of public office and promises whatever pleases his constituents in order to get elected. James and John apparently felt the stirrings of ambition when they asked Jesus for the places of honor in His coming kingdom. (Mark 10:35-37)

Ambition is unquestionably a powerful force in human society. Does it have a place in a Christian's life? Or is it wholly bad? The Greek word for "ambition" occurs three times in the New Testament. (Rom. 15:20; 2 Cor. 5:9; 1 Thess. 4:11) Twice Paul claims to be ambitious; once he exhorts others to be ambitious. Ambition in Paul, however, was not a strong desire for personal advancement. He may have felt that way once as a rising star in Judaism, but Paul the Christian was not self-centered. He was completely Christ-centered. And that made a world of difference.

Dr. Hollis Abbott

Ambition and Preaching the Gospel (2)
Romans 15:14-21

It was Paul's ambition to preach the Gospel of Christ. He says, "It has always been my ambition to preach the Gospel where Christ was not known." (Rom. 15:20, NIV) In other passages he says he was EAGER to preach; (Rom. 1:15) he was CALLED to preach; (Gal. 1:15-16) he was SENT to preach; (1 Cor, 1:17) and he felt that he MUST preach the Gospel of Christ. (1 Cor. 9:16)

Note how Paul's ambition had changed. Once he was a persecutor of the Christians with a burning desire to destroy the church. (Acts 8:3; 9:1-2) Now, however, we see him as a preacher of the Gospel, a builder of what he once tried to destroy. Why? Because he had a life-transforming encounter with Jesus Christ and his life had been completely turned around. The persecutor had become a preacher.

Paul was also ambitious to be a pioneer preacher, to proclaim the Gospel where it had not yet been heard. He tells us in Romans 15:19 that he had fully proclaimed the Gospel in the eastern provinces of the Roman Empire; now he says he wants to go to Spain (Rom. 15:24, 28) in the western part of the Empire. Interestingly enough this is the only reference to Spain in the Bible. It appears because a pioneer preacher had it on his heart.

Many who read this devotional will say, "God has not called me to be a preacher, pastor, evangelist, or missionary." However you can still be a proclaimer of the Gospel, a witness in the school where you teach, the office where you work or the business in which you are involved. Many in our own land have never heard a vital Christian testimony; have never seen a truly transformed, Spirit-filled life. You can reach into areas where a pastor/preacher cannot. You, too, can be a proclaimer of the Gospel. Is that your ambition?

Dr. Hollis Abbott

Ambitious To Be A Body Builder (3)
1 Thessalonians 4:9-12

Paul's third use of the word "ambition" is found in 1 Thessalonians 4:11, "Make it your ambition to lead a quite life, to mind your own business and to work with your hands." (NIV) This is really quite a striking exhortation. Ordinary ambition seeks to be seen and heard, that is to be VISIBLE and VOCAL. Paul says, "Be ambitious to be quiet."

To understand the significance of the exhortation we need to be aware of a problem in the Thessalonian church. Apparently some had misunderstood Paul's teaching on the Second Coming of Christ. They thought His Coming was so imminent there was no need to keep busy with their regular work, to carry on with normal activities. As a result instead of being busy they became busybodies, that is, instead of being occupied with their own work and household responsibilities, they got involved in other people's affairs. They were minding everybody's business but their own. This always leads to tension and conflict within the Body of Christ and results, further, in a negative witness to the world. There is nothing attractive about a group of people who spend their time meddling in each other's affairs.

Two reasons for obeying Paul's exhortation are given in verse 12. 1) Instead of discrediting the Christian faith, they would win the respect of people who were not Christians, and 2) they could earn enough money to pay their own bills and therefore would not need to depend on others. (Note Paul's statement in 2 Thessalonians 3:10, very appropriate for today)

The purpose of Paul's exhortation then is to encourage people to so live that the Body of Christ is built up and not torn down.

Dr. Hollis Abbott

Ambition and Pleasing Christ (4)
2 Corinthians 5:9-11

Paul was not just attached to a CAUSE, the cause of preaching the Gospel; he was supremely attached to a PERSON. He says next that his ambition was to please the person of Christ, "So we make it our goal to please Him . . .." (NIV). We could very well use the word "ambition" instead of "goal" for that is the meaning of the term.

This involves a very basic choice. Whom shall we please? We are born with a powerful bias in favor of pleasing ourselves. Human relationships are very real, very demanding. We want to please people – family, friends, employer, etc. But pleasing God should have top priority. Paul had made his choice: Christ first.

Why should pleasing Christ take top priority? First, because we love Him. (vs. 14-15) We have a personal relationship with Him and want more than anything else to live the kind or life that pleases Him. Second, because we represent Him. We are His ambassadors and an ambassador does not do his own thing but speaks on behalf of the one who sent him. Third, we want His approval. We want His approval NOW. Therefore when He speaks, we obey. When He reveals His will, we do it. Nothing can compare with the inner sense of well being which comes when we know we have pleased God.

We also want His approval THEN, that is, on the Day of Judgment. Note carefully verse 10, "For we must all appear before the judgment seat of Christ . . .." When we face Him at the judgment it is His approval that is decisive. How good it will be to hear the "well done" of the Lord.

To please Christ is a worthy ambition. How do we reach this point where Christ is absolutely first? By surrendering fully to His Lordship and then by walking in step with Him day by day. (Rom. 12:1; Gal. 5:25)

Is pleasing Christ your ambition?

Dr. Hollis Abbott

On Wells And Buckets
Mark 12:24-34

"What's in the well comes up in the bucket."

Haven't you heard that? Many times?

But, you ask, is <u>that</u> in the Bible? Of course! Several times! Well, the meaning is there, as we shall see presently.

My thoughts return to a well just a few feet east of the front porch at my grandparent's home. There was an open well with a bucket and a long chain and a windlass to unwind and let the bucket down for water or wind it up and bring it to the surface. And, sure enough, what was in the well came up in the bucket – good, clean, cold, fresh water. Oh, it tasted so refreshing.

Of course, if the well had been polluted, the water in the bucket would have been too. Isn't that logical?

But what about the Scripture? It says that out of the heart are the issues of life. (Proverbs 4:23) Again, it says that as a man thinketh in his heart, so is he. (Proverbs 23:7) And Jesus said, "out of the abundance of the heart the mouth speaketh." These, and other references, tell that the heart is the <u>wellspring</u>, the <u>fountain</u>, (James 3:11), the <u>source</u> and the origin of our outer lives, in thinking, in speaking, in acting, in all our motivations. Surely it follows, then, that whatever is in the heart, whether evil (Mark 7:21) or good (Matthew 12:33) will give moral color and quality to all of life.

Thus, by now we see the importance of heart purity (Matthew 5:8) and of the pure, humble love of Christ flooding the heart and flowing through the life. (Mark 12:24-34) So I turn again to read, "The end of the commandment is charity (love) out of a pure heart . . .." (1 Timothy 1:5) I am convinced, "What's in the well comes up in the bucket." What's coming up in your bucket?

Dr. Eldon Fuhrman

The Extravagance Of Love
Mark 14:3-9

Some months ago, I had the opportunity to tour the homes on what is billed "The Street of Dreams" in Portland. These are brand new homes that are open to the public before their occupancy. They are to be examples of the finest in architecture, materials, and craftsmanship, and are filled with what latest technology has to offer. I remember that the master bedroom suite in one of homes was almost as large as most of the homes that I am acquainted with. The price tags were really beyond my comprehension.

A few months later, I attended an Auto Show for the first time. I noticed several cars with $100,000+ price tags. I couldn't afford to buy a house at that price, so extravagance came to mind with the thought of buying one of those cars.

From the viewpoint of others, however, I imagine that all of us have some extravagances in our lives. If we look carefully, we will find that these extravagances have to do with things or people we love.

The woman in our passage today was thought by some to be extravagant, because she broke that alabaster vial and devoted its costly contents to Jesus, but notice that Jesus said the deed she had done was good.

It seems to me that the world accepts extreme devotion to sports ("fans"), but not extreme devotion to Christ ("fanatics"). In fact, I have come to believe that Satan will promote just about any and every extravagance except the extravagant love for Christ.

What we should not miss is that God is the best example of extravagant love. Does God really love us? Jesus, the best that God had, was broken and spilled out for us. "For God so loved the world, that He gave His only begotten Son, that whosoever believes in Him should not perish, but have eternal life." (NASB)

Rev. Glen Boring

I Don't Like Surprises
Mark 14:43-52

One of our country's premier holiness preachers was Morton Dorsey. He used to tell of a time when he so envied his grade school chums who had the measles. No going to school, no homework, no chores – to have the measles was to enjoy a grand vacation. So he thought – until the day he was so favored. True, there were benefits, but there were inconveniences as well. And, as he told it, the latter out numbered the former by far: confinement, medicine, no playtime and, of course, the physical discomfort itself. So one day he said to his mother, "If I'd a known it was going to be like this I sure never would a wished to have the measles!"

I suppose that is what the disciples were thinking as they fled the scene of our Lord's arrest: "If I'd known it was going to be like this I would have never have become a disciple."

This was not their first rude awakening; they who had envisioned a place of prominence in an earthly kingdom among God's favored people. Rejection, oppositions, sacrifice, poverty, persecution and now the arrest of their Leader would compel them to lament, "I sure didn't expect discipleship to turn out this way!"

And that is a common complaint among the sanctified – we just thought living the life of holiness would be a lot more comfortable than it has turned out to be. It is a case of conjured images being replaced by concrete realities. And it is a rude awakening.

But God knew all about the events ahead of you when He sanctified your heart. Indeed, holiness is His loving provision for all grace for all situations. Holiness people are not conquered by their circumstances – it is their victory in every situation which is their most effective witness.

PRAYER: "Dear Lord, I'm glad you are in charge and that is my confidence for this day. Amen."

Dr. Merne Harris

Advent Fruit
Luke 1:67-79 (vs. 74-75)

In a day when so many professions of faith seem to make so little difference, it is refreshing to be instructed by the spiritual understanding of Zacharias as he pours out his praise to God. Through the Holy Spirit he recognizes that the glorious redemption that God was providing would result in wonderful fruit.

The commandment to be holy did not originate with Peter in 1 Peter 1:15. Holiness was God's requirement for all of Israel as seen in Lev. 19:2, and the nature of holy living as described in the remainder of that chapter. In fact, we learn in Eph. 1:4-5 that God's intention for His people before the foundation of the world was that they should be holy and blameless before Him.

Now, with marvelous spiritual clarity, Zacharias recognizes that what God has required, He is providing. The fruit of the redemption that Zacharias heralds is that we "might serve Him without fear, in holiness and righteousness before Him all our days."

Even though our righteousness is as filthy rags, Advent leads us to the One in whom we can live and serve in holiness and righteousness all our days.

What wonderful fruit! "Holiness" suggests the Godward and "righteousness" suggests the manward aspects of our conduct, or from another perspective, "holiness" may relate to the inner life and "righteousness" to the outward walk.

At any rate, this glorious fruit is to be enjoyed now. It is not just for what my grandparents called, "state days and holidays," and it is not just reserved for some time way off in the future. It is for all our days. I want to be sure to enjoy Advent fruit now – and always.

Rev. Glen Boring

How To Be Like The Master
Luke 1:74-75

Jesus gives the unerring rule for holy living; "Except your righteousness shall exceed the righteousness of the scribes and Pharisees, ye shall in no case enter in the kingdom of heaven." (Matt. 5:20) The religion of the Pharisees was outward show. Christ begins the work of saving grace by the regeneration of the heart. The sinful heart can be renovated, renewed, and made fit for the indwelling of the Holy Spirit. When the Spirit comes in, a new life begins.

A minister, watching a man tune an organ, asked the question, "How do you tune so many pipes so perfectly?" The answer was simple: "I tune every pipe to a perfect middle C." Friend, is your life tuned with the teaching of Jesus Christ? If it is, there will be fewer false notes and less discord!

There are trends among professed Christians, which should be avoided at all costs. Protect the soul against complacency and laxity. The sin of being at ease in Zion is luring far too many into forbidden paths which lead away from God. To keep blest and follow in the stage of Jesus, keep a constant vigil and a tender conscience, with Jesus always in full view!

When Mr. Hudson, the great missionary, was forced to retire, due to sickness, his wife sought to encourage him by reading some clippings from the newspaper, which compared him to Peter and Paul. This annoyed him, and he said, "Wife, I don't want to be like Peter or Paul; I want to be like Jesus!" Ah, my friend, may this be our earnest prayer!

"Be like Jesus, this is my song.
In the home and in the throng:
Be like Jesus, all day long;
I would be like Jesus." (James Rowe)

Rev. Gene Moyer

The Right Place
Luke 2:41-49

Jesus thought it incredible that Mary and Joseph had not known where to find Him. "Why is it that you were looking for Me? Did you not know that I had to be in My Father's house?" (Luke 2:49, NASB) Evidently they had wasted a lot of time looking when they should have known where to find Him. Before we feel too superior, however, maybe we ought to examine our own practice more carefully.

God is not playing some kind of hide and seek game with us. Jesus told His disciples where He would be after the resurrection, and He has told us, "For where two or three have gathered together in My name, there I am in their midst." (Matt. 18:20, NASB) If you are looking for Jesus, you will find Him wherever two or three have gathered in His name. Could it be that this is why the writer of Hebrews says that we should not forsake our own assembling together? Jesus is still found in His Father's house.

A.W. Tozer said that everyone "is as holy and as free of the Spirit as he wants to be." People who are more familiar with the TV room than the sanctuary, who are better acquainted with the Top 40 than the Psalms, hymns, and spiritual songs, and who allow almost anything to take precedence over the Sunday evening service – let alone the prayer meeting – may wish for holiness, but can hardly be said to want it.

Paul's instruction for Timothy is good for us as well. "Now flee from youthful lusts, and pursue righteousness, faith, love and peace, with those who call on the Lord from a pure heart." (2 Tim. 2:22, NASB)

Rev. Glen Boring

Christ Condemns Carnality
Luke 9:46-62

One of the greatest reasons we have for seeking a clean heart is because Christ continually condemned the manifestations of the heart of sin. I think it would be fair to say that the traits of the carnal heart grieved Him greatly.

In this one passage we see verse after verse the manifestations of carnality and the immediate condemnation by Jesus of such attitudes.

There were SELFISH AMBITIONS – "which of these should be greatest." There was BIGOTRY – refusing to fellowship with God's people outside one's own group. There was RESENTMENT – a desire to call fire down and destroy people who had never-dying souls. There was SELF-CONFIDENCE – "I will follow with Thee whithersoever Thou goest," but when they saw there was no resting place and that the work was continuous, they turned back. There was the trait we see so much of in our churches today, SOCIAL BEFORE SPIRITUAL (yes, this is a carnal trait!) -- "Lord, let me first bury my father" is not as important as "follow me." Finally we see the HUMAN BEFORE THE DIVINE – let me do this or that first before I serve Thee.

These are all traits of the yet-carnal heart. Jesus, in every instance, immediately condemns. Friends, power to cast out devils or to cure diseases are no evidence of a pure heart, nor can they cure the carnal heart. Only Jesus can destroy in the inward work of the devil in our souls! And when that is done, the manifestations are done too!

"But the fruit of the Spirit is love, joy, peace, longsuffering, gentleness, goodness, faith, meekness, temperance: against such there is no law. And they that are Christ's have crucified the flesh with the affections and lust." (Galatians 5:22-24)

Rev. Rodger Moyer

Meeting Fire With Fire
Luke 12:49; Acts 2:3

During some of the wildfires in California it was discovered once again that the best way to fight fire is with fire (backfires). This reminded me that our world is on fire and the best way to fight it spiritually is by the fire of God.

What does fire do?

1. It destroys. So the Holy Spirit deals with sin.
2. It purifies. So the Holy Spirit cleanses.
3. It illuminates. So the Holy Spirit reveals the things of God.
4. It guides, even as in the ancient days of the Hebrew tabernacle. So the Holy Spirit shows the way to the people of God.

The sparks of the flames in our world shoot up into the sky today. Fires of destruction are all around. What is the supreme answer of the Church of Christ in this portentous hour? She must meet the fire of international chaos with the fire of the Spirit of God!

Friend, every believer should be involved in this hour of crisis! Let not one of us lag behind! The Holy Spirit has not changed – He is still the fire of God. Then let us, as never before, yield to His blessed control. Let us commit ourselves unreservedly to His infilling and direction. Let us allow Him to rekindle our devotion to Christ on the altar of dedication. Let us eliminate by confession any practice or mode of thought, which might dampen His flame or lessen His glow in our hearts.

Let the Holy Spirit refresh us and fill us and overflow us. Let Him be our personal Fire as we confront the world's advancing flame. Let us fight fire with God's fire.

Rev. Gene Moyer

What God Is Looking For
Luke 13:6-9

Many are familiar with the classic question, "If a tree falls in the forest with no one around to hear it, does it make any sound?" The answer may well hinge upon whether the respondent has a background that is strong in physics or one that is strong in philosophy.

A more pertinent question for the professing Christian is, "Can a tree that bears no figs be a fig tree?" In this parable, the fig tree that does not bear fruit will be cut down. It certainly will not be a fig tree then. The principle is the same in Isaiah 3 where the vineyard that does not produce good grapes is laid waste.

Jesus could hardly be any clearer than when He says in John 15 that He takes away every branch in Him that does not bear fruit. The fruit bearing branches He prunes in order that they may bear more fruit. God is looking for fruit.

We look for fame and finances – God is looking for fruit. We look for fantastic gifts and forceful personality – God is looking for fruit. In Isaiah 3, God was looking for the good grapes of justice and righteousness. In our lives, He is looking for love, joy, peace, patience, kindness, goodness, faithfulness, gentleness, and self-control – the fruit of the Spirit. God is looking for figs from fig trees and Christlikeness from Christians.

The world around me needs to see what God is looking for in my life today. It is not enough to say that I am filled with the Spirit, I must bear the fruit of the Spirit.

Rev. Glen Boring

Discipleship
Luke 14:25-35

Not everyone can be a disciple of Jesus Christ. Startling as it sounds, it is true. That which disqualifies, however, has no relation to race, culture, or intellectual attainment. Some people cannot be disciples because they do not meet the spiritual conditions laid down by Jesus for discipleship.

Who, then, cannot be a disciple? Jesus, in Luke 14, clearly says that:

(1) He who puts family before Jesus cannot be His disciple. (v. 26) Family loyalties are normal and good. However, if a conflict arises, loyalty to Jesus must come first or one cannot be a disciple.

(2) He who does not bear his own cross cannot be Jesus' disciple. (v. 27) Bearing the cross means complete and continuous submission to the will of God. The cross was an instrument of death. Here it means death to the claims of self and an aliveness to the claims of Christ. For a disciple, Jesus is Lord – absolutely.

(3) He who does not give all he has to God cannot be Jesus' disciple. (v. 33) There must be a yielding up of possessions, time, talent – everything. Jesus then becomes not only the mediator between God and me, but between my possessions and me. This means that all I possess is mine by the grace of God. It means I must hold loosely to all I claim to be mine.

Salvation is free but discipleship costs everything.

Dr. Hollis Abbott

A Great Gulf
Luke 16:19-26

During the "Gulf War," the term "Gulf" became an everyday word in our vocabulary. Today's Scripture speaks of a "gulf," but in an entirely different context.

Jesus speaks of this "gulf" through Abraham's conversation with the "rich man" in Luke 16:25-26. The conflict between good and evil has raged for ages making this gulf necessary. This gulf separates heaven from those experiencing eternal punishment. For the child of God, should we not create the gulf now?

To do this we need to become more determined in the declaration of our holiness message. We must be more fanatical in our devotion to Christ! We must "come out from among them, and be separate, and touch not the unclean thing." (2 Cor. 6:17) The church has too often accommodated itself to the world in an effort to make Christianity palatable. Real Christianity will never be palatable to this world. If Christians were as devoted to Christ as many ball fans are to their favorite team, the world would quickly be evangelized.

The gulf separates holiness from the world even as Christ against Belial; light against darkness; and holiness against sin. Christ's holy Church must speak against Baal worshippers who masquerade as Christians within the church. Unless the church accepts her responsibility for establishing the gulf between holiness and sin now, multitudes will never understand that "great gulf fixed," that separates the righteous from the wicked for all eternity. The power of the compromising Church wraps herself in the robes of holiness (mental assent and all the right terms) and allows what Christ forbids.

Let us seek God's will and do it and thus frustrate the forces of evil. Let us live holy lives in Christ Jesus and press the battle for holiness.

Rev. David Weinert

Clarified Vision
Luke 24:13-27; Acts 1:1-8; 2:14-40

Entire sanctification will clear up our vision regarding Scripture. As new believers we are able to see things in God's Word but the presence of carnality hinders our "depth perception." We seldom see the deep and temporal understanding of the Bible.

This hindered vision is evidenced in the lives of the disciples prior to Pentecost. On the road to Emmaus, Jesus rebuked the two He walked with for being "fools and slow of heart to believe all that the prophets have spoken." Notice, their dull vision was not due to an intellectual deficiency, but to hearts slow to believe. Just prior to His ascension Jesus told His disciples of an experience "not many days hence." What response did he get from them? "Lord, wilt thou at this time restore again the kingdom to Israel?" This was irrelevant to Jesus' statement, and shows that they still had an earth bound view of the kingdom and a selfish view for the positions they might occupy in this coming kingdom. They were dull and had no depth perception.

But on the day of Pentecost, Peter suddenly had a new ability to see into and expound the Scriptures. From the very scriptures in which the disciples had previously seen little, Peter drew the truths of the suffering Servant, the resurrection, the atonement, the intercession of Christ, the promised Holy Spirit shed forth by Jesus, repentance and faith, with such anointing that the hearers were struck with conviction.

If Peter and the other disciples needed purification of their hearts to clarify their vision of God's revealed truth and give them "depth perception," so do we.

Rev. Dan Morgan

Holiness, Revival and Missions
Luke 24:19, Acts 2:1-4, and Matthew 28:19-20

"I wish I could send you all to Hell for two weeks," cried William Booth. He felt the terrors of torment might sting us wide awake to the lostness of the lost. But, really would it? I believe it's true for saints, as for sinners, that if we hear neither Moses nor the "Go ye" of Christ's command, neither would we be persuaded though one rose from the dead! For no messenger from the other world could make goodness more lovable, or Hell more terrible, or Christ more divine, or duty more clear, or decision more urgent, or eternity more solemn than do the Scriptures we hold in our hands. What we need is simple submission to the Word and Spirit of God – we just need revival, real revival – revival with an overflow!

I fear the trouble is that we are filled with the "Lord, Lord" of lip service, but have little intention of obeying His last command. We are so glued to our gods of worldliness and material prosperity that doing the will of God means to us little more than a sentimental singing of "Have Thine Own Way, Lord."

Our basic problem is identical to that of God's people of old. Did they not in their double-mindedness pretend to serve both God and their idols? Were they not perpetually halting between two opinions? Like Israel, we continue to "fear the Lord and serve our own gods."

Friend, it is fatal to us as God's people when we suggest to Christ what He meant by the Go' ye" of His last command. When the Captain of our salvation commands, it is not ours to "reason why," but to obey and "go." And "Go" means to be on the march as soldiers – soldiers, not of "occupation," but of "conquest!" So, the only question is, "Am I totally His or am I not?" If I thus belong to Him, His Word to me is "Go." And every obedient servant responds, "Here am I, Lord, send me." To such a servant it matters not where or when or at what cost, it is only that he get going!

Rev. Gene Moyer

Holiness And Missions (1)
Luke 24:45-49

All through Scripture there is an obvious relationship between the message of full salvation and the church's responsibility to evangelize the world. Our text for today is just one of the five appearances of the "great commission" in the New Testament. Three of those five (Luke 24:49; John 20:21-22; Acts 1:4,8) include a very direct reference to the necessity of the Holy Spirit's sanctifying work for accomplishing our task. How sad it is then, that on one occasion missionary statesmen, Eugene Erny, felt compelled to comment: "80% of all mission work today is being done without the Holy Spirit!" We dare not let that be the case in our local church, or in any of our endeavors to reach the world.

How then are holiness and missions related? First, holiness releases the pocket books of God's people. If we are going to reach the world for Christ, it will cost a lot of money. Three or four decades ago we could send a couple to the mission field for about $4.00 a day. It now takes about twenty times that. In order to accomplish this expensive task, we must have people who have surrendered everything to Jesus – including their pocket book.

Second, holiness raises up unselfish prayer warriors. There has never been a greater need for God's people to pray. There are places and lives that we will only touch through prayer. There is greater opposition than ever before – opposition we cannot successfully overcome without much prayer. The task of world evangelization depends on people who can be freely led of the Spirit to pray at any time for the great need (emotionally, physically, spiritually, financially) before us.

Dr. Bruce Moyer

Holiness And Missions (2)
Acts 1:1-8

Yesterday we looked at two important relationships between holiness and missions. Today we will focus our thoughts on four more.

Third, holiness <u>remedies</u> the problem of too few workers. I don't know of a holiness mission board today that isn't facing the problem of not having enough missionaries to meet the challenges and opportunities before us. One of the few things Jesus taught us to pray for was workers. (Matt. 9:39) The unsanctified person will often rebel at a missionary call, because the heart has other plans.

Fourth, holiness <u>removes</u> carnal prejudices that would make a missionary ineffective, and even worse, divisive. The missionary is called to serve (aren't we all!), and the only thing that will really make him or her a great partner on the team of other missionaries and nationals with whom he/she ministers, is a sanctified heart.

Fifth, holiness <u>results</u> in changed lives. I have heard other missionaries testify to it, and I found it to be true in my own experience – the message that brings the best results is the message of full salvation. When we preach the whole counsel of God, sinners will be saved, believers will be sanctified, and the saints will continue to grow in grace!

Finally, holiness <u>retains</u> the fruit of world evangelism. So many fall away (some rather quickly, others over a period of time) if they are not urged to go on into the experience of heart cleansing. Unsanctified leaders, as well as laypersons, never seem to reach their full potential without this marvelous grace.

Think about it today: *The doctrine we preach, affects our worldwide outreach!*

Dr. Bruce Moyer

Power In The Inner Man
Luke 24:45-53

The last words of a person are considered very significant and, in this instance, they are doubly so. The use of the personal pronoun is significant. "YOU" is used four times, indicating that this enduement with the Holy Spirit is a personal and individual experience. It is "power from on high," something outside us, a power from above. It is power in the inner man. It is a spiritual power, not physical or psychological.

There is a danger in using physical force to gain spiritual ends. Peter drew his sword in the garden and cut off the ear of the servant of the high priest. The disciples wanted to call down fire upon the Samaritan innkeeper to avenge his rejection of Jesus and the group.

After Pentecost it was spiritual power. Prayer in the face of persecution, love in the face of law and legalism, forgiveness in the face of criticism, faith in the place of fear.

"Tarry in the city." Why not in the mountains or a quite place by the seashore? The city is the place of congestion, corruption, conflicts, with problems of storm, stress, and tension. The Holy Spirit is adequate for the hard places of life. "Tarry in Jerusalem." Why not in Nazareth, Bethany, or Capernaum? Jerusalem was the place of tragedy, crucifixion, denial, and defeat. It was the place of hostility and prejudice. The Holy Spirit wants to prove master of the difficult places of life.

There is a difference between a sailboat and a steamboat in navigation. The sailboat is dependent upon the circumstances of wind and weather. But the steamboat has inner power that is not dependent upon outer conditions. This should be our experience when the Holy Spirit fills us.

Rev. Roy Clark

Do It God's Way
Luke 24:49

There they were in the Upper Room in sight of a perishing world seemingly wasting time in prayer while the world went to Hell! Ah, but they were there fulfilling a commission – a commission to tarry so that they could then enter the battle in effectiveness of power. This "pause" should shout at us today that there is a "pause that refreshes." It stands at the forefront of our history the Lord's most memorable protest before hand that no authority under heaven could qualify men to propagate the gospel without the Baptism of the Holy Spirit!

Each solemn day of those ten days they waited for the one and only source of power that would make them effective witnesses. Without that same "wait" before the Lord, our wealth, influence, and facilities are mere ships of war and ammunition without guns or men! Friends, we should want in our age, above all other wants, God's holy fire, burning in men's hearts, impelling their emotions, vibrating in their actions. Without this, every instrument of usefulness the Church now has, becomes an instrument of weakness. I believe that if we will obey, tarry, and let this Baptism descend, thousands of us who, up to now, have been but commonplace or weak in our witness would then become the "mighty army" of which the songwriter speaks! Man would wonder at us – and we would wonder – not at ourselves, but at the grace of God that could thus transform us.

"Tarrying" will not be easy – especially when the people all around us are perishing. Nevertheless, let us answer, "We are awaiting to be endued with power from on high – to be baptized with the Holy Ghost and with fire." Let's "do it God's way!" No other will suffice!

Rev. Gene Moyer

You Are Clean!
John 1:29, "Behold, the Lamb of God."

One morning I defrosted and cleaned my freezer. A short time before that, a plastic container of wheat had slipped out of my hand and kernels of wheat had scattered everywhere -- between and under boxes of strawberries, peaches, and vegetables. Though I had tried to remove the grains by teaspoon, hand, and vacuum, I could not get them all.

But now the freezer is sparkling clean, orderly, and ready to meet the needs of unexpected guests -- ready to receive additional fruit, meat, and vegetables. From the freezer I may "send portions to them for whom nothing is prepared." (Neh.8:10) I may share with a neighbor who says, "A friend of mine in his journey is come and I have nothing to set before him."(Luke 11:6) Now when I look into the freezer, I am not irritated by disorder.

How like our lives! Seeds – hard seeds scattered through, around, below, and above our hearts; seeds of sin, selfishness, rebellion, jealousy, pride, love of money, love of the world. No matter how hard we try, we cannot, by human means, remove all of these hard kernels from our hearts.

BUT THERE IS ONE WHO CAN! "Behold, the lamb of God who takes away the sin of the world." (John 1:29) He removes the hard, hindering seeds, our sins. And if they are taken away, they are no longer there! Hallelujah!

"The blood of Jesus Christ cleanses us from all sin." He defrosts the iciness inside. Yes, removal of sins and cleansing from sin! Re-arranged priorities! Our souls clean, sparkling, unencumbered, and orderly. And He Himself, the Holy Spirit, resides within as Cleanser, Keeper, Guide, and Friend.

Jesus, thank You for taking away our sins. Thank You for cleansing our hearts through your Word. (John 15:3)

Mrs. Alice Fisher

Fitness For The Kingdom Of Heaven
John 3:1-15 (verse 3)

It has rightly been said by numerous people that the new birth is holiness begun, or initial sanctification. One who is genuinely born again and walking in all the light he has, should he die, will go the heaven. He will have been made fit by the blood of Jesus, shed on Calvary.

The new birth in itself does not give us fitness for heaven in itself even though we have title to it. We have family rights. It prepares us to be made clean and fit for heaven. Let me illustrate in a way in which every parent will understand, especially mothers.

Two children are playing out-of-doors after a wonderful refreshing rain. Puddles and mud abound everywhere. One child is yours and one is the neighbor's child. As truly as sparks fly upward, mud attracts children. Need more be said concerning their play? Mother has just cleaned the house including the scrubbing of floors. The children are through with their play and come to the house. Their mother meets them at the door. Is she going to deny her child entrance to a warm, comfortable home where love abounds and every need is met? Not at all. However, before her child enters he will need to submit to a cleansing. He is her child, he does belong to the family, he has every right to the comfort and joy of that home; but before he can enter he must be cleansed and be made pure. The small child cannot do this himself; he must let the mother do it. The mother is responsible for her child, as God has chosen to be responsible for His children and to "provisionally" cleanse them because they are in the family of God. Mother is not responsible for the other child. He is not in the family and thus not subject to her cleansing.

The new birth gives us the title to heaven but only cleansing by the blood of Jesus makes us fit for heaven. This is done in entire sanctification.

Rev. David Weinert

Disciples At The Crossroads
John 6:48-69

"From that time many of His disciples turned back and no longer followed Him."

These words have to be among the saddest in the Scriptures. Consider that there were those who saw, heard and perhaps touched the Lord in person and still turned back from following Him. There were disciples who began the journey well but, because the cost was more than they were willing to pay, they turned back to the world.

Is it possible that some followed Him for the wrong reason when He walked on the earth? Is it not a reality that many are involved in the Church today for reasons that are not pure? The portion of Scripture that precedes our reading of today indicates that there were those who followed Jesus because He had recently fed them at the miracle of multiplying bread. They wanted to be fed again.

Instead of giving them more bread, Jesus began to outline His death and called these disciples to identify with Him. He related the importance, as well as the cost, of living a holy life. Although they may not have understood all that Jesus was calling them to, there was earthly comfort and bodily satisfaction. Some said in verse 60, "this is a hard teaching." And then they made the decision to "follow Him no more."

Every follower of Jesus must come to this same crossroad where the decision is made as to whether or not he will identify with Christ at all cost. Too often, even today, the call to holiness is a "hard saying" that causes many to turn back. May our souls be encouraged today to answer, as did Simon Peter when Jesus asked if he too would turn back? His reply: "To whom shall we go? You have the words of eternal life."

Rev. Duane Erickson

The Hard Places Of The Gospel
John 6:60-71

Millions are looking for an easy way, yet there are many others who know that nothing worthwhile will ever be accomplished on beds of ease. Things worthwhile do not come in an easy manner. Certainly this is true in the matter of salvation. Have you ever wondered how large the multitude that followed Jesus would have been if none had ever turned back? How large would your church be if none had ever turned back?

The gospel is not a light thing. It does have its hard places. The devil and his influences in the world are constantly seeing to it that people turn back. He offers an easier way. It is easier only in that it takes no effort to initially follow him. Man's nature is naturally inclined to evil. If he does nothing he will go the devil's way. The end result is that the devil's way will be much harder than to go God's way with all its apparent difficulties.

Jesus told them that they must go the way He went and then they would abide in Him. His way was route Calvary -- crucifixion, the cross, and death. Many cease to follow when they face the need of a clean heart. Many people would not think of quitting church, but they will find one where they will not be so often reminded of the need of a clean heart, or one where they will be told, "you can't have a clean heart in this life." They won't go the way of Mt. Calvary and thus, they are not a disciple in the way Jesus said they must travel.

More and more routes are becoming available in these last days, but there is only one route that leads to God and that is route Calvary. Jesus said, "Except those days be shortened no flesh would be saved." (Matt. 24:22) Jesus asked his disciples as they saw others leaving, "Would ye also go away?" Jesus is looking for those who will go all the way to Calvary and be useful servants for Him.

Rev. David Weinert

159

Reach Out And Touch
John 7:37; Acts 1:8

The scripture for today's devotional: "Streams of living water will flow from within … in Jerusalem and in all Judea and Samaria, and to the ends of the earth." (John 7:37; Acts 1:8)

So before beginning this day let us think about two things, beginning with our world.

Your world and mine consists of that sphere of contact and influence which is uniquely our own. While all of us have family, friends, neighbors, church community and work-study environments, the commonality ends there. For within those groupings are people with whom we have regular contact in a way denied to other people. In a very literal sense, then, there are "worlds" which are distinctly ours with all of the responsibilities that statement implies.

Among the responsibilities so suggested there is one that becomes the second focus of our devotional thinking for today: We are to impact our world as a river of living water! Not just be there or announce our presence there. We are to register a positive, beneficial presence in the world that is especially our own.

So as we move through this day and that part of our world we will occupy this day, may the Lord help us leave in our wake positive evidences of our presence – love, joy, peace, patience, kindness, goodness, faithfulness, gentleness and self-control. These expressions of personality are, as you have recognized, the fruit of the Spirit. And that brings us back full circle to what Jesus said on the last day of the feast – this river of living water would be the consequence of the Spirit's powerful abiding presence.

To think seriously about my world becomes a powerful motivation to live conscientiously the Spirit-filled life today. I may be the only one in my world to do so.

Dr. Merne Harris

Like a Mighty River
John 7:37-39

What do Jack Horner and many holiness people have in common? Well, at least three things. To begin with, Jack was comfortable and secure in the corner he had found, isolated and insulated from the rest of the world around him. And we often take refuge in that sanitized and safe refuge we call the holiness movement – even though that posture does remove us from the real world all around us.

Then, Jack was so delighted with the special treasure he had come by – a delicious piece of Christmas pie. But the thought of sharing that joy with anyone else seems not to have bothered him. Now, we who often talk about our joyful possession – the best thing this side of heaven – but are seldom troubled by any serious concern that the blessing ought to be shared.

Finally, Jack was proud of the kind of person he was. It is unbelievable that such an isolated and selfish person could actually say, "What a good boy am I!" And we are similarly guilty when we consider it God's good fortune that he has such theologically correct and circumspect people as we holiness people are.

This is not the picture of the Spirit-filled life that emerges from Jesus' great sermon on "that last day of the feast." No, it is not some blessing to be treasured in a remote, safe place. It is instead like a mighty river, reaching out to touch all who come in its path.

And remember – it is like a river. Not a trickle, not a rivulet, not even a stream. It is a river – and rivers THAT ARE IN FULL SUPPLY touch everything within range and are adequate for every need within that range.

Today, be a river. Not a pond or pool of collected spiritual blessing, but a MIGHTY RIVER bringing power, beauty, satisfaction and healing to our world.

Dr. Merne Harris

Pleasing Father
John 8:12-30 (verse 29)

Did you ever do something just because you wanted to "please someone"? I recall an incident during my years at home on the farm that involved my father. There were six girls and one boy in our family and, since the boy was the youngest, we girls had to help with the milking…the old fashioned way!! When I was in the 7th or 8th grade on a certain given evening I was to help my father with this particular task. He came home from the office sick that evening but he was going to help anyway. As he rested awhile, I was to go on down and start milking. We were milking eleven cows at that time. I wanted to get as many done as possible so my father wouldn't have too many to do. I milked as fast as I could and when he came in I was on the eleventh cow. Of course he was surprised and you may ask, "Why on earth did you do that?" And I would reply, "Just to please my father." There was no other reward than words of thanks and I wasn't even asking for those. I just wanted to please my father.

I believe it would touch the heart of God if we did things for our Heavenly Father just because we wanted to please Him, thinking nothing of what would be gain for ourselves. Pray to Him, asking not for ourselves, but what can we do just to please Him. Enter into the Lord's House on His day, not just because He said so, but to please Him. Give of our tithes and offerings, not just because we're afraid not to, but to please Him. Jesus Himself said in John 8:29, "and he that sent me is with me: the Father hath not left me alone: for I do always those things that please him." We can say that, too. Our Heavenly Father will not leave us alone IF we do those things that please Him.

I have a feeling that my hands look the way they do today partly because of milking but they serve as a gentle reminder of wanting to do something to please my father.

Mrs. David Weinert

June 7

Freedom Through Truth
John 8:25-36

I have a brother who spent a number of years associated with a bank. Part of his training was to learn to detect counterfeit money. You might expect that the employees spent a lot time examining counterfeit money in order to be able to spot it, but they were not shown any counterfeit money until relatively late in their training which primarily consisted of spending much time with the real thing – becoming thoroughly acquainted with legitimate currency. Once they were familiar with the real, the counterfeit was easy to spot. Freedom to detect the counterfeit came from intimate knowledge of the real.

So it is in the spiritual realm. Freedom to detect sin and error comes from an intimate knowledge of the truth. Is it any wonder that worldliness goes unchecked in much of the professing church where entertainment flourishes and Bible study languishes? I need to spend less time examining the counterfeits and more time examining the truth. Then the false will be clearly seen.

Knowing the truth not only gives me a freedom to detect sin, but also a freedom from sinning. In vs. 34 Jesus said, "everyone who commits sin is the slave of sin." Thank God, however, that in vs. 36 He said, "If therefore the Son shall make you free, you shall be free indeed."

In v. 32 Jesus said that "the truth shall make you free," and in v. 36 He said "the Son shall make you free." This should come as no surprise, for Jesus is the One who said, "I am the … truth." Truth is not just an abstract concept – it is a Divine Person. Let us become intimately acquainted with Truth that we might experience the freedom that only He can give.

Rev. Glen Boring

Free Indeed
John 8:31-36

As a student as the University of Oregon in the sixties, I remember the "Free Speech Platform" being an important focal point for many on the campus.

At another part of the campus stood the huge library. There are two sets of main doors to the library – one at the east end and one at the west end. Over the doors on the east are the words, "You shall know truth," and over the doors on the west end you will find, "And the truth shall make you free." Since those words are taken from the Bible, I doubt that they will find their way on any new building on a state campus, but in reality, the state had already secularized the words in two ways. First of all, as I recall, there was nothing to indicate that the words had been spoken by Jesus and came from the Bible. Secondly, the implication was that a university library was filled with truth, the knowledge of which would provide freedom. There are probably few who would doubt the connection between freedom and truth, but modern man is not really much different from Pilate who asked, "What is truth?" (John 18:38)

Jesus makes it clear, however, that real freedom – freedom from sin – is a product of knowing the truth; truth that comes from discipleship that abides in His Word. Is it any wonder that He prayed for His disciples before His crucifixion, "Sanctify them in the truth; Thy word is truth?"

Real freedom comes from the truth, but not just prepositional truth about facts and figures. The truth that brings freedom from sin comes by relationship – discipleship that abides in God's Word. This is the truth bringing glorious freedom, and that freedom can operate behind iron bars, within failing bodies, and surrounded by adverse circumstances. Regardless of the situation, praise God, we can be free indeed!

Rev. Glen Boring

The Price Of Fullness
John 10:10; Galatians 5:18b

The difference between the Spirit-filled life and the life that is not filled with the Spirit is the difference between a life abandoned wholly to the will of God and a life that wants to have its own way and please God too. Abandonment is that of which it is most easy to speak, and yet it is the one thing from which all men shrink. Men are quite prepared to sign pledges, do any amount of work, even to sign checks or give money, if only God will let them have their own way somewhere in their life. If he will not press this business of abandonment on them, if He will not bring them to the cross, they will do anything; but they draw back from the place of death.

Yet it is only in that place that the Holy Spirit is able to slay the rebellion, to then flow out into every part of life and energize it, until in all conduct of life is Jesus crowned Lord, and the fruit of the Spirit manifest in man's character. Nothing can take the place of abandonment. There are some who attempt to put prayer where God has put abandonment. Others there are who profess to be waiting until God is willing to fill them. Both are wrong! While they think they are waiting for God, the fact is God is waiting for them – at the cross –the place of abandonment. At the moment they yield to the Holy Spirit, He will sweep through every gate and avenue and into every corner of the life and "life more abundant" will be realized.

The price of fullness? "My all for God's all – all of the time!" (E.R. Fuhrman) My friend, your "abundant life" Giver is waiting for your abandonment. Will you give so that he may give?

Rev. Gene Moyer

Dead To Sin
John 10:17-18; Romans 6: 8-11

In our first Scripture, Jesus is emphatic that he laid down His life in freedom. It was totally voluntary and "no man took it from Him." Also, we see that He laid it down <u>in order that He might take it again.</u> His awful, solitary, voluntary death issued forth in a glorious resurrection.

In our second reading, Paul exhorts that, just as Christ died unto sin, we are to "reckon ourselves dead indeed unto sin, but alive unto God through Jesus Christ our Lord." We do not have the power to lay down our physical life as did Jesus, but His voluntary death in the physical realm is meant as a pattern of the voluntary death to sin we must experience in the spiritual realm. When, as believers, we come face to face with carnal mind, it is our obligation to willingly go to our own Calvary and die out to sin, committing our spirit to the Father in faith just as Jesus did. We must have the aid of the Holy Spirit to do this, but it is <u>aid</u> not force or compulsion. We must choose to die to sin.

Too often, believers who ought to be pressing into the blessing of heart holiness, explain their stalled condition with a shrug of the shoulders, "God just hasn't talked to me that much about it." While God must and will help us, everywhere in the New Testament believers are exhorted to "seek," "follow," "hunger and thirst," etc. As Jesus freely died and rose in a glorious resurrection, we must deliberately choose to cooperate with God and die to all sin and by faith be resurrected to walk in a new and holy way.

Rev. Dan Morgan

Fruit From Dead Things
John 12:17-32

I want papaya trees in my garden in order to have an abundance of this nutritious fruit. I saved seeds from one delicious papaya and have let them dry completely. I will plant them in a bed of fertile soil, expecting them to germinate. When they have grown sufficiently, we will plant them in the garden in anticipation that they will become fruit-producing trees.

Two facts predominate in John 12:24: First, "if it die" and second, "bringeth forth much fruit." The two states of condition and result are inseparable. It is impossible to have the fruit without the death. Equally, the death brings the fruit.

Does the "corn of wheat" rejoice in being dead? Is there exhilaration in cessation of life in the certain anticipation of the more glorious state – abundance of fruit?

The implication to my heart is that, after fully experiencing Romans 12:1 ("present your bodies a living sacrifice"), my only desire is Christ and His will. He then uses that "dead thing" to produce eternal, spiritual fruit.

The dead thing can do nothing. It is not expected to do anything – only be dead, useable, and submissive in the hands of the Fruit Producer. When I have done my part (dying), the promise is that the only One Who can produce fruit will do so, through the "dead thing" that is yielded to Him. This relieves me of trying to produce fruit (the salvation of souls) by my own effort. It can't be done! My ingenuity, no matter how sincere, how coercive, how clever, can never produce spiritual fruit.

BUT the true Fruit Producer, the Holy Spirit, can and will produce fruit through the "dead thing" that is completely surrendered to His control.

Oh, the glory of being dead! Of being ALL HIS!

Miss Jeanne Seager

Self-Crucifixion
John 12:23-27

There is a well-known song that we love and often sing, the third stanza of which challenges us to the very heart: "Yes, 'tis sweet to trust in Jesus, Just from sin and self to cease." There are many in our churches today who have well ceased from sin who know very little or nothing of having ceased from self. Self is a very real enemy for bearing much fruit or glorifying the Father.

Jesus gave us a very clear and positive statement as a requirement for bearing much fruit. "Except a corn of wheat fall into the ground and die, it abideth alone; but if it die it bringeth forth much fruit." We need not be so concerned about the fruit as about the dying. If the dying is a reality then the fruit is sure. Just as surely as we need a "new birth" into new life in Christ, we also need to follow Him to the cross and testify with Paul, "I am crucified with Christ." The new birth that gives pardon from the guilt of sin is the first and right step in the right direction, but depraved self that remains will give us all kinds of trouble.

There is no better example of this than what we see among church people today in the number of broken homes. It is possible to be truly converted, join the church, serve on church boards, or even preach something of the Gospel, but if pride, anger, jealousy, selfishness still remain, we have all the potential for a broken home. These things in the lives of our church people will also rob the church of its power to reach the lost outside and render it in a great measure unfruitful. Have you ceased from self?

Prayer Suggestion: Pray that God's children will not stop short of a clean heart, filled with the Holy Spirit and perfect love.

Rev. Marshal Cavit

The Telling Mark Of Christianity
John 13:12-35 (verses 34-35)

This is a definite command, "love one another, even as I have loved you," which means that this is not open to opinions, options, or objections. But Jesus not only commanded that we love one another, he clarified what He meant, by adding, "as I have loved you, that you also love one another." He considered this the telling mark of Christianity: "By this all men will know that you are my disciples." What makes this mark so distinct?

IT IS CLEAN   There is simply nothing as attractive and effective as "love out of a pure heart." This kind of love is not tainted with sinful nor selfish motivations in its devotion to God and service to others. It is delightfully, transparently, genuinely, and thoroughly clean.

IT IS CARING   This love is expressed in a deep and genuine care of others. Much that passes for "care" today is nothing more than a fulfillment of what we know to be socially acclaimed and acceptable. It simply feeds our egos, but has its limits. All too many are "good Samaritans" until it becomes a matter of taking the hurt one to the inn, because this calls for personal sacrifice.

The distinctive mark of a spiritual man is a true, selfless care for others that rises from their love for God. This is what caused Esther to say, "If I perish, I perish;" Ruth to say, "Whither thou goest, I will go;" Paul to say, "and whether we be afflicted, it is for your comfort and salvation;" and Jesus to say, "nevertheless not My will, but Thine, be done."

IT IS COURAGEOUS   Selfless love will rise in the face of opposition and danger, and will, if need be, lay down its life. Jesus said, "No greater love hath any man than this, that he lay down his life for his friends." Perfect love takes timid, shy, backward and cowardly souls, and puts fire in them. They live by the power of love, the kind that Jesus has: perfect love.

Dr. Hubert Harriman

The Holy Spirit (1)
John 14:15-18

It is easy for us to sit back and meditate on all that the Holy Spirit does for us – He applies the redemptive work of Christ to our lives in salvation and sanctification, He indwells us, He teaches us, He gives us joy, He keeps us, He helps us to pray, and so much more. However, today I would like you to consider with me a few scriptural thoughts about Who He is.

He is the <u>Spirit of God</u>. (Eph. 4:30) He is God in all of His Deity and omnipotence. He is the <u>Spirit of Christ</u>. (1 Pet. 1:11) This not only means that He was sent by Jesus (as we saw in our Scripture reading), but that He speaks of Christ. He is the One Who really shows us Who Christ is. Paul tells us (Rom. 8:2) that He is the <u>Spirit of Life</u>. He is both the Communicator and Sustainer of spiritual life. In our reading for today Jesus said that the Holy Spirit is the <u>Spirit of Truth</u>. He stands in opposition to all that is false and speaks to us only that which is true – He is totally dependable! According to Zech. 12:10, He is the <u>Spirit of Grace</u>. He not only bestows upon us the grace of God, but He makes us gracious, like our Lord. In some of the last earthly words of Jesus (Acts 1:8) we are promised the <u>Spirit of Power</u>. He takes that which is weak and ineffective and causes it to become powerful and productive. What good news that is for us! And though we could go on, let us stop with Rom. 1:4 which teaches us that He is the <u>Spirit of Holiness</u> – the only One Who can sanctify and make us like Himself!

Dr. Bruce Moyer

The Holy Spirit (2)
Exodus 30:22-33

There are many types or symbols of the Holy Spirit throughout Scripture, but one of the most significant is that of oil. The anointing of oil in Ex. 30 gives us a beautiful picture of the Person and ministry of the Holy Spirit. Today we will simply look at some of the restrictions for the use of this oil.

First, this oil was not to be poured on men's bodies. (v. 32) The oil was not to be used for men's goals and desires, but only for spiritual purposes. In the same way, we cannot expect the Holy Spirit to come and anoint that which is being done "in the flesh." If we are to expect this anointing we must learn to operate under His motivation (perfect love!), according to His methods, and in His might. His words, His works, His compassions, His holiness – they must all become ours.

The second restriction placed upon the use of the anointing oil was that they were not to make any imitation of it. (v. 33) It was sacred. Oh, how God hates imitations (just look at what He has to say about idolatry, which is substituting an imitation for the real thing)! How many times do we find ourselves, or others, (either knowingly or unknowingly) substituting the organization of man for the operation of the Holy Spirit?

The third restriction mentioned in the text is that the oil was not to be put upon anyone outside of the priesthood. (v. 33) Concerning the Holy Spirit, Jesus said, "The world cannot accept him, because it neither sees him nor knows him." (John 14:17) [Comp. Acts 8:18-24]

Dr. Bruce Moyer

The Holy Spirit (3)
1 John 2:26-27

Today we want to continue looking at the Holy Spirit as our Anointing. There are several purposes in Scripture for anointing.

Men were <u>anointed for sanctification</u>. (Lev. 8:10-12) We also have available to us an Anointing that sanctifies. We are not inherently holy, but are only made so as we are totally possessed by the Holy Spirit. The Scriptures also speak of being <u>anointed for seeing</u> (or perceiving, understanding) – as in our text for today. The Holy Spirit is the One who enables us to know and understand the truth (just look through 1 John for all that we can know!). Acts 10:38 reveals that Jesus was (and we may be too) <u>anointed for serving</u>. He "went about doing good." Anyone can participate in great humanitarian efforts, but only those anointed of the Spirit can truly serve. 2 Cor. 1:21-22 teaches us that we may be <u>anointed to stand firm</u>. Without the Spirit, we are doomed for failure. In 1 Sam. 9:16 we read about King Saul, "Thou shalt anoint him to be captain, that he may save My people." Saul was <u>anointed to save</u>. There is a sense in which we are saved to save. We need His anointing in order to pray, to give, and to go as we ought. Finally, we may be <u>anointed to speak</u> (preach, minister). Jesus Himself said, "The Spirit of the Lord is on me, because He has anointed me to preach good news . . .." (Luke 4:18) The effectiveness of our witness is directly related to this holy anointing!

Dr. Bruce Moyer

Before And After
John 14:15-20

Like me, you've seen those "before and after" pictures. In one advertisement we see someone who lost 65 pounds in just a few weeks. In another we see a man who quickly grew hair on his formerly balding scalp. Sometimes it's a car that looks like new overnight, or cabinets that make your whole kitchen shine. In every case there is a dramatic difference between the "old" and the "new."

As we read the New Testament we also get something of a "before and after" picture. Pentecost made a dramatic difference in the lives of the apostles. The "old" is seen in the Gospels, and the "new" is seen in the books of Acts. We have space enough for just a few examples; you will want to find others on your own.

In John 18:15-27, Peter denies his relationship to Jesus on three occasions. After Pentecost he boldly proclaims the truth (Acts 2) and stands firm for Jesus even in the face of persecution (Acts 4 & 5). Here was a new power!

In Luke 9:46 we find the pre-Pentecost disciples arguing over position. Read the "after" picture in Acts 4:32, "All the believers were in one heart and mind. No one claimed that any of his possessions was his own, but they shared everything they had." Here was a new peace.

Again, look at John's fiery spirit toward the Samaritans in Luke 9:54. After Pentecost it is John who accompanies Peter to minister to the Samaritans. (Acts 8:14-17) Here was a new purity of heart.

Pentecost does make a difference!

Dr. Bruce Moyer

Following Jesus
John 14:15-31

How many times have you heard the old cliché, "Do as I say, not as I do!" Even the best of us make mistakes and may have used that phrase a time or two ourselves. However, that was not the case with Jesus. In this passage He is teaching us a vital principle for Christian living, which He Himself lived up to and modeled for us.

In John 14:15, 21, 23-24 and 15:10, 14 Jesus repeats the principle (not always in the exact words) that our love for God is to be proven by our obedience to God – "If you love me, you will obey what I command." It's a concept that runs contrary to much of what I observe in the contemporary church. Obedience sounds too much like legalism. It sounds too contrary to "freedom." So the church today decides it will define for itself how love is really expressed and, in the process, forgets that Jesus has already stated and modeled the definition for us.

When Jesus gave us this eternal principle he testified (v. 31), "The world must learn that I love the Father and I do exactly what the Father has commanded me." His love was evidenced by His obedience! He never had to say, "Do as I say, not as I do."

When I talk to others about loving God – in a Bible study, a sermon, a Sunday School class, an opportunity for personal witness – do I have to say "Do as I say, not as I do?" Or, is that love also being evidenced in my life by obedience and holy living?

Prayer: "Lord, I do love you! Help me today to discern the difference between legalism and obedience and to evidence my love for you through genuine obedience to Your Word."

Dr. Bruce Moyer

Our Faithful Helper (1)
John 14:16-18, 26; 15:26; 16:7-15; Acts 1:4-5, 8 (NASB)

The Holy Spirit would help them to see what they could not see on their own.

Jesus referred to this Helper as "the Spirit of Truth" (Jn. 14:17), and stated very strongly in John 16:13, "… when He, the Spirit of Truth comes, He will guide you into all truth.…"

Truth has to do with reality, or what is real and what is right, as opposed to what is not. To be guided into all truth is the ability to face reality as shown to me by the Holy Spirit, and to make that evident in my life.

"When He comes…" Friends, there are simply some things we will never see, as we ought to see them, until He comes. It is the Holy Spirit who helps our helpless spiritual grasp of life and causes us to see and come to grips with things no man could have taught us in a thousand years.

It was after Pentecost (Acts 4:5-6) that Peter and John demonstrated this truth. It states simply, "Now as they observed the confidence of Peter and John, and understood that they were unlearned and untrained men, they were marveling, and began to recognize them as having been with Jesus." (Acts 4:13) These men had not only gotten a hold of truth, but truth had gotten a hold of them. They saw it as never before and it transformed them.

Daniel Steele states that unregenerate men may be trained from infancy… to assert with the lips the supreme deity of Jesus, but it is like the talk of an educated parrot till the Spirit of truth, or the Spirit of reality, makes the dogma which has been drilled into the intellect real to the heart." Steele concludes emphatically, "The Holy Spirit in the believer preserves, vitalizes and makes real to the consciousness all the essential truths of the gospel." (*The Gospel of the Comforter*, 274)

Dr. Hubert Harriman

Our Faithful Helper (2)
John 14:16-18, 26; 15:26; 16:7-15; Acts 1:4-5, 8 (NASB)

<u>The Holy Spirit would help them to be what they could not be on their own.</u>

It's with a sense of urgency that Jesus commands His disciples "not to leave Jerusalem, but to wait for what the Father promised …" stating, "but you shall receive power when the Holy Spirit has come upon you…. (Acts 1:4,8)

If there is anything that describes the great help of the Holy Spirit, it is this word "power." It comes from the Greek word *dunomai,* which means "to be able," or to "enable."

Following the promise of power, Jesus states that, as a consequence, "you shall <u>be</u> my witnesses." To be " speaks of a condition, of constancy and what they were would speak louder that what they said, simply because the Holy Spirit would enable them to be what they could not be without his help. This required the "baptism with the Holy Spirit." (Acts 1:5)

It is in this baptism that we are washed of that which won't let us <u>be</u> a witness; that is, of inbred sin firmly planted in a self-centered heart. This cleansing will include things that are totally contrary to the fruit of the Spirit, which is "Love, joy, peace, patience, kindness, goodness, faithfulness, gentleness, self control." (Gal. 5:22-23) What a Helper! A Faithful Helper!

Dr. Hubert Harriman

Our Faithful Helper (3)
John 14:16-18, 26; 16:7-15; Acts 1:4-5, 8 (NASB)

The Holy Spirit would help them to do what they could not do on their own.

To any student of Scripture it soon becomes apparent that the Holy Spirit was not given as our helper simply for us to sit back and be served, but rather to help us serve. This service would take these early disciples, and those who would follow, from Jerusalem, to all Judea, through Samaria, and "even to the remotest part of the earth." (Acts 1:8)

There was no way anyone would be able to do this task without the faithful help of the Holy Spirit. If souls were to be moved and churches established it would require Spirit-filled men. The task was too great, otherwise, for both evangelism and edification.

Church history attests that vain are the substitutes for the might of the Spirit. The early disciples were so convinced of their deep need of the help of the Holy Spirit to do the work of God, they stipulated that even men chosen for what might be considered the more menial tasks, were to be men full of the Spirit. (Acts 6: 1-3) Why?

First of all, men who are not filled with the Spirit of God won't do the work of God. They will do their own work for their own sake, according to their own feelings. Secondly, as A.W. Tozer states, "You can write it down as a fact: no matter what a man does, no matter how successful he seems to be in any field, if the Holy Spirit is not the chief energizer of his activity, it will all fall apart when he dies." (*Tragedy in The Church*, 13)

Dr. Hubert Harriman

"My Father … prunes every branch."
John 15:1-8

When Spring comes, I get out the gardening tools. First on my list is "prune" the grape vines. I admit using that word loosely. I'm not sure a real gardener would recognize it as pruning. He would probably use to word "butchering."

I'm not the only one having trouble with the word. Even the translators had problems since each one gave a slightly different reading. John said, "My Father is the gardener … He trims clean every branch so that it will be even more fruitful." (NIV) Phillips and the RSV both translate the word "prune." One says, "He cleans," another uses "purgeth," and so it goes! Dr. Erdman, commenting on this passage notes, "both figures refer to the process of pruning; dead wood is cut away, even living shoots and fruit bearing branches are cut back in order that the cluster of grapes may be more rich and full." (*Erdman's Commentary*, p. 132) And with this I heartily agree.

As I pruned away, I started thinking about my life. I can look back to the time when God, by His Holy Spirit and through the Word, cleaned me up. What a day that was! John did not use the past-tense for prune in this place. He used a tense that says God prunes us in a continuous going-on act in the present. Past experiences won't suffice. As a branch in Christ wants to bear fruit, I must right now experience His loving hand cutting away whatever prevents me from bearing fruit in abundance – prolific.

I'm not entirely sure what this means in practical terms, but I realize that my relationship to Jesus Christ is all-important, "without me ye can do not one thing," – present tense, up-to-date spiritual communion with Him, the vine. And wonder of wonders, He wills to manifest His life, not only in me, but through me!

So my prayer is, work on me, Lord! Cut away whatever is hindering Jesus being seen in me. Amen.

Dr. Gerald Dillon

Without Jesus I Can Do Nothing
John 15:1-11

My little girl recently learned to ride her bicycle without the training wheels. With a false sense of self-confidence based more in the old training wheels than in real ability, she initially rejected my offer to assist her. A few embarrassing falls soon cured her of self-sufficiency! In a much more humble frame of mind, she soon came to me imploring, "Daddy, I <u>need</u> you to help me, I can't do this without you!" Well, now we were getting somewhere! With only a few back-breaking runs down the sidewalk with old Dad helping hold her upright, pretty soon she was off on her own!

In our reading for today, Jesus tells us something most basic to the life of faith: "without Me you can do nothing." A simple truth, but one so often overlooked in practice! How often do we err in striving to be holy through religious discipline? How often do we read and pray more out of a sense of duty than need? How often do we serve out of a sense of obligation rather than privilege?

It is a fine line that divides between self-righteousness and the righteousness which is from God by faith. Self-righteousness boldly presumes "I can do this!" The righteousness which is from God by faith humbly confesses "Jesus, I <u>need</u> You to help me, I can't do this without You." In this spiritual climate of humility, faith can function. By faith the grace of God can be appropriated. And by grace we are enabled to be holy and righteous and truly spiritual.

Friend, how long has it been since, from the heart, you prayed, "Jesus, I <u>need</u> You?"

Rev. Chris Neilson

Holiness: Abiding In Christ
John 15:1-17

There's nothing like a hot bowl of oatmeal accompanied by cinnamon raisin toast on a cold winter morning. So, one snowy Saturday morning in January, I got up to prepare just that kind of breakfast for my wife and me. I pushed the toast down in the toaster and went to rouse Ruth from her sleep. We sat at the table and prayed. I wondered why the toast hadn't popped up. I poured the oatmeal into our bowls and covered it with just the right amount of brown sugar. Still no toast. After adding just a touch of milk and still not hearing the toaster pop up, I decided to check it. You guessed – it wasn't plugged in. I could have waited all day and that toast would have never been done!

Later that same day I recalled the incident with the toaster and I thought about how much like the life of holiness that is. We can have everything ready, our intentions can be good, and we can even be involved in a multitude of programs – but if we aren't "plugged in" to The Source of power, we can go all through life and it will never amount to anything.

God's gracious work of entire sanctification is both preceded and followed by growth in grace. That growth is contingent upon our "abiding in Him" – that is, staying plugged into Him. That means a year-by-year, day-by-day, moment-by-moment commitment to draw close to Him and live in obedience to Him. It's a wonderful joy, and a great responsibility. Next time you make toast, make sure the toaster is plugged in . . . and that you are too!

Dr. Bruce Moyer

"You Also Must Testify"
John 15:18-27

There are certain portions of Scripture that I go to again and again. I guess you could say that they're my "favorite passages" – John's Gospel and Epistles and Paul's letter to the Ephesians. Recently, while reading through the Gospel of John again, I was struck by this thought found in verse 27 of chapter 15, "You also must testify."

As I went back over the book of John I discovered that there are many "testimonies" with respect to Jesus. In John 5:31-40 we see that there was a human testimony of John. (v. 34) There was the practical testimony of the works which Jesus had done. (v. 36) There was the Divine testimony of the Father. (v. 37) And there is the written testimony of the Scriptures (v. 39). Then, in John 8 (vs. 14, 18) we see that Jesus Himself testified about who He is – a personal testimony. In our reading for today we are told (v. 26) that the Holy Spirit bears witness about Jesus. That is followed by Jesus' words to His disciples, "You also must testify."

As I pondered the significance of this for me, a contemporary disciple of Jesus, I realized that it is not enough that others testify, or that the Father, the Spirit, the Word, and Christ's own works all testify about Jesus. He commands that I too should bear witness of Him! I am to be a vital part of His total program to declare to the world who He is.

I was also struck by the reason Jesus gave, "You also must testify, <u>for you have been with me</u> . . .."

Prayer: "Lord, help me to spend time with you today quality time that will cause me to be a quality testimony of your grace!"

Dr. Bruce Moyer

The Comforter Has Come!
John 16:1-16

I still think that plain, soft-spoken Quaker lady paid me a high compliment when she said, "Thank you for that simple-minded preaching." For is it not incumbent upon us to present the great truth of full salvation as simply as we can? Jesus did – He often simplified unfamiliar truth by the use of familiar ideas.

For example, who among His disciples would not have at some time or other experienced the need of a comforter – someone who could stand by during one of life's difficult experiences? So He spoke of the Holy Spirit as THE Comforter. Richard Taylor has said: "The one called alongside to help."

As a pastor, I came to appreciate the role of the comforter. While I was sometimes called upon to stand by people as they weathered a particularly stressful storm, I was never once asked to deny the existence of the storm or to somehow drive it away. But I was asked to help them survive the storm – I had been "called alongside to help."

What followed confirmed that it had worked. They wrote or spoke words of gratitude: "Your presence was such a source of strength … your words were a comfort to us … we really needed you."

Rev. Jim Diehl used to say, "Life isn't always fair … but God is always faithful." His faithfulness is communicated to me through the abiding presence of His Holy Spirit – the one called alongside to help. That truth enables me to face the unpleasant aspects of this day optimistically. And it helps to sing:

O spread the tidings 'round
Wherever man is found,
Wherever human hearts and woes abound;
Let ev'ry Christian tongue proclaim the joyful sound:
The Comforter has come!

Dr. Merne Harris

It Sure Helps To Have A Helper
John 16:5-16

The moment I saw it I knew I had to have it – that bright red ring on David's finger. David was my neighborhood friend, and although we were both eleven at the time he was considerably taller than I. He had come to my place that morning wearing his new, prized possession, which had probably cost all of ten cents. The spirit of covetousness gripped me, but I had no money to buy it and nothing that David would accept in trade – except my mother's lone laying hen which was nearby. I offered that hen and David accepted the deal with an enthusiasm that should have been a warning to me.

No matter, the ring was mine! But my joy was short-lived, for about that time my mother called me in for lunch. Of course she saw the ring and seemed unreasonably determined to find out how it had become mine. She was not pleased when she finally learned that her chicken had bought the ring! "As soon as you finish your lunch," she said, "you will take that ring back to David and bring my layer home."

That was a long meal, with David growing in stature by inches as I thought about asking him to trade yet again. But the time finally came and I was on my way. I sat on our back porch trying to figure out what happened to such a wonderful day. Eventually I was aware of something standing on the step near me. It was my Dad, and I heard him say, "Come on, son, I'll go with you." What a change in my whole day those words made. We walked together those few blocks to David's house and I knew no fear. With Dad's looming presence it was no trick at all to persuade David that we should undo the deal we had made earlier.

I've had occasion to remember this incident when life had become bigger than I am and its demands frightening. But if I listen I can hear the Spirit saying, "Come on, son, I'll go with you." And it makes a difference, every time.

Dr. Merne Harris

The Spirit Convicts
John 16:7-11

We taught in three different Bible Schools in three different countries. We leaned on the Holy Spirit to reveal the hidden things in the lives of the students. Only He could convict and bring deliverance. Mr. Su quarreled with another student over onions on the menu. Su was the buyer and he liked lots of onions and they were cheap. His fellow student from South China was objecting to the onions. They parted still mad. Mr. Su climbed to the tower room for his daily devotions, but strange to say, the whole room smelled of onions! He caught on to the Spirit's nudging. He went down and made an apology and the matter was settled. When he went back up to the tower, strange to say, he did not smell onions anymore!

Another student was the buyer for the men's dining room. Wang was a sharp bargainer, but the money he saved went into a new watch on his wrist. He argued with the Spirit that he had saved it by his wits and he had earned it. How creative the Spirit is! He made the tick-tock of the watch get very loud to Wang and it kept saying "you steal, you steal" in his ears. We know the story because Wang stood up in chapel holding the watch and made a detailed confession in penitence. He paid back the money and then the watch did not accuse any more.

Even the faculty kept tender before the Lord. The dean returned a key to a former school where he had taught, another professor returned a hymn book, I had to confess I had told an illustration as a happening in my own life, and so we learned to all work in humility before one another. Holiness testimony gets hard and brittle without the melting, probing presence of the Holy One, and obedient responses from us.

Mrs. Laura Trachsel

The Holy Spirit
John 16:7-16

Recently I asked in a Sunday School class these questions: "What is the Holy Spirit?" "What does it do?" "How can we experience it?" After various responses I informed the class that the questions I had asked were impossible to answer. Do you know why? It is because the Holy Spirit is not an "it," but a "whom." The questions would have been correctly asked, "WHO is the Holy Spirit?" "What does HE do?" "How can we experience HIM?"

I am finding this great error more and more as I talk to people within the church. Yes, within the church. People seem to be seeking for more power, more gifts, more signs, more anything, instead of seeking the person of the Holy Spirit who is the source of all true spiritual power -- the source of power in prayer, the source of power in preaching, the source of power in testifying, and the source of all power to live a holy life in an evil world.

So if we seek, "How can I be more filled?" or "How can I get it so I can do more of this or that?" we are asking amiss and our prayers are futile. But if we seek the person of the Holy Ghost, our seeking will be "How can He, the Holy Spirit, get hold of me and use me?"

I'm so glad that there is no Divine Power that I can get hold of and use according to my own will. In my ignorance and foolishness of mind there is no telling what I might do. But I thank God that there is a Divine Person who can get hold of me and use me according to His all-knowing, perfect, and loving will.

Seek HIM, and then you shall have power to be all that God would have you to be.

Rev. Rodger Moyer

Holy People In An Unholy World
John 16:33

This present age is waxing worse and worse, because evil men and seducers are waxing worse and worse, deceiving and being deceived. (2 Timothy 3:13) Perilous times are upon us, and as long as this present age is so deeply steeped in sin, God's holy people can expect three things.

There will be a significant contrast. If an unholy world is mastered and motivated and molded by the devil, then we can expect it to be an ease-loving, time-serving, pleasure-seeking kind of life and death. But Christians, especially entirely sanctified Christians, are mastered and motivated by the Lord Jesus, who is their model and in whose image they are being molded. Then we can expect to find a self-denying and Christ-serving people whose joy is to do God's will, not their own. What a contrast.

There will be serious conflict. The World of light is in conflict with the world of darkness. (Jn. 1:5) The world of love is in conflict with the world of hate. (1 Jn. 3:13-14) The world of righteousness is in conflict with the world unrighteousness. (1 Jn. 3:7-8) The world of holiness is in conflict with the world of sin. (1 Thess. 4:3-8) The world of humility is in conflict with the world of pride. (Jn. 13:1-17) The world of faith is in conflict with the world of unbelief. (Heb. 3:12-4:11) The world of Christ is in conflict with the world of Satan. (Eph. 6:10-18) Yes, and these conflicts are very much with God's holy people today; and Jesus warned us that, "In the world ye shall have tribulation." (Jn. 16:33)

There will be Spirited conquest. In John 16:33, Jesus went on to say "...but be of good cheer; I have overcame the world." Because He overcame, we may overcome through Him. We may "overcome evil with good." (Rom. 12:21) God's grace is still greater than sin. (Rom. 5:20-21) Through grace we will conquer the world, with its false appeals; the flesh with its lusts' and the devil, no matter how maligned he may be. (1 Jn. 2:15-17)

Dr. Eldon Fuhrman

186

Why Jesus Prays For Sanctified Disciples
John 17:9-26 (verse 17)

We must remember that these eleven disciples had forsaken all to follow Christ. They had forsaken the old life of sin. Jesus Himself testified (v. 16) that they were not of the world, even as He was not of the world. Verses 9, 10, 12, and 14 all verify that these eleven disciples were all clearly converted men and, yet, Jesus was praying to His Father that they would experience a second definite work of God's divine grace. This prayer of Christ's was clearly specific and holy. The word "sanctify" used here means, "to make holy" in an instantaneous work. This prayer of Christ's is effectual for all believers for all time. (v. 20)

What practical reasons lay behind our Lord's prayer for sanctified disciples? First, it is for the **purpose of purification.** (v. 17) Jesus says in Mathew 5:8, "Blessed are the pure in heart for they shall see God." Sanctification makes us fit for heaven. (Rev. 21:27) Secondly, it is for the **purpose of perfection.** (vs. 21, 23, 26) The work of sanctification rids the believer of his double-mindedness and brings unity in the church, oneness with the heart of God, and perfect love toward fellowmen. (1 John 4:17) Thirdly, it is for the **purpose of proclamation.** (v. 18) The negative aspect of sanctification is cleansing from inbred sin, but the positive aspect is the filling with the Holy Spirit. This filling endues with a new power and authority to witness of Christ to others. (Acts 1:8) Fourthly, it is for the **purpose of preservation.** (v. 15) Sanctification is indeed an establishing grace. A sanctified soul can live in this wicked world without being tainted with its evil influence because the inclination for its allurements is gone. It seems clear that Jesus was praying for the precise need of every believer.

Has Jesus' prayer for sanctified disciples been fulfilled in your heart?

Rev. John Yoder

Keep Them From The Evil (1)
John 17:13-26

One of the reasons why Jesus wanted His disciples sanctified was that they might be kept from evil (evil one). Of ourselves we are no match for the enemy of our souls. We are not capable of directing our own lives. Jeremiah had it right, "O, Lord, I know that the way of man is not in himself: it is not in man that walketh to direct his steps." Only in the power of the indwelling Holy Spirit can we find safety for direction in our lives.

It was not to be kept from lying, stealing, murder, or drinking that He wanted them sanctified. Common sense will cause us to avoid these things. But there are many things that we cannot see as evil that the Lord wants us to avoid simply because they are not His will for us and not for our best good.

The year before we went to the mission field I was pastoring a church in a small town in Utah, and because of a shortage of teachers during the war, I was also teaching in the high school. For the following year I was offered the same work with a salary of a teacher with a master's degree. I could have accepted that and earned two or three times what I was to receive as a missionary and no one would have criticized me in any way. But God had called us to the mission field and the door to go was now opened. It was only by the power of the indwelling Holy Spirit that I turned a deaf ear to the voice of money, the voice of pleasant circumstances, and the voice of friends, and said yes to the voice of God. This opportunity was not evil in itself, but it would have been evil for us simply because we knew it was not the will of the Lord. We would have missed the tremendous blessings the Lord had in store for us by serving Him on the mission field.

If the devil can get the children of God sidetracked even to do perfectly good things and keep them out of the center of God's will and away from His blessings and fruitfulness, he has won a great victory and our defeat.

Rev. Marshal Cavit

Keep Them From The Evil (2)
Matthew 13:18-23

Many are prone to look at the parable of the sower as the story of four kinds of soil, or four different conditions of the heart. Really there are only three: the hard heart (the unconverted); two illustrations of hearts that have received the truth and started in the way of righteousness, but still with obstacles for spiritual growth and fruitfulness; and a third type of hearts that are pure and right for bearing fruit to the glory of God.

Carnality is that obstacle and is the cause of born again Christians to fall back into sin and unfruitfulness and the loss of their soul. The first illustration is soil with stones just beneath the surface. Jesus said, "This is he who hears the word and immediately receives it with joy (born again); yet he has no root in Himself (no power alone); but endures only for awhile. For when tribulation or persecution arises – immediately he stumbles." But there are many who never face tribulation or persecution, but are like the seed sown among the thorns. "The cares of this world and the deceitfulness of riches" are their downfall. How true it is that the worries and burdens of life, and the loud voice of riches that is so very deceitful, are the downfall of many Christians who fail to find the help of the Holy Spirit to meet life.

Only the soil that is cleansed from all obstacles is fit and ready to bear fruit to the glory of God. Only by the merits of the cleansing blood and the power of the Holy Spirit can we be free from the temptations of the carnal heart.

"Herein is my Father glorified, that ye bear much fruit; so shall ye be my disciples." The secret of this is the abiding life and the only way to know the abiding life is to be single minded (the mind of Christ). "The double minded man is unstable in all his ways." (James 1:8) The carnal mind must go; the carnal heart must be cleansed. Then, and then alone, can we bear fruit and bring joy to the heart of our Heavenly Father.

Rev. Marshal Cavit

189

Keep Them From The Evil (3)
Luke 12:1-5

Fear of man and fear of death have been the cause of many persons to surrender to Satan and finally lose their souls eternally. The only remedy is the power of the Holy Spirit to cleanse the heart and fill it with His presence, casting out fear. "Perfect love casteth out fear," but nothing else can do it.

The thought of what people will say or do is forever a temptation to those who have not crucified self and are set on protecting their pride and self esteem. There is nothing the matter with trying to act right, dress nicely, and present ourselves as a pleasant person to fellowship with others, but when it is a matter of pleasing people or obeying God, then our will needs to be the will of God without fear of the consequences. We need the help of the Holy Spirit to keep us from reaction to the contrary. Pride and self-esteem can easily be a trap for us.

When Daniel faced the lion's den, or obedience to the king contrary to the command of God, he feared neither the lions nor the king, but followed the will of God. The three Hebrew children faced obedience to the king or a furnace seven times hotter than usual, but they chose to be faithful to God even if God let them burn. Elijah stood alone to challenge prophets of Baal and without fear made sport of them concerning their prayers and their god. Joshua and Caleb saw the giants of Canaan but fearlessly said they could possess the land only because they had faith in God and did not trust in their own strength. Paul faced a mountain of persecution (2 Cor. 2), but feared nothing of it, not even death itself, because he trusted God and stood on God's promises, having a heart that was cleansed and filled with the Holy Spirit.

If you mean to walk with God and gain heaven for your eternal home, there will be giants ahead, a mountain of trials and temptations, and no chance of victory unless fear be cast out and perfect love for God fill your heart.

Rev. Marshal Cavit

Keep Them From The Evil (4)
Ezekiel 3:17-18; Matt. 7:21-23; 25:41-46

Many times we are deeply concerned and make great effort to be sure and not do the wrong thing, but what about our failures to do the right thing, the sin of omission? The word of God by the prophet Ezekiel tells us that if we fail to warn the wicked from his evil ways that his blood will be required at our hands. In the Sermon on the Mount, Jesus made it plain that we could do a lot of good things, but if we failed to do the will of God we would be banished to outer darkness. It's very clear that we not only need to give attention to the things that we shouldn't do, but also think of the urgency of doing what we are commanded in the Word.

In Eph. 5:14, Paul writes, "Be not drunk with wine, wherein is excess; but be filled with the Spirit." There is as much disobedience in refusing to be filled with the Spirit as there is in being drunk with wine. There are a host of Christian people today that would never think of committing the sin of getting drunk, but have no concern whatever about being filled with the Holy Spirit. To refuse to be filled with the Spirit is to leave us powerless to do the service that God desires of us. Serving the Lord acceptably is not by might, or power, or education, or money, or great plans and organized programs, "but by my Spirit, saith the Lord."

He commands that we love God with all our heart, soul, mind, and strength. Can we do it while the carnal mind remains, which Paul says is "enmity against God: for it is not subject to the law of God, neither indeed can be?" He said, "Love your enemies." Can you do it while vengeance and anger are in your heart? He said, "Go ye into all the world and preach the Gospel." Can you have a missionary vision and burden of love that will lay the world on your heart while selfishness reigns? Only the Spirit of God can make a missionary out of you and do the will of God in this matter.

Don't think only of the things you shouldn't do, but think of what He has commanded you to do.

Rev. Marshal Cavit

Don't Be A Crab Apple
John 17:17-26

My daily routine of physical fitness is a leisurely jog down Clark Road. For the past year I have observed the activity of a certain crab apple tree. In the spring it flowers, brings forth fruit in the summer and by October it's crop of ripened crab apples have fallen to the ground. The entire process is managed with no help from the farmer on whose land the tree grows. The crab apples grow wild.

A few miles east of the crab apple tree is a family run orchard. The owners have a roadside sign that advertises many varieties of apples. The trees require the gardener's care and the results are delicious!

Years ago, as new Christian, I made a decision to unite with a small holiness congregation. It is a decision I do not regret. I did not want to be a crab apple, if I could help it. I got inside the orchard.

In the local church, my soul was fed and the Christian fellowship strengthened my walk. I heard testimonies of God's glorious second work of grace and I saw first hand "fruit" from serving the Lord. There are advantages to being a member of the local church!

Being in "the orchard" increases your sense of responsibility, interest, and love for those around you. It lends to that sense of oneness in Christ, unity of purpose, and life with members of the church. In a sanctified walk with Jesus, you are united with other saints in doing His will. Jesus expressed this: "That they all may be one; as thou, Father, art in me, and I in thee, that they also be may be one in us: and that the world may believe that thou hast sent me." (John 17:21)

Why would anyone want to be a "crab apple Christian" when joining a "holiness orchard" is part of God's wise plan?

Rev. William Kren

The Promised Power
Acts 1:6-8; Acts 7:54-60

The promised power was for witnessing to Jesus Christ. This witness would be by word and by life. Life-style evangelism is the most effective form of witnessing. What we are goes farther than what we say. The demonstration of a Christ-like spirit under pressure is more persuasive than the fine-spun arguments of an orator. The essential power therefore is moral and spiritual.

But it also is power to witness by word of mouth. We are given grace to stand up for Jesus, and the Holy Spirit makes our faithful word effective. Not all Spirit-empowered Christians will preach or become eloquent. They may remain timid and shy by temperament. But as they honor the Spirit they will find themselves dropping a word here and there, and discover the truth that "a word fitly spoken is like apples of gold in pitchers of silver." (Proverbs 25:11)

The most common misunderstanding about the promised power is the notion that it is primarily charismatic in nature. The disciples had already been given this – read Matthew 10:1.

It is true, of course, that signs and wonders did accompany the witness of the apostles in the Early Church: "And with great power the apostles were giving witness to the resurrection of the Lord Jesus." (Acts 4:33) But it is easy to ignore the rest of the verse: "and great grace was upon them all." Not all possessed the power of miracles but all possess the power of great grace – which is far more essential.

When modern Christians begin to chase after external signs of power, they elevate this form of power above the power of holiness and the humble ordinary word. This is to stand the divine order on its head. Let us be holy in heart and life, and be faithful in the simple word, then leave the more spectacular forms of power totally up to the sovereign will of the Spirit. (1 Corinthians 12:11)

Dr. Richard S. Taylor

My Witnesses
Acts 1:8

It is inescapable! Christians who are filled with the Holy Spirit will find themselves doing works of God, which will amaze people, dismay the devil, and display Jesus.

Undoubtedly, heart purity and fullness of love are the primary results of the Holy Spirit's work in our hearts. Yet, we cannot deny that powerful witnessing is also a work of the Holy Spirit. It is attested in the Scriptures and by the testimonies of Christians through out history since.

Powerful witnessing through preaching, teaching, counseling, singing, writing, testifying and soul-winning should be expected, because Jesus promised it would take place when we are baptized with the Holy Spirit, and New Testament accounts demonstrate it. Of course, we will never seek to be filled with the Spirit for that reason. But once we are filled with the Spirit, we can and should pray for Him to exercise His sovereign power through us for the glory of Jesus.

As you prepare for living today, tomorrow and next week, first be sure that you are filled with the Holy Spirit. Then pray for His work to be powerful in you for making Jesus Christ known to people.

No one may write your experiences in a book, but you will praise God, the world will know they have met a Spirit-filled person, the demons and the devil will tremble and Jesus Christ will be glorified.

Rev. Ken Friesen

His Witnesses
Acts 1:8

Jesus spoke to His disciples of His suffering, death, and resurrection and declared, "Ye are witnesses of these things." (Luke 24:48) More than witness to historical facts they were to witness the reality of Christ in their lives. Christ's plan is for the Holy Ghost to indwell every Christian. He makes Christ real.

We are to witness about Christ and for Christ. We witness His divinity, atonement, death, resurrection, ascension and soon return. The Holy Ghost testifies of Christ, and so should we.

The disciples were cowards before Pentecost. Afterward, they were courageous and fearless. The dynamic of the Holy Ghost made the difference.

We are His witnesses verbally and silently. We consciously witness to glorify Christ, make Him known, and overcome Satan. John Wesley said, "It requires a great deal of watchfulness to retain the perfect love of God; and our great means of retaining it is, frankly, to declare what God has given you and earnestly to exhort all the believers you meet and follow after full salvation." Unconsciously we witness by the places we go, the attitudes we take, the company we keep, and the things we do and say.

The Holy Ghost creates an inner urge to witness. Thomas Cook said, "How I wish I could tell of the sweetness, the richness, and the indescribable blessedness of this life of perfect love. I cannot tell the story; but I cannot let it alone. O for a thousand tongues to proclaim Jesus to men, the mighty Savior, who is able to save them to the uttermost who come to God by Him."

Witnessing is the direct outflow of a Spirit-filled life.

Rev. J. Eldon Neihof

Keep The Blessing
Acts 1:8; 2:1, 6; 4:27, 31

The outpouring of the Holy Spirit on the day of Pentecost was the beginning of the Christian Church. Christians empowered by the Holy Spirit began a task that will continue until the return of Christ. Christians with hearts set aflame by the "cloven tongues of fire," strengthened by the power of the "rushing mighty wind," went forth to witness with loosened "tongues." Men of "every nation under heaven" (Acts 2:5b) heard and understood them that day.

On the day of Pentecost 3,000 people were saved. In a short time multitudes found Christ as Savior. The leaders of the Jews resented this and began to persecute them. Peter and John were arrested and commanded not to speak or teach in the name of Jesus. (Acts 3:18)

Instead of backing down, we find the disciples praying for boldness in Acts 4:29, "And when they had prayed, the place was shaken wherein they were assembled together; and they were all filled with the Holy Ghost, and they spake the word of God with boldness." (Acts 4:32, KJV)

These disciples who were filled with the Holy Spirit on the day of Pentecost were refilled on several occasions throughout the book of Acts. The fire of Pentecost must be refueled or renewed. We need to keep in close contact with our Lord so that we can be refilled with the Holy Spirit as we need it, and ready to meet the challenges of everyday life.

Jesus spoke of the Holy Spirit being like "rivers of living water" flowing out of our innermost beings. (John 8:38) A river must flow or it becomes a stagnant pool.

In our day, we too must determine that our hearts will be open, surrendered channels, through which the Holy Spirit can flow. We need His power to speak the word of God with boldness and to keep blessed.

Rev. Ivan Olson

The Day of Pentecost – the Wind
Acts 2:1-4

There are three expressions of the Holy Spirit manifested on the Day of Pentecost – the wind, the fire, and languages.

The wind symbolizes power for the new life that the Spirit brings in His filling. All of us encounter people, even in the Church, who believe all the right things and even believe they are trusting in the work of Christ on the cross as the basis for their salvation, but they lack the kind of vital aliveness that can come through total surrender to the ministry of the Holy Spirit. There are people who have all the forms of godliness but seem to lack the spiritual dynamism that distinguishes the Christian from the world.

John Wesley was conscious of this condition in his own life as he served as a missionary to Georgia. He knew he lacked assurance that he belonged to God and the joy that comes along with being in Christ. But one evening at a prayer meeting in a small building on Aldersgate Street the Spirit came upon him. From then on Wesley knew of the new life that the Spirit generates in the Christian and how the Spirit can take the deadness of the soul away. The Holy Spirit had come upon Wesley like a wind.

The Holy Spirit took impotent, willful, frightened, discouraged disciples and made them effective instruments to live the Christian life abundantly, a life that let others see Christ in the disciples and cause them to want that kind of life for themselves. What happened to Wesley can happen to all of us if we are willing to be surrendered to what the Spirit wills to effect in our lives.

Rev. John Moyer

The Day of Pentecost – the Fire and Languages
Acts 2:1-4

The fire on the day of Pentecost reveals the purifying work of the Spirit that delivers us from the effects of depravity. So many of us need this fire in our lives. We need to have the uncleanness of our hearts burned away.

It needs to burn to the depths of our hearts. It needs to go beyond the surface of just acting more decently and upright. The chaff needs to be burned up with "unquenchable" fire. (Lk. 3:17) And we need to be filled with a burning love that will warm those who come from the dark, cold world they are living in. It's a purifying work that will cause the gifts of the Spirit to be used unselfishly and sacrificially for the sake of God and His kingdom.

Then, communication was another work on the day of Pentecost by the Spirit of God. We all want relationships in which there are no barriers to honest communication. We all want to be with people who understand us. And that's what happened on the day of Pentecost. People from different ethnic backgrounds discovered a oneness in the Holy Spirit that met their deepest need for fellowship. The Holy Spirit created clear communication that day.

In our workplaces and in the Church there are occasions that cry out for real communication. Words are spoken. Sermons are preached. Statements are made. But little understanding occurs. The need for Spirit-filled communication is all too obvious. But it is the Spirit-filled that can communicate the Gospel the best. The real soul-winner, the real communicator of the Gospel is the Holy Spirit. But He needs clean instruments that are empowered with abundant life in order to speak to others.

Pentecost will empower, purify, and lead to Spirit-filled communication when it really takes place in our hearts.

Rev. John Moyer

The Holy Man Under Pressure
Acts 6-7

We are introduced to Stephen in Acts 6 and we bid farewell to him in chapter 7. In these two chapters we learn about Stephen and about how a holy man reacts under pressure.

He had experienced the fullness of God. Some people are full of sin and self, but what a testimony to be known as a man full of the Spirit. In Acts 6:5 it states that Stephen was full of the Holy Spirit. In Acts 7:55 it shows that he was. It's what comes out when the pressure is on that will tell what we are truly full of.

He excelled in the Word of God. Stephen knew the Word and he used it effectively. Our greatest strength in the promotion of truth still lies in our ability to relate the Word of God. We have nothing to prove, just something to reveal. But we can't reveal effectively what we don't know. We don't need arguments, we need authority.

He expressed the love of God. While Stephen was being stoned, he cried, "Lord, lay not this sin to their charge." (7:60) This is love "that thinketh no evil." That is, it does not nurse personal ills, and it does not keep a list of old ills done against it.

He felt himself expendable in the work of God. A.W. Tozer wrote, "We languish for men who feel themselves expendable in the warfare of the soul, who cannot be frightened by threats of death because they have already died to the allurements of this world. Such men will be free from compulsions that control weaker men. They will not be forced to do things by the squeeze of circumstances; their only compulsion will come from within – or from above. This kind of freedom is necessary if we are to have prophets in our pulpits again instead of mascots."

Dr. Hubert Harriman

199

God's Coronation Gift – The Holy Spirit
Acts 2:33-38

Nansen, a Norwegian explorer, took a carrier pigeon with him when he went to explore the North Pole. Arriving, he wrote a tiny message and fastened it securely under a wing of the pigeon. It flew over a thousand miles of snow, another thousand miles over ocean before it flew into the lap of Nansen's wife. The descending dove was eloquent testimony that her husband had arrived at his destination.

Peter explained Pentecost by saying, "Exalted to the right hand of the Father, Christ has received from the Father the promised Holy Spirit and has poured out what you now see and hear." Before He left this world Christ promised "another Comforter." The word "another" in the original language meant another just like Jesus. This other Comforter arrived at Pentecost to usher in the church age.

By the age of thirteen I was deeply convicted over my battle with the carnal nature. At a youth conference at the altar, I settled my consecration by, in effect, signing my name to a blank page and saying an eternal "yes" to let God fill in the page with the rest of my life. That "right-to-myself" was put to the cross – God's will was to be my will always. I had entered the door to the highway of holiness to learn obedience by the things which I would suffer. (Heb. 5:8)

Unlearning selfishness is a slow process unless we allow the Holy Spirit to sensitize our conscience and then quickly obey His directions. He allows us to suffer failure, loneliness, and losses in order to crowd us to Himself. "Anything, Lord" is a heart cry that ratifies on a daily basis our earlier covenants in the crisis hour of sanctification.

The Word became a new book to me after I was sanctified. Prayer was more real and personal – the checks of the Spirit more easily recognized and obeyed.

Mrs. Laura Trachsel

Not For Sale
Acts 8:9ff

Simon was ready to offer hard cash for the power of the Holy Spirit. While we cringe at the crass commercialism, it is to his credit that he at least wanted power. A disturbing number of Christians nowadays are apparently content not to consider it a major issue.

Power! How are we going to obtain it? The Apostles put Simon straight – the Holy Spirit was not for sale. He was, Peter said, "the gift of God." He is to be obtained on God's terms alone.

The Holy Spirit is available to those who wait for Him. "Tarry ye in the city of Jerusalem until ye be clothed with power from on high" (Lk. 24:49) was the Lord's command to the disciples. We need to wait for Him. The length of time is not the crucial matter, but the manner of our waiting. We must search our hearts diligently and deeply. We must come to sincerely see our helplessness and hopelessness apart from His enabling, and so surrender ourselves completely to Him. "Blessed are all they that wait for Him." (Isa. 30:38)

The Holy Spirit is available to those who ask for Him. Waiting is not an interminable process. Waiting must lead to asking. This, too, is the word from the Lord, "… how much more shall your heavenly Father give the Holy Spirit to them that ask Him." (Lk. 11:13) Waiting for Him will reveal our deep need and inspire a longing for His fullness in our entirely surrendered heart. But then we must ask for God's good Gift.

Waiting and asking. And then? The Holy Spirit is given to those who obey Him. (Acts 5:32) An obedient Christian cannot help but be a powerful Christian.

Power is not for sale, but is obtainable to all who wait, ask, and obey.

Rev. Gene Moyer

Tricked By Our Faith
Acts 9:1-16

We must be careful about letting our faith boost us too much. Faith may try to make it easier for us by reminding us of these basic truths: we needn't fear; we can trust the will of God. Faith reminds us of the song which we have often sung, "God's way is the best way!"

Faith says: "Is not God all-wise? – so He couldn't be mistaken. Is He not all-righteous? – so His will couldn't be evil. Is He not all-loving? – so His will is bound to be kind." Faith reminds us that when all is considered we just can't lose. But may I surprise you by insisting that all of these can be the wrong reasons for deciding to obey God.

So tell faith to go mind its own business and not try to dilute the authenticity of your obedience. May I explain further? If you allowed faith to provide the basis of your decision, so that you said to yourself, "I know that if I obey God I will be happier in the long run," you would still be acting primarily out of self-interest. Self would still be first and God perceived to be our way of getting the best out of life.

Now it is undeniably true that God's way is the best way. It is true that obeying God is the surest way of being happy in the long run. But I must insist that these are not the right reasons for embracing the will of God. There is only one right reason: because <u>God is God</u>, and therefore to obey Him is <u>right</u>. Cross out the prospect of God's will being either pleasing or promising.

Settle the acceptance of God's will on that basis and you will never wobble as long as you live. Settle it on any other basis and you will never stop wobbling.

Dr. Richard S. Taylor

When Saints Disagree
Acts 15:35-41

Here is an incredible story of two Spirit-filled men, Paul and Barnabas, having controversy over John Mark, and parting company. Is it possible for sanctified people to have a falling out? Here is the problem of personal feelings and emotions. It is a case of human opinion. Note the words, Barnabas "determined," Paul "thought it not good."

Let's face it – sanctified people do not always think alike. It is perfectly human to differ over policy and procedure, and not grieve the Holy Spirit. We have to believe that their contention was not carnal or unchristian. And we can see that it led to the furtherance of the Gospel and the growth of the church.

There are lessons we can learn from this difficult story. First, there is a difference between unity and uniformity. God's people often do not see things alike, yet there can be love and oneness among them. Secondly, there is a great difference between humanity and carnality. We all have our human preferences, our likes and dislikes. But these should not overlap into personality clashes. Thirdly, we should be able to disagree without being disagreeable. We should be able to contend without being contentious. This is where the help of the Holy Spirit comes in.

There is one thing about this story that bothers me. In Acts 13:2-4 it was emphasized that sending out Paul and Barnabas was specifically the leading of the Holy Spirit, after much prayer and fasting. But there is no mention that sending John Mark with them was led of God. They did not even pray about it. Perhaps that is one reason for the conflict; why he quit them in the midst of the first missionary journey. Paul and Barnabas did not even suggest praying about their difference. How much we need to make areas of conflict a matter of earnest prayer!

Rev. Roy Clark

The Life To Live
Acts 20:18-38

There are two aspects of Paul's life that are worth noting in this passage: (1) that he lived what he preached, and (2) that he proclaimed the whole counsel of God. We shall look at the first one today.

Paul could honestly point to his life among the Ephesians and say, "You know . . . in what manner I always lived among you." He did not set standards for others to live by, if he himself did not live them. So what standards do we find? Titus is full of them. Just a few of them are found in 2:6-8: "be sober-minded, in all things showing yourself integrity, reverence, incorruptibility, sound speech that cannot be condemned, that one who is an opponent may be ashamed, having nothing evil to say of you."

What a marvelous testimony! Paul could say, "You know that my life has been one of doing good works, and I didn't twist the Bible to fit me but I taught it honestly and forthrightly. I have lived a holy life and no one can point at me and say 'hypocrite.'"

Our outward life is to be a manifestation of the inward working of the Holy Spirit. Can there be spiritual life if there is not fruit? The answer found in Titus 2:11-12 is no. Salvation brings us to a turning away from worldly lusts and implants a desire to live a godly life.

But Paul's life was one of consistency too. Notice the phrase, "in what manner I always lived . . . ." With Paul, we do not see a life run by the emotions of the hour. Reliance upon emotions makes for unsettled attitudes and erratic decision-making. Paul's life was stable - solid, because he had faith in an unchanging God.

God calls us today to live consistent, godly lives. Can we do it? Not by ourselves, but it is possible, if we allow the Holy Spirit to cleanse us of carnality ... if we ask Him to work that gracious work of full-salvation.

Rev. Roger Schoenborn

Unmovable
Acts 20:22-27

A great need in our churches today is for men and women who know what they believe, both by head knowledge and heart experience, and know why they believe it. It is possible to read and study and come to a knowledge of what is right, but if there is a lack of inner spiritual strength it is easy to surrender to contrary pressure from friends or from those who have authority over us. The only solution to the problem is self-crucifixion, a complete consecration to God, allowing the Holy Spirit to cleanse and fill our hearts with His presence and power.

The Holy Spirit had warned Paul that bonds and affliction were waiting for him, but his testimony was, "I am crucified with Christ." (Gal. 2:20) You can bind or beat a corpse, but there is no response in return.

John the Baptist could have saved his head if he hadn't told Herod that it was not lawful for him to have Philip's wife. Stephen could probably have avoided being stoned to death had he not been so faithful in his preaching. Daniel could have avoided the lion's den by finding a more secret place to pray and being a little quieter in his praying, or just asking of the king instead of his God, Whom he knew to be the true God. The three Hebrew children would never have seen the fiery furnace if they had only consented to worship the king's idol. The list is long of martyrs who preferred to die rather than be unfaithful to God and to the souls of men. To have been unfaithful was to lose their own souls and also to have the blood of other lost souls on their hands on the Day of Judgment.

We have the same decision to make today. We may not suffer physical death by the wrong decision, but what of the judgment day? Can you say with Paul, "I take you to record this day, that I am pure from the blood of all men, for I have not shunned to declare unto you all the counsel of God?"

Rev. Marshal Cavit

The Christian's Full Inheritance (1)
Acts 26:12-18

I would call your attention to two points found in our text (v. 18), a distinct people and a distinct inheritance.

There is a people who have met God's requirements and are now in the line for the inheritance. Those distinct people are the sanctified. The question comes, "What is sanctification?" As taught in the various holiness denominations we can probably best describe it as "to be made a partaker of the Divine nature." (2 Peter 1:4) As seen in Scriptural context it is "the will of God" (1 Thessalonians 4:3), that God's people should be "holy" – pure, chaste, clean – cleansed from all the filthy lusts of the flesh, and all manner of uncleanness both of heart and life, soul and body. It is God's will that our sanctification is true in both the permissive and authoritative sense. He is willing we should be holy, and He commands and requires us to be holy.

You will find it was Paul's commission to preach and exhort believers to obtain this experience. It was the climax of Paul's preaching that believers be led into their "full inheritance." It is an established fact, regardless of the unrighteous acts of professed Christians who do not have the experience.

Let me say it unequivocally. It is not what man says that makes a thing true. Every man may be a liar; God is true! It is not the profession of a doctrine that establishes its truth. It is the will of God, from whom it has proceeded. Man's experience may illustrate it, but it is God's truth that confirms it!

Holiness, like truth, is a simple uncompounded element or quality and continues unchangeable; the same at all times and under all circumstances. It can never be made anything else in its essential nature, being the absence of moral iniquity. It is expressive, not of an advancing growth, but of moral quality and has respect mainly to kind or quality, rather than degree.

Rev. Gene Moyer

The Christian's Full Inheritance (2)
Acts 26:12-18

Now another question arises, "Who are the sanctified?" The person in who is sanctified is one whose heart here has taken place the expiration of all that is opposed to grace. They are those who are "cleansed from all sin," who are made "perfect in love," who are "without spot," who are "cleansed from all filthiness of flesh and spirit," and who have thus perfected holiness in the fear of God." Simply put, the sanctified are those who have a pure heart. Jesus said, "Blessed are the pure in heart for they shall see God." Having considered the point of "a distinctive people," let us now consider the phase of the inheritance of the sanctified.

One outstanding point to be noticed is that this inheritance is to that group of people who are known and identified as being sanctified. Not growing into the experience, not longing for the experience, but those who are sanctified now, in the present tense. These are in possession of and manifest the nine graces of the Spirit of Galatians 5:22-23. Notice these groups of three: (1) love, joy, peace – character as an inward state; (2) long-suffering, gentleness, goodness – character in expression toward man; (3) faith, meekness, temperance – character in expression to God. These graces or fruits of the Spirit come only to those who are Christ's, who have crucified the affections and lusts. (Galatians 5:24) The word "flesh," as used, is the same as the word "flesh" of Romans 8, meaning "the carnal mind." Friend, carnality cannot inherit the Kingdom of God because carnality is enmity against God and is not subject to the law of God, neither indeed can be!

Rev. Gene Moyer

The Christian's Full Inheritance (3)
Acts 26:12-18

The final test of the successful Christian life is this: "Are you sanctified?" Some may say "Yes," and point to the power and success of the disciples before Pentecost. That is true, but when the test was on, where were they? Where was Peter when Jesus was being led to Pilate's judgment hall? The Bible says he was "afar off." However, after the Day of Pentecost, we have no record of them being powerless.

Let's look at what Jesus has done for us. He took upon Him our sins and gave us His holiness. He took our death and gave us His life. He was despised that we might be honored. He was rejected that we might be received. He took our griefs that He might give us His joy. He gives us beauty for ashes, the oil of joy for mourning, and the garment of praise for the spirit of heaviness. All this has Jesus done that He might lead us into everlasting life and the inheritance of the sanctified.

One day I noticed a bank advertisement that said, "When you think of banking, think of...." My friend, is it not a fact that when we think of eternity and the welfare of the soul, we think of God? And when one thinks of God in His holiness and His eternity, it produces a similar effect as it did on Isaiah, "Woe is me." When this is done, it will cause us to do one of two things: either turn one's back on God, or fling ourselves upon the mercy of God and plead the blood. If we follow the Holy Spirit He will lead us into the inheritance that belongs to the sanctified. The promise to the Christian is that they are heirs of God and joint heirs of Christ.

You may have an earthly inheritance pending, but you may never live to receive it. Not so with the inheritance of the sanctified. This inheritance is for "you who are kept by the power of God." It is yours, if you are sanctified. If you are not, press forward and claim that which God desires to give you.

Rev. Gene Moyer

A Heart For The World (1)
Acts 26:13-19

Paul is making his defense before king Agrippa and at the heart of that defense is Jesus' commission to reach the world with the gospel. When Jesus mastered Paul, he was compelled and propelled to reach those who know nothing of the great salvation Jesus had provided all people through His death and resurrection.

Some time ago I was standing by the train station in Uvinza, Tanzania about 9:30 at night. Since there is no electricity, the town was dark. The houses and trees were silhouetted against the light of a full moon. Out of the darkness came the sounds of drums and chanting. A spirit worship ceremony was in progress. This is part of what verse 18 means by the "power of Satan." Not only was there physical darkness but spiritual darkness!

It's hard for us to imagine how Satan has kept people in spiritual darkness. 2 Corinthians 4:4 speaks of those who the god of this world has blinded so the light of Christ won't break through to them. But these people are searching and crying out for help. All they go through is a desperate attempt to silence the fear, loneliness, guilt, and emptiness in their lives. The Africans in the spirit ceremony, the sacrifices at rocks and trees, the charms, rituals, burning incense, offerings, and ritual prayer; the religious who go through the sacraments, works, penance, and self-imposed hardships – all are seeking for something to break them out of the darkness, though they may not be able to pinpoint their trouble as spiritual darkness.

When our hearts have been cleansed of self-will, we begin to have an interest in others. In particular there is a deep concern for their spiritual welfare. The spiritual darkness of others burdens our hearts and propels us to action to see that they too have an opportunity to hear the good news and make a choice.

Rev. Nevin Williams

A Heart For The World (2)
Acts 26:13-19

The first task in this troubled world is to bring the gospel to bear against the awful bondage of Satan. People's eyes must be opened to the truth that there is a better way; that God has deliverance for them. They must see that the blood of Christ can do what they've been trying to accomplish in so many other ways.

When we were exploring a new area in Burundi, pastor Isaka read from Isaiah 9 to the curious who were watching. Verse two says, "The people that walked in the darkness have seen a great light...." That was the beginning of opening their eyes. Today there are over a thousand people in the church established in that area.

While in Kenya I had the chance to counsel with a father and his two grown sons who requested prayer after the message. They had a deep hunger for the Lord. As I shared God's Word with them, you could see the truth taking hold in their hearts and minds. After praying, all three left the church as new Christians. Psalm 119:130 says, "The entrance of thy words giveth light; it giveth understanding unto the simple."

Sanctification clarifies the vision and enlarges the heart to reach around the world. When the media reports natural disasters there is usually a great outpouring of sympathy and material help. Only men, women, and young people who have died to self and become bondservants of Christ see the far greater disaster enveloping the world – spiritual darkness. We have the means to penetrate that darkness. We have the message that can open their eyes and present them with Jesus Christ who can forgive their sins, make them new creatures, sanctify them wholly, and fit them for heaven. Now that's exciting!

Rev. Nevin Williams

A Heart For The World (3)
Acts 26:13-19

Even salvation can become selfish. This was Israel's problem. They walled themselves off from the gentile world even though God had told them they were to be a light to the gentiles. Sanctification takes the focus off of ourselves and gives us the desire to be instruments of God in bringing that light to others.

Do you remember when you were born again? When Jesus became real in your life? When you were made a new creature in Christ? There was that release from guilt and a new purpose in living. Things really were made new! How could we ever deny this life changing opportunity to needy hearts around the world? I wish you could see what happens when many of these people enter into the joy of sins forgiven. The darkness is rejected as they embrace the light. The power of Satan is broken in their lives as, in repentance and faith, they allow Christ to come into their lives.

I can still see the elderly woman at the Kapsimbiri Christmas service in Kenya. With a radiant smile she testified about how the Lord had kept her from the time of her conversion. Or what about the 70 year old man in Mexico who rose from his knees, tears streaming down his face, a new creature in Christ, after hearing the gospel for the first time? Space doesn't permit telling about the sorcerer, rainmaker, schoolteacher, government official and scores of others who have turned from darkness to light, from the power of Satan unto God, and received forgiveness of sins.

In this country of light, it's hard for us to understand how radical this turning really is. Yet as the gospel is preached, it has the supernatural power of God breathed into it by the Holy Spirit that produces that turning. As holiness people, there can be no greater task to which we can give ourselves than getting the gospel to all people. A holy heart cares. A holy heart reaches out.

Rev. Nevin Williams

A Heart For The World (4)
Acts 26:13-19

The whole gospel message has as its end goal holiness of heart and life. As hearts cry out around the world, their real, deep, ultimate need is deliverance from inbred sin that exalts self against the Creator and seeks its own good rather than the will of God. Therefore "getting them saved" simply isn't enough. They must hear and understand that not only does Christ provide for forgiveness of sins but has a work of grace that cleanses the heart from the root of sin. The peoples of the world need the opportunity to find their inheritance among those sanctified by faith in Jesus. In an age that glorifies self, people everywhere must be told that self is at the heart of the world's problems; it's at the heart of their own problems.

One of my greatest sources of satisfaction has been the preaching of holiness not only in North America but also in Africa. A man in Kenya came to me in tears after a message on holiness. There were three areas of his life that needed to be straightened out before he could be sanctified. After confessing and asking the Lord to forgive him, he committed himself totally to the Lord, died to self and trusted Jesus for cleansing. He was radiant! Before the meeting was over, he asked me to pray for him and his wife as he felt the Lord might be dealing with him about fulltime service. In December of 1988, I watched as he and his wife were commissioned by the church to be missionaries among another people in Kenya. The first of the year he quit his good paying job with the government and moved to that remote part of the country to bring the message that will open their eyes and change lives!

That's the way it works! Sanctified children of God will always see the need and desire to reach out around the world in one way or another.

Prayer: Father, help me that when I stand before you I may be able to say, "I was not disobedient to the heavenly vision."

Rev. Nevin Williams

Easy Access
Acts 26:15-20

Asuncion, Paraguay, unlike the rest of the country, is a bustling metropolis bursting with business places and busy thoroughfares. Mariscal Lopez Avenue, with its bumper-to-bumper traffic, is especially hard to gain access to. One may wait interminably only to give up and go hopping down a narrow side street to reach a larger intersection where there are traffic lights.

Easy access. Why do we make it so hard and drawn out to receive holiness of heart? The Israelites could have used God's easy access to go into the Promised Land. Not to decry the giants and the fierce battles that would have taken place, it still would have been easier to enter in right then and there, immediately after their deliverance from Egyptian bondage, if they just had **believed**. "All things are possible to him that believeth." (Mark 9:23)

Israel chose man's way and as a result, the entering in became insurmountably difficult. So difficult, in fact, it was impossible. So many times we have seen seekers after holiness trying to enter in "man's way" digging away at the mountain of carnality with a pitifully small pick and shovel, picking up a rock here, a piece of debris there, looking at the difficulties, trying harder and harder to be perfect or die out to something or other, presumably procuring to push their miserable wheelbarrow of a vehicle by brute force into the main stream. Impossible!

In the final analysis God's way is always the easiest way, the **only** way. We must let go of our way and let God do it His way. To believe is to let God do the heavy work. "That they may receive...(an) inheritance among them which are sanctified **by faith** that is in me (Christ)." (Acts 26:18)

Rev. Harold Harriman

Holiness And Faith
Romans 4:18-25

For a long time I have responded to the question, "What is faith?" by quoting the well-known words of Hebrews 11:1, "Now faith is the substance of things hoped for, the evidence of things not seen." I am not anticipating trading that definition in on a new one, but I recently came across another Scriptural definition of faith that I enjoy as well. It is found in Romans 4:21 where Abraham is described as "being fully persuaded that God had the power to do what he had promised." What a marvelous definition of faith!

Anyone who ever has been sanctified, or ever will be, will receive that marvelous blessing only by faith. (Acts 15:8-9) We must come to the point where we are <u>fully persuaded</u> that God has power to do what He promised. And surely He has promised, "I am going to send you what my Father has promised; but stay in the city until you have been clothed with power from on high."
(Luke 24:49; Acts 1:4-5)

I recall my own personal experience. I had come to the realization that, though a child of God, there was still a battle raging in my heart. At times there seemed to be no hope of victory when, with very little provocation, anger, pride, and lust would spew forth their rotten fruit. The night I sought heart cleansing I struggled for nearly an hour with the enemy of unbelief. Could God cleanse a heart as desperately wicked as mine? The blessing finally came when I was <u>fully persuaded</u> that indeed He could. And then He did!

Dr. Bruce Moyer

Consecration (1)
Romans 6:1-14

We must always be careful not to confuse consecration (man's responsibility) and sanctification (God's work of grace) when we speak about being made holy. However, we still recognize that consecration necessarily precedes sanctification. This makes it vitally important for us to understand what consecration is.

Consecration is, according to Scripture, <u>confession.</u> It is confessing that Christ alone has the right to govern and rule in my life. (1 Cor. 6:19-20) This is where consecration really begins – recognizing that Jesus must be King of my life.

The Scriptures go on to say that consecration also involves <u>separation.</u> (2 Cor. 6:14-7:1) A consecrated person is one who has made a decision to take on a new life-style. He/She, though still living in this world, is no longer a part of it.

Consecration is not only "from" something (sin and the world) but also "to" "Someone" (God). Thus it may be further described by the word <u>dedication</u>. It is a dedication of all my life and service to Jesus. He becomes my first concern. (Matt. 6:33) I have set my mind on the things above. (Col 3:2) A consecrated person is one who has dedicated him or herself fully to the service of the King.

Tomorrow we will look at three more characteristics of consecration. Perhaps the following words of A.M. Hills (*Holiness and Power*, 242) will summarize what we've seen thus far: "Consecration is the actual present surrender to God of the whole man and all we possess."

Dr. Bruce Moyer

Consecration (2)
Romans 12:1-2

We saw yesterday that consecration may be partly defined as confession, separation and dedication. Today we shall touch on three more distinct aspects of consecration, which are found in Scripture.

Consecration may be described as a <u>presentation</u> of my entire being to God. (Rom. 6:13) It is a handing over of my life to God, without condition or reservation. There can be no "dickering" over the price – it is a total surrender. There can be no strings attached to this presentation of life and possessions if it is to be true consecration.

A fifth aspect of consecration is <u>submission</u>. It is a decision to submit my will to God's on every occasion. It is a commitment to obey God at all times and in all situations. (Acts 5:29; Luke 22:42)

Finally, consecration involves <u>determination</u>. I determine in my heart to follow God at any cost. (Luke 14:27) The Apostle Paul had this kind of determination. He wrote, "This one thing I do...." (Phil. 3:13-14) He was determined to follow Christ at any cost. Nothing (afflictions, sufferings, failure, temptation, etc.) could deter him from this determination!

Dr. Lowry has written:

"When we give all to God we make a summary transfer of ourselves to Him...Do it so really that ever after it would strike you as an act of trespass to use any member of your body, or faculty of your mind, or affection of your soul, or portion of your possessions against God, apart from God, or for any selfish motives, that would offend God, and take you or yours any way out of His hands." (*Possibilities of Grace,* 310)

Dr. Bruce Moyer

Overflow Not Overwork
Romans 6:1-14 (verse 13)

Machinery that is operated without oil will soon become useless. The life that endeavors to do God's work without the oil of the Holy Spirit will soon discover that mere human strength is insufficient for doing soul-winning work.

Here are some prerequisites of the overflow life. I trust they will be helpful.

1. Purity of heart. Any selfishness, unholy ambition, personal resentment against another soul will stop the joy of the Lord's presence and will cause a blight to settle over the soul. If you would overflow, the Living Christ must indwell you. If you want the overflow you must separate yourself from persons, places, and things that in the slightest manner shut Him out, weaken His touch upon your life, and loosen your grasp upon Him.
2. A full and utter confidence in the power and authority of God's Word. God wants us to trust Him and not to rely upon feelings, fancies, or appearances. He would save us from the peril of testing our victory, or testing His indwelling, by any preconceived notion of ours as to how His presence shall be felt or manifested.
3. Live independently of the opinions of others. He who lives for the good opinions of others will never know the glories of the overflow life. To live the overflow life, ever keep in mind that the work to be done is His work - the harvest to be gathered is His harvest - the church to be built is His church. He is the power, the glory, and the victory.

Rev. Gene Moyer

Fruit Unto Holiness
Romans 6:12-23

Our attitude toward sin is the keystone of Christian theology. Tell me what your belief is regarding sin, and I will identify your doctrine. Your belief concerning sin defines whether or not you can have spiritual victory.

In this chapter Paul deals openly and honestly with the problem of sin. More than a dozen times in this chapter he speaks of having victory over sin in our lives: "Dead to sin, free from sin, sin shall not have dominion over you." There is an experience of divine grace that lifts us above the domination of sin. Praise God!

This climax of "fruit unto holiness" is the culmination of four concepts in this chapter. All of them are experiential and apply to Christian living. Our relation to sin is the emphasis of v. 7. The body of sin is destroyed and we are freed from sin. It is not that it is impossible to sin, but that it is possible not to sin. God wants to give us an experience of divine grace that settles the sin problem in our lives.

Our relation to God is the theme of v. 13. The secret is total yieldedness and surrender to God. The pictures of servanthood and instruments in the hands of God are the secret. A tool is the extension of the worker's skill. When we yield ourselves as tools in the hands of God, we become useful in building His Kingdom.

In v. 19 the emphasis is upon life. Fruit unto holiness is the result of total surrender. "Servants to righteousness unto holiness" is the wording of the verse.

Relation to death is the thought of v. 23. The end is everlasting life. What a difference in our concept of death. There is no fear of dread, but a glad anticipation of eternal reward. Praise God!

Rev. Roy Clark

I Didn't Want To – But I Did
Romans 7:14-25

At best, my wife and I are novices at snow skiing. We just learned a few years ago and we seldom go. The last time we went I was reminded of the day we had learned to ski. It was a Thanksgiving weekend as we visited friends in Denver. At least we were smart enough to pay for the beginner's instruction. One thing the instructor kept stressing was that, as beginners, we should never point our skis straight downhill and get into a tucked position – that would almost certainly bring disaster and end our skiing for life!

After the training period we were allowed to ski on our own for two more hours. Being the athlete that I am, something inside me just wanted to go faster ... so finally I did it – I tucked and headed straight downhill. It wasn't long until I was out of control and you can guess the rest of the story. It's only by God's grace that I'm not a part of the permanent art collection on the wall of the ski lodge.

In Romans 7, the apostle Paul looks back on his life before entire sanctification and is reminded that carnality operates just like that. It is that urge within the heart to do something other than what the Master Instructor has told us to do. It makes a battlefield of the heart. No matter how much we grow and mature in the Lord, if it isn't cleansed from the heart by a radical work of God's grace, it will eventually result in a spiritual downfall. How I praise God, as Paul does in verses 24-25, that there is victory over that bent toward sin through Jesus!

Dr. Bruce Moyer

It's "The Sin," Not The Will
Romans 7:15-8:4

Holiness is now a popular subject for Christian speakers and writers. I applaud efforts that inform Christ's Church about the holiness of God. I appreciate those whom God uses to inspire Christians in the pursuit of holiness. I am alarmed, however, whenever holiness advocates set forth a standard of holiness, raise aspiration for attaining it, then let sincere seekers down.

One letdown is telling the seeker that holiness is a goal to strive for, but it can only be attained finally in heaven.

Another letdown is found in the words of the writer who says that holiness will begin to be our experience when we begin choosing consistently to do God's will.

This is exactly what Paul says is neither the problem nor the answer. His will wants to do God's will. His desire is to please God. His delight is in God's law. So, what's the problem? The problem is what lies behind the will. The problem is a will that is affected by "the sin living in me."

In the Greek New Testament the word "the" appears before the word "sin" in Romans 7, indicating that sin here is not an act I perform, but a condition or principle which pollutes my heart. My will can choose holiness, but it cannot stop "the sin" from prompting it to choose evil. Unattained holiness is a problem of "the sin," not a problem of the will.

The good news, Paul wrote, is that Jesus Christ by His blood and His Spirit can rid me of the prompting, captivating principle of sin. My efforts at attaining holiness fall short, my will fails; but the power of the blood and the presence of the Holy Spirit can free me from "the sin" and fill me with holiness.

Rev. Ken Friesen

A Foreign Element
Romans 7:21, 23, 24; 1 John 1:7

I had just returned from a trip that had kept me away from home for several days. As always, after such a trip, I was catching up on the news from my family. One of the news items was that our dog "Willie" was acting as if he were gagging and seemed to not feel well.

As I was petting him, I noticed a lump on his neck and under his long, floppy ear. The lump was about two inches in diameter.

The next morning we took Willie to the veterinarian, who took X-rays and then preformed surgery. How surprised we were after the surgery when the vet showed us the problem. "I have found a foreign element that pierced Willie's throat," the vet told us. Willis had found a sewing needle with about eight inches of black thread and had tried to swallow it. How he must have suffered! However, surgery removed the foreign element, and today Willie is energetic and well.

Paul, when writing to the Romans, told about his spiritual foreign element. He desired to be all God wanted, but a law in his members warred against God. This was a foreign element that was not in God's will for man. But how man suffers because of this foreign element! Paul calls it the carnal mind and goes on to say that "it is not subject to the law of God." (Romans 8:7) There is only one way that God can deal with this foreign element. He must destroy it by cleansing the heart of His child. (1 John 1:7)

For this reason God's Spirit "x-rays" our hearts and wants to perform the purifying surgery of cleansing so that we are not sickly but healthy and energetic Christians. Our part is to let Him search our hearts, then yield to the work of His Spirit cleansing us from all sin.

Rev. David Kushman

Freedom From Rebellion
Romans 8:1-9; Romans 6:1-13

Rebellion is one of the hallmarks of carnality. Self-interest doesn't yield gracefully to those things that block it from having its own way. While riding with one of our police officers, he told me about stopping a speeder and found that neither the man nor his fourteen year old son were wearing their seat belts. Upon pointing this out, the man shot back, "Nobody tells me what to do!" "That's fine," replied the officer, "but it just cost you $22.50 a piece for that privilege."

Even God is a target of this rebellion. The carnal mind will never yield to the laws of God. This means there is a battle going on in the life of the carnal Christian. His loyalties are divided. Part of him wants to be obedient to Christ and follow Him; another part of him wants his own way. Things pop to the surface in his life along the line of feelings, relationships and attitudes that cause him sorrow, taking him to his knees before God.

This state will not go on forever. Either we will seek the remedy for carnality or it will lead us down the path of gradual decline into a lukewarm religion that has the name Christian tacked to it but no real life. Romans 6:6 is clear that "the" sin, as it says in the Greek, can be cleansed from our hearts! This bias toward self with which we're born can never submit, it has to be removed. As we yield totally to God in a deliberate act of consecration and trust Jesus to cleanse our hearts, the work is accomplished we are freed from the rebellion of the carnal mind. Someone has said that everything on the inside must be on God's side. Praise God for the deliverance that brings everything in line with Him!

Rev. Nevin Williams

The Holy Spirit And Prayer
Romans 8:26-27

For the true child of God the fullness of the Spirit is imperative for an effective prayer life. Carnal motives will prohibit an answer from God. "You ask, and receive not, because you ask amiss, that you may consume it upon your lusts." (James 4:3) A clean heart is essential for faith that receives an answer to prayer.

We need the Holy Spirit to help us to know how to pray and what to pray for. We need the Holy Spirit to teach us the will of God. "If we ask anything according to His will, He heareth us." (1 John 5:14) Because of the weakness of our human nature, we know not how to ask as we ought, and we need the help of the Holy Spirit to help our infirmities. Knowing our hearts, He makes intercession for us in accord with the will of God, and what is best for us. If our hearts are completely given to God and we love Him perfectly, the Spirit knows this, and knows that we will be satisfied and grateful to receive what God, out of love, gives to us. There have been times in my life that I have asked the Lord for what I thought was in accord with His will, but He didn't give it to me. He even gave me what at the time seemed to be much worse than what I asked for, but I accepted it with thanksgiving, and later realized He had given me what was much better than what I had asked for. The finiteness of my mind and inability to see the future, kept me from asking for what was best for me and the glory of God. But the Spirit, knowing my heart's desire, interceded for me in accord with God's will, to give me something that turned out to be best for me.

We need the Holy Spirit to open up the Scriptures to us, that we may know better what the will of the Lord is. He will also give us a better understanding of God's faithfulness to give us His best, out of love and care for us.

Rev. Marshal Cavit

223

Praise Under Any Circumstance!
Romans 8:28-31

Worn out on a hot September day, a tired farmer sat under a walnut tree to rest. Relaxing, he looked at his pumpkin vines and said to himself, "How strange it is that God puts such big heavy pumpkins on a frail vine that has so little strength it has to trail on the ground!" and then, looking up into the green branches of the tree above him, he added, "How strange it is that God puts small walnuts on such a big tree with branches so strong they could hold a man!"

Just then a sudden breeze dislodged a walnut from the tree. Falling to the earth, the walnut found its mark directly on the farmer's head! The tired farmer wondered no more as he rubbed the knot on his head…and he thought: "It's a good thing there wasn't a pumpkin up there instead of a walnut!"

Living the sanctified life is no guarantee that we will be free from great trials and tribulations! The clouds of adversity will blow our way and we may be tempted to moan and complain – wonder why we must suffer or face such a great test. We may even go so far as to question God and His wisdom of allowing us to face our "especially difficult test!"

When the winds of trial begin to blow, remember that God, who is great and wise, makes NO mistakes! He deserves our praise under any circumstance. And that is why the Spirit baptized Christian can claim that wonderful promise, found in Romans 8:28: "and we know that all things work together for good the them that love God, to them who are the called according to His purpose."

Rev. William Kren

The Life Of Victory
Romans 8:28-39

The Bible pictures a life of daily victory for the Christian. God does not tease us with goals so high they are unreachable. He gives enablement with every command, even the command, "Be ye holy." The light that reveals our need is the light that heals.

My father, as a young man in Iowa, felt a lack and prayed for a clean heart and the Holy Spirit filled him. He did not know the holiness terminology until years later when he heard it preached in Oregon. His hunger led him into the fullness of the blessing.

Suppose a turkey dinner is displayed in a restaurant window. A very hungry man sees the display, has the amount of the price, and searches eagerly for the door. His hunger drives him to the feast. Our Bible School students would tell me that they wanted to be filled with the Spirit, but I would say, "You are not deeply longing for it." There must be a groan in the soul and a surrender of all things. "If He is not Lord of all, He is not Lord at all."

We do not accidentally stumble into the second blessing. We don't go to sleep with reservations in our consecration and wake up in the morning fully sanctified. "Anything Lord" is a short, but comprehensive prayer for a desperate seeking heart. Just as Christ was wholly given up to Christ, we must go down before we can go up. There must be a dispossessing before there is a possessing. There must be poverty before there can be riches. There must be death before there can be life.

Mrs. Laura Trachsel

What Consecration Did You Make?
Romans 12

There are many people who are consecrated to certain lines of religious work who are not wholly sanctified. Our consecration to receive His sanctification is not for us to do something for Him, but for Him to do something for us; to cleanse and fill with His Holy Spirit and empower us for his service. We are to present our bodies a living sacrifice "unto God." This is a complete love gift of our all to the will of God, as clay in the potter's hand.

This is "our reasonable service," the only reasonable thing to do, knowing that even "as the heavens are higher that the earth, so are HIS WAYS higher than our ways, and HIS THOUGHTS higher than our thoughts." (Isaiah 55:9) Therefore the only, and most reasonable, thing to do is to consecrate our all, "a living sacrifice," not to some work of righteousness according to our own thinking or planning, but to God, to "prove what is that good, and acceptable, and perfect, will of God." (Romans 12:2)

Some have said, "I have given Him everything I know." That is not enough. We must also give Him everything we do not know. Our consecration must include a very large bundle of the things that God has in store for us that He will reveal to us in the future. It is for our good that He does not reveal them all to us now. If He did, and they were hard and difficult things, it could be hard for us to say a "yes" to it all. If they were a lot of good and wonderful blessings, we would be prone to be boastful and proud. Thank the Lord that He has chosen to reveal things step by step and give sufficient grace to meet each day, and in such a way to keep us in complete harmony with His own will.

We need to be willing to receive what He gives, lack what He withholds, give what He takes, suffer what He allows, be what He requires, do what He commands, go where He sends, and say what He wants us to say.

Rev. Marshal Cavit

Our Medium of Exchange
Romans 12:1

By the nature of things as God created them, our spiritual personages must live out our days in a material world, and in a physical body, all the while under a commandment to love God with all of our heart, soul, mind and strength and our neighbor as ourselves. How can the love of my spirit, soul, mind and strength by expressed to God and my neighbor? It can be done through the medium of my physical body.

My heart's compassion, love and sympathy for another can be expressed through my body, by going to those in need of that which I can give, "for I was an hungered and ye gave me meat; I was thirsty and ye gave me drink; I was a stranger and ye took me in; naked and ye clothed me; I was sick and ye visited me; I was in prison, and ye came unto me. Inasmuch as ye have done it unto on of the least of these my brethren, ye have done it unto me."

Other common ways to express our love and devotion to God is by reading His word, praying, and attending the stated services of the church. These things can only be done through the medium of the physical body.

A very simple and practical way to express our love to God is to exchange my physical energy and time that God has given me into the most needed medium of exchange in the church, **MONEY**; then in turn give God first tithe, and any amount beyond the tithe that God requests of me, that the work of God may go forward.

This, I believe to be the intent and purpose for presenting our bodies to God as a living and holy sacrifice that is acceptable to Him.

Rev. M. Max Morgan

Our Part In Sanctification
Romans 12:1-8

The title almost sounds heretical doesn't it! After all, sanctification is a work of God's grace in the heart. There is nothing we can do to sanctify ourselves. But we must remember that God can only do what we allow Him to do. That means there is something we must do to prepare the way for God to work.

Paul is reminding us in these verses that our part is a complete consecration of everything, everyone and ourselves to God. It is really the submission of our wills to the Lordship of Jesus Christ. When we are born again we surrender our sins. When we are sanctified we surrender self. I give up the right to myself. I am no longer in control, Jesus is.

The battle is always fought along the line of surrendering self-will. I must come to grips with the issues, even, "What if God should _____?" And I must face that possibility until I can say, "Not my will, but Thine be done!" The symbolic picture of consecration is an ox standing patiently between an altar on the right and plow on the left with the inscription. "For service or sacrifice." That must become a reality in my life!

But the carnal mind will always look for an easier way. It will cloud the issues and confuse the seeker. "I can't seem to get through." But the battle is never with God, it is always with ourselves. If we're not getting through it is because something isn't surrendered. Often just one, last sensitive issue blocks the way. But when we let go of whatever or whoever it may be, God will come and do the work as we trust Jesus for cleansing. He sets us free from bondage to self-will; free, gloriously free to be His and His alone.

God yearns for your total surrender; yearns for you to invite Him to come with cleansing and deliverance from the carnal mind. Trust Him today.

Rev. Nevin Williams

Is Our Consecration Alive Or Dead?
Romans 12:1-10

Some people go through a form of presenting their bodies to God, but it proves to be a dead sacrifice rather than a living. Their daily lives are not actually lived entirely for God.

To present our bodies is to consecrate ourselves to God for His total control and His total direction. We no longer belong to ourselves. We no longer think of ourselves as our own. We no longer run our lives, or have any remaining disposition to do so.

We seek God's will in everything. We are willing to accept God's employment and His deployment. We are willing to live by God's timing.

We want God to choose for us our location and our vocation, our spouse and our house.

If spouse and house are already chosen then we say to God: "They are yours. They are on the altar. I will live with them according to thy law and for thy glory."

To present our bodies a "living sacrifice" means to acknowledge our stewardship. Our talents, time, energy and money will not just be available but actively devoted to God's service. We remember that the one-talented servant, whom the master called "wicked and slothful," (Matthew 25:26) kept his master's goods available. But that was not acceptable. He should have devoted himself to the task of increasing his master's goods. If our consecration is truly a "living sacrifice" this kind of whole-hearted initiative will mark our stewardship. Languid passivity will not do.

Dr. Richard S. Taylor

Giving A Present To God
Romans 12: 1-21

The epistle to the Romans is the apostle's masterpiece. It is a logical, irrefutable treatise on the fundamental doctrines of the Christian faith. In the first three chapters he establishes the fact of the universality of sin, and proves that all men are alike – condemned under its guilt. Following this the apostle clearly outlines the doctrine of justification by faith, which is opened to all men. His argument culminates in a grand climax on the doctrine of sanctification, the inheritance of the believer.

Chapter twelve in which our text is found consists of a series of practical instructions governing the life of the believer. The Christian religion is a practical one. These exhortations are based on the appeal given in the first two verses – an appeal to entire consecration. Doing must follow being. Paul first presents the doctrine of the Christian, then the duty of the Christian, thus, basing duty upon doctrine, and conduct upon character. You see, what a person believes will be revealed in what he does!

Now, in order for our consecration to be acceptable with God, the following five elements should characterize the offering:

The offering must be a **voluntary** one. – God presses no one into service. The offering must be **complete**. – Nothing can be held in reserve. The offering must be made **deliberately**. – Man has deliberately rebelled and gone away from God, and it is due to Him as a rational being to deliberately return to God. The offering must be made for **all time**. – It must never be modified nor taken back. The offering must be made **in faith**. – Experimental consecration will not satisfy God and therefore cannot satisfy man. Believe that God will receive what He has required.

Remember, my friend, all that we give up for Christ is incorporated in what we receive from Him – and infinitely more!

Rev. Gene Moyer

Are You A Chicken Or A Duck?
Romans 12:2

Some of you may have heard the late Dr. John Logan tell his amusing "chicken and duck" story. If you have you will enjoy it again; others will appreciate the important truth is conveys.

As he told it, an egg from a chicken's nest rolled out of its place into the nest of a mother duck. Unaware of what had happened, the duck hatched the chicken along with her own. While the chick realized he was, in many respects, unlike his siblings it really did not bother him – until the day mother duck took her ducklings down to the pond to swim. The chick knew he was supposed to swim, but it was not his nature to do so. For that reason he was heard walking along the pond with one foot in the water and another on the ground saying; "cockle-doodle-doo, quack quack; cockle-doodle-doo, quack quack." He just was not sure who he was or where he belonged.

This is true of too many Christians today. The standards of holy living are clearly evident in the Word of God, and those genuinely born of God know those standards are for them, but it is just not their nature to do so. So begins the frustrating task of trying to be what you really cannot be.

But there is more. What a confusing picture that bewildered chick presented to spectators: how were they to know whether he was a chicken or a duck? Which suggests a critical element in the matter of our witness: what is a Christian REALLY like? Is a Christian totally free of any conformity this world, or does a Christian dabble in two worlds?

The question is mine, and yours: Am I a chicken or a duck? I must know, so that others will know.

Dr. Merne Harris

Load And Fire
Romans 15:18-29

In *Helps to Holiness*, Commissioner Samuel Logan Brengle tells of his strong desire to lead others into the experience of heart holiness. So he asked a brother in whom he had great confidence in these matters how to go about it. The answer: "Load and fire, load and fire."

The principle is clear – if we are "loaded" with the truth of holiness we will "fire," prompted by a compelling sense of reality and urgency. It's the process we need to be concerned about; how do we get loaded in the first place?

To begin with, we need to note some background factors that do not help in the loading process.

Certainly there is little in the public media that will prepare heart and mind for an effective witness to holiness. The same can be said for popular publications that reduce the message of heart purity to a glitzy program of self-improvement. A freewheeling intellectualism, void of stabilizing absolutes, leaves few certainties upon which any effective witness to holiness must be based. Preaching which is indifferent to the importance of holiness in the life of the Christian will scarcely inspire those Christians to experience and then share that blessed life.

But there are ways to "load the gun" and one is selective reading – significant writings which stir the soul and generate an enthusiasm to witness to heart purity. Holiness classics such as Brengle's works will do much to strengthen our commitment to this great truth. There are also many good contemporary authors and recorded messages on holiness.

Above all, tarry in His presence. As the marvel of God's cleansing grace refreshes your soul you will know the gun is loaded and ready to be fired!

Dr. Merne Harris

We Preach Christ Crucified
1 Corinthians 1:18-25

The holiness message has often been confused and misinterpreted. Or, perhaps we should say, it has been interpreted at times to fit the expectations and hopes of men. It was that way in the Apostle Paul's day, and it holds true today. Paul was constantly facing the challenge of bringing the Jews and Gentiles together. One of the differences between those two groups is brought out in today's text. The Jews were always looking for a miraculous sign. On one occasion (Matt. 12:38-39) Jesus rebuked the Jews saying, "A wicked and adulterous generation asks for a sign!" Then there were the Greeks who thought that reason and knowledge was the highest prize in life. They lived for the day. They had nothing to do but spend their time discussing philosophical "mumble-jumble" on the street corner with their neighbors.

Things haven't changed much! A lot is being said today about the Person and ministry of the Holy Spirit. There are those "Jews" who are still looking for signs and wonders and who are present every time the terms "Spirit-filled" or "Baptism with the Spirit" are mentioned. We still have the Greeks who are content to discuss to unbearable lengths the significance of each gift of the Spirit, but who find little time to practice them.

Somewhere there must be a balance! Paul said there was: "We preach Christ crucified … Christ the power of God, and the wisdom of God." Yes, our message will prove to be a stumbling block to some, and to others it may seem like foolishness – but it is still God's Word to a dying world! Let us sing with the hymn writer: "My hope is built on nothing less than Jesus' blood and righteousness!"

Dr. Bruce Moyer

The Law of the Carnal Heart
1 Corinthians 6:12-20; 10:23-33 (NASB)

This law is characterized by two syndromes:

1.   The "I can have it" syndrome:"all things are lawful for me," and this is supported by two arguments: "there's no harm in it," and "I can't help it." This is an open door for Satan to feed our desires while making us feel secure even in sin.

Paul made a strong castigation of immorality being allowed, within the church, under the umbrella of the "I can have it" syndrome. But many things are sometimes excused, within Christian context, which may not be immoral as such, but are simply not proper, expedient or conducive to Christian values, ethics, and testimony. Its root is the same: "I can have it." Its dangers are very subtle, in that our arguments can sound so reasonable, and even religious, but they end up robbing us of spiritual life.

2.   The "I can handle it" syndrome: The carnal mind always likes to think that it is in complete control, but, in fact, this syndrome is driven by permissiveness and pride, and there is nothing more out of control. The fact is we can't handle some things, and the sooner we admit and accept that, the safer we will be. It doesn't matter how sanctified, or Christian, we are, there are certain things that we must close the door to (and the sanctified man will) or they will soon master us.

Paul's rule was "all things might be lawful, but I will not be mastered by anything." He wrote, "Abstain from all appearance of evil." (1 Thess. 5:22) Jesus said, "If your eye offend you, pluck it out. If your hand offend you, cut it off." If you can't handle it, and there are things you can't handle, cut it off. No one can play at sin's door and not be burned. We must set rules, standards and convictions for ourselves! These aren't binding, but rather a blessing. We are free to not have to have.

Dr. Hubert Harriman

The Law of the Christian Heart
1 Corinthians 6:12-20; 10:23-33 (NASB)

The Christian heart is governed by a different law than that of the carnal heart. There are three basic questions he is always concerned about concerning anything he does:

1.   Does it identify me with Christ? (Read 1 Cor. 16:15-19) A man who thinks like a Christian is always conscious that his body is the temple of the Holy Spirit, so, therefore, he will always be choosing on the basis of that which identifies him with the One who indwells him. He will not be mastered by any lesser drives, and although it may be argued "lawful," that which is spiritually profitable governs him.

2.   Does it glorify God? Paul tells these Corinthians "For you have been bought with a price: therefore glorify God in your body." (1 Cor. 6:20) In writing to Titus, Paul speaks of Christians living so to "adorn the doctrine of God our Savior in every respect." (Titus 2:1-10)

3.   Does it edify? In 1 Cor. 10:23, Paul writes, "all things are lawful, but not all things edify."

We need to ask ourselves two questions before we do anything that we might argue for: "will this help or hinder my spiritual life?" and, "will this help or hinder someone else's spiritual life?" It is this principle that Paul lays down in 1 Cor. 10:23-33, and if this principle doesn't govern us and check us, we are not governed by Christian law, but rather carnal law.

Dr. Hubert Harriman

Dead And Alive
1 Cor. 9:24-27; Eph. 6:10-18; Col. 3:12-14

In the process of seeking for the cleansing of our hearts, we die to self and to sin. God then sanctifies us by putting the old sin nature to death and filling us with His Spirit. But we must remember that there are still some things that are alive.

OUR BODY DID NOT DIE. We must still discipline our bodily desires and deal with our weaknesses. The body must, by will power and Spirit power, be kept the servant of Christ. Allowing our bodies to usurp the Lordship of Christ will allow sin to reinfect our natures. Our bodies are very much alive, even while we are dead to sin.

SATAN DID NOT DIE. Peter pens the warning that the devil, like a roaring lion, is on the prowl. (1 Peter 5:8) Paul says the demons hurl fiery darts at us. James tells us to resist Satan and he will run from us. (James 4:7) John says we can overcome him by faith in Jesus' blood, by testifying to God's sanctifying work, and by obeying even if it means death. (Rev. 12:11) The devil is very much alive, trying to get us back into sin.

OTHER PEOPLE DID NOT DIE. Working and worshipping with people is easier when we are dead to ourselves and to sin. But the people around us are still alive. They will fail us, attack us, ignore us, use us, or praise us. We must serve them, forgive them, and watch out for them.

In order to maintain sanctified hearts, our bodies must be disciplined, Satan must be resisted, and people must be reckoned with.

Rev. Ken Friesen

God's Plan For Victory
1 Corinthians 10:1-13

In our passage for today the Apostle Paul relates a bit of the history of Israel and how the people of that nation fell to a variety of temptations. Here he specifically mentions idolatry, (v. 7) immorality, (v. 8) impertinence, (testing God, v. 9) and ingratitude. (v. 10) How glad I am that the Apostle went on to explain God's plan for victory over these temptations and the many others we face almost daily! That plan includes the following steps:

1. Remember who you are. (v. 12) Avoid overconfidence. Never get to the place where you think you are above falling. As soon as we think we have made it – we've begun to lose it!

2. Remember that you are not alone. (v. 13a) As soon as we begin to think (with Elijah) that we are the only one left or that no one understands what we are going through, we are in trouble. Learn to lean on the One Who has already faced it all!

3. Remember that God is faithful. (v. 13b) "He will not let you be tempted beyond what you can bear!" What a beautiful promise! He not only knows about my temptation, but He also gives me enough strength to resist it no matter how severe it may seem!

4. Remember that there is always a way of escape (v. 13c) – "a way out." The idea of the original language here is that when it seems that we are surrounded completely by the mountains of temptation, God will help us to discover a pass, a way out, a means of escape! Keep in mind that the full weight of temptation comes just before a moment of victory. So, "keep hangin' on!" God has a plan for victory!

Dr. Bruce Moyer

Watch The Weak Spots!
1 Corinthians 10:12

All of us have weak spots in our lives. And of course this is exactly where the devil aims his attacks on us. Early one morning while we were still in Africa, the commissioner sent for me so I could help them with some lions that were killing livestock and attacking people. When I arrived at the home where the cows had been killed, I could see that the lions went for the weakest part of the house – the grass roof. Jumping onto the roof, they had clawed through the grass and bamboo, dropped down inside, grabbed the cows and carried them back through the hole in the roof. Just so, Satan always goes for the weak spots in our lives.

That being the case, we must be honest with ourselves and set a special guard in those areas. It may mean denying ourselves certain things, pastimes, or places with which others have no difficulty. It will certainly mean daily prayer for God's strength and discernment. The familiar promise found in verse 13 of this same chapter is always true. God will provide for us in time of temptation. But he also expects us to do our part in avoiding those areas that lead to certain temptation.

The other side of this coin is that our strengths can become weakness if we wrongfully feel we are safe in those areas and have no need of vigilance. I remember when grandpa was trying to trap a rat in the barn. The rat would come to the entrance of its hole and jump over the first one. WHAM! That's all it took. Never think you're too clever for the devil. True, he is a defeated foe, but still a foe. While we need not fear him, we must respect his abilities and keep a constant watch lest we fall.

Rev. Nevin Williams

It's Not The Apple But The Pair
1 Corinthians 15:20-28

A friend of mine once said, "The problem in the garden of Eden was not the apple on the tree but the 'pair' on the ground!" And that's right, because it was the pair on the ground that made a fateful choice – a choice which has involved us all. (1 Cor. 15:22)

Thus acquainted with the importance of the choices we make, it is imperative that we understand the process involved. A simple illustration will bring that process into sharp focus for us.

Healthy people know and understand the natural and necessary desire for food. But if that desire is accompanied by others – the desire to finish a job, see a friend, or take a nap, for example – there is a conflict situation that has to be resolved for we cannot respond to more than one stimulus (desire) at a time. And the vote for action will be cast in favor of that desire which has the strongest appeal – a value judgment.

Enters the mind with its comprehension of and evaluation of those values of greatest importance to the person confronted by a choice. And while we cannot predict the ultimate decision (to eat, work, visit, or sleep) we can know the decision reflects the paramount value in the situation at hand.

What meaning, then, we should assign Paul's statement that the carnal mind is not subject to the law of God, neither indeed can be. It does, in fact, take an adversarial role – the carnal mind is enmity against God. (Rom. 8:7)

Unsanctified Christians, faced with choices that involve their relationship to the law of God are in an impossible situation: the mind – the source of value judgments – is fixed in its enmity against God and is in a position of immutability in its opposition to the law of God.

Thank God for deliverance from the carnal mind that Paul found, and that is our privilege as well.

Dr. Merne Harris

Commands For Godly Living (1)
WATCH
1 Corinthians 16:13-14

In these two verses the Apostle Paul states four imperatives, which come with hammer-like blows, or staccato military commands. Then the fifth command is a terse sentence. A noted preacher once termed these, "Five Rules for Godly Living." While Christianity is different from other religions in putting away any thought of self-salvation, we must remember that when first salvation is received by faith, then comes the obligation to work it in our lives.

The first sharp imperative is WATCH YE. This is a note of warning like that red signal in the traffic light. A good translation would be, "Be on your guard," or, "Stay awake!"

A truism is that this is a dangerous world physically. But how much more is it to remember that this is a dangerous world spiritually. Mountain climbing has been defined as the "art of going safely in dangerous places." So it is in the Christian life. We are on the upward road and a hard one. If we are to go safely towards our heavenly goal, we need to stay awake, to be on guard spiritually.

Because we live in enemy territory, Paul has urged us to watch. At times we have taken lightly what the Bible says about evil and Satan. We dare not do so today in light of current evils, which too often show a God-defiant aspect. Thus the Apostle Peter writes in his first letter, "Be vigilant, because your adversary the devil, as a roaring lion, walks about seeking whom he may devour." Paul speaks to us through his word to the Ephesians, "We wrestle not against flesh and blood, but against principalities, against powers, against the rulers of darkness of this world."

Lord, help us to be watchful in the Spirit this day. Amen!

Dr. Arthur Climenhaga

Commands For Godly Living (2)
STAND FAST
Ephesians 3:14-19; 1 Corinthians 2:2

How then are we to watch, to be on our guard? Here is the answer – Standing fast – being in a certain place and staying firm there; having spiritual convictions and sticking to them.

So many people today are getting mixed up. They think in order to grow one must discard his or her beliefs and take on some different ones. That makes sense only if beliefs were untrue in the first place. Also that is not what Paul means when he says, "Stand fast" – not in any one of a number of beliefs, but "Stand fast in Faith."

Trees can be used to portray a godly person. I have visited the Sequoia National Park and have seen the trees that were old when Columbus discovered America; yes, even old when the Apostle Paul wrote to Corinth; some were even there when Nebuchadnezzar conquered Jerusalem.

Some say Sequoias never die unless struck by lightning or felled by some outside force. What is their secret? Well, they are rooted in the right place; planted firmly to the right soil; grow in an upward direction towards the light; and at the same time spread out their branches.

And that's the way the Christian should be. Standing fast in the faith that the Apostle Paul declared in 1 Corinthians 2:2, faith in a crucified Christ, faith in a risen Lord.

Lord, help us to so stand fast firmly today. Amen!

Dr. Arthur Climenhaga

Commands For Godly Living (3)
ACT LIKE MEN – BE STRONG
1 Timothy 6:11-16

The Apostle Paul's third and forth statements in 1 Corinthians 16:13 stand together. Quit yourselves like men; be strong. When he said this, Paul evidently meant we are to be brave in spirit as well as in the body. Bravery in sport or in other activities of life may be splendid, but there is a higher courage – MORAL COURAGE.

The story is told of Henry Martyn who, as a brilliant young Cambridge man, went to Persia to be a pioneer missionary in the beginning of the nineteenth century. He wanted to present a New Testament to the Shah of Persia and went alone into the outer court to do so. When received by the Vizier, he found himself surrounded by an angry crowd demanding that he repeat the Islamic creed. "God (Allah) is God and Mohammed is his prophet." The court awaited in silence. Suddenly young Martyn's voice rang out clearly, "God is God and Jesus is the Son of God." That was moral and spiritual courage.

So today we need such courage in the market places of life. We depend not on ourselves but on the Lord Jesus Christ. "For when I am weak, then I am strong," says Paul. To be strong requires self-discipline. There is no other way to strength spiritually than through nourishment [reading/study of the Bible] and exercise [prayer] combined with faith in the Lord Jesus Christ.

Oh Lord, help me to quit myself and to act like your servant and in you be strong. Amen!

Dr. Arthur Climenhaga

Commands For Godly Living (4)
LOVE
1 Corinthians 13

We have seen in the three previous devotionals Paul's four commands for Godly living as stated in 1 Corinthians 16:13. Then in verse 14 Paul states further the climax of all four commands in the injunction, "Let all your things be done with love" (charity – KJV). This is a reaffirmation of the great passage on love in the same letter, Chapter 13.

Paul is reminding us that the basis of a godly life, one rule that never fails, is LOVE. He said before, "Love never fails." Or again, "The love of Christ constrains us." But if we do not have love, we see the following:

Without Love – <u>Watchfulness</u> may become narrow, selfish; looking out for number one.

Without Love – <u>Standing Fast in the Faith</u> may be nothing more than cold, doctrinal correctness.

Without Love – <u>Courage of Conviction</u> may be obstinate stubbornness.

Without Love – <u>Strength</u> may be wasted and ineffectual.

LOVE is the hallmark, the distinguishing feature of the Christian. It comes not from us but from God. If we love HIM as we ought, it is because ever and always He first loved us. And if we love our fellowmen, it is because we love Him and because His Spirit, which is the Spirit of love, entirely sanctifies and dwells in us.

Dr. Arthur Climenhaga

Holiness And Money
2 Corinthians 9:6-15

One of the beautiful things about holiness is that it is so practical. It affects every part of life and every aspect of the ministry and work of God's church ... including the finances. You see, when we "sell out" to God, that means He governs when and where my money goes as well. In today's Scripture, the Apostle Paul left us with several principles to help us be truly joyful givers. Here are just four of them:

First, remember the resource – "God is able." (v. 8) He is able to supply not only what He asks me to give, but for all the other needs I may incur because of my having given something away. Actually, I become partners with God as He provides the ability and I provide the obedience.

Second, remember the reason for our riches is so that we can be generous – responding to Kingdom needs. (v. 11) The sanctified Christian has committed <u>all</u> his resources to the King.

Third, remember the results of our generosity. (vs. 11c-14) Thanksgiving and praise are given to God. (vs. 11c, 12b) The needs of others are met. (v. 12a) Those who are helped may begin to pray for me. (v. 14)

Finally, remember the response. Generosity is simply my response to the greatest gift of all – Jesus Christ. (v. 15) When I recall all that He has done for me, how can my giving hundreds or thousands or even millions of dollars compare?

Elisha Hoffman wrote ...

You have longed for sweet peace, and for faith to increase, and have earnestly, fervently prayed;
But you cannot have rest or be perfectly blest until all on the altar is laid.

Dr. Bruce Moyer

Spiritual Weapons
2 Corinthians 10:3-6

Two distinct and separate activities are mentioned in these verses. One is physical and human, the walk. The other, the warfare, is spiritual. Warfare needs weapons. These are presented here.

As to their character, we see that they are not carnal. This word in Greek, *sarx*, may mean "human as opposed to the divine." Our weapons are not human, but divine. Secondly, we see their functions: 1) pulling down strongholds, 2) casting down arguments, 3) casting down every high thing that exalts itself against the knowledge of God, and 4) bringing every thought into captivity to the obedience of Christ.

Satan capitalizes on every means of keeping souls from the knowledge of God. For some this is a lifetime of belief that all will eventually be saved. Others seek escape in arguing about certain points of Scripture or of doctrine. The crucial point is the thought life where there is both obedience and submission to Christ, or disbelief and disobedience. God's divine weapons are able to work in these realms, for Paul says that they are "mighty through God."

Let us bombard the strongholds, the arguments, and the high things with the divine weapons of praise, prayer, the blood and the name of Jesus, and bring all into captivity to the obedience of Christ.

PRAYER: God, allow us the experiences which force us to use our weapons and gain full spiritual victory in our warfare. Teach us to know and use our full weaponry.

Miss Jeanne Seager

Satan Is Out To Get You
2 Corinthians 11:3, 13-15

I believe the church world today still takes Satan too lightly. The tendency is to look at him as a myth, or just some kind of evil influence, but he's not! Satan is real, he is active, and he is the ruler of this world and he's after us!

The devil is described to us in God's Word as a lion, a wolf, and a serpent. His power is shown to us in the Book of Job; he had power over people, over their minds, over the elements, and over the body. And that same devil is sitting by the pathways of our lives waiting, ready, ever watching for that opportunity to poison our souls with sin. He is after us!

But in all his power and ability the devil really has one basic purpose: to keep us from full surrender to God, and the true sanctifying grace of God.

He is an "angel of light!" He says "go to church, join the church, be active in church, read your Bible, do everything you want, but just keep back yourself; don't let Christ rule completely in your soul."

He says, "I have something better." To Christ he said, "kingdoms, riches, prosperity. Do it yourself, make bread, you can do it. I'll make you popular, jump off the pinnacle, be spectacular -- just don't go to the cross!"

Remember, the one great purpose of Satan is to keep us from the cross of sanctifying grace. His purpose is the reason this grace is the most fought against, least preached, and most confused doctrine in the entire world. It's the only thing that allows nothing to be held back, and no substitute is allowed.

Friends, my greatest concern for the church is that we never let down the banner of the need of every soul to be sanctified. It's the clean heart God loves most; no wonder it's what the devil hates most!

Rev. Rodger Moyer

Center Of God's Will – Sufficient Grace
2 Corinthians 12:9-10

Living in Wilmore, Kentucky, while my husband was attending Asbury College, I took a few months of piano lessons from Mrs. Betty Gibson. She was the wife of the well-known and well-loved evangelist, Jimmy Gibson. In my contact with her, I marveled how cheerfully and graciously she tolerated the long absences of her husband while she stayed at home with their two school age sons. I remarked about this to her one day. This was her reply, "God gives one grace to do whatever He asks us to do." That impressed me as a young Christian. Little did I realize that I would one day need that same kind of grace for that same kind of need!

But this is not a restricted or narrow promise. It encompasses anything and everything that God's Spirit leads us to do. Whenever we are in the center of God's will, His grace is sufficient for our need. If He asks us to start a youth group, He gives us the grace and direction we need. If He asks us to visit some lost soul and give a witness for Him, He will give us boldness and ability as we obey Him. If He directs us to change jobs in order to serve Him better, He will go with us. If His will leads us into a less comfortable lifestyle, His grace is sufficient for us to do it cheerfully. If His will is to lie on a bed of affliction for a while, His promise is just as sure then. The list is endless just as His grace is endless – and sure!

Mrs. Clarice Moyer

Where Am I?
2 Corinthians 13:5

It is great to know the time you were saved. It is also great to be able to look back and know when you were sanctified. But neither of those matters much if you cannot look at today and say, I know I'm saved and sanctified, up-to-date, and walking with God right now.

A true Christian ought to be growing in the Lord. The walk with God should be better right now than it has ever been before. Is yours? Here are some thoughts to help you know where you are with God.

1. Do I have an increasing interest in reading, studying, and obeying God's Word?

2. Do I have an increasing desire to pray -- a continued desire for that intimate fellowship with God? Am I at men's prayer, women's prayer, and Wednesday prayer meeting?

3. Do I have increasing desire for the salvation of souls and the sanctification of believers? Am I testifying, inviting to church, and finding a greater boldness to share holiness even with those who might disagree?

4. Do I have an increasing desire to glorify God in word, thought, and deed? More than anything, do I want to be holy?

5. Do I have maturing interests -- "putting away childish things?" Is God first, above sports, job, money, or anything else?

6. Do I have a greater enjoyment of the Lord's Day? Do I love going to church, because it is the Lord's Day?

7. Do I have an increasing willingness to stand up, to stand alone, and to truly bear the reproach of the cross of Jesus, and suffer for His sake, at home, at work, or anywhere else?

Is your one and only main desire in this life – Jesus?

Rev. Rodger Moyer

Walking In The Spirit (1)
Galatians 5:16-25

The life of holiness is not a life of abstract idealism. The Scriptures make it clear that holiness is the only practical way to live if we are going to live for God. Walking (or living) in the Spirit is the Biblical terminology for the life of holiness. But, just what does it mean to "walk in the Spirit?"

It means to <u>walk by faith</u> rather than by sight. (2 Cor. 5:7) The entire Christian life, from start to finish, is a life of faith. We dare not trust our emotions or our decisions to circumstances – that which we can see. The holy life is a life of quiet trust and confidence in God and His Word – in spite of all that I see around me.

To walk in the Spirit is to <u>walk in the light</u>. (1 Jn. 1:7; Eph. 5:8) That simply means that I am to walk obediently. The sanctified Christian is one who has determined to obey God in everything and at all times – not just when His will and plans happen to coincide with ours. In Acts 5:32, Peter describes the Holy Spirit as One "Whom God has given to them that obey Him." Jesus describes Him as the One Who guides us into all truth – but He will not guide those who are unwilling to obey.

To <u>walk in love</u> is another aspect of keeping in step with the Spirit. (Eph. 5:1-2) There is probably no greater word than "love" to sum up what holiness is all about in practical terms. Holiness is loving God with all my heart, soul, mind, and strength; loving my neighbor as myself; loving my family and friends; and, yes, loving those who are unlovely and cannot find it in their heart to love me.

Dr. Bruce Moyer

Walking In The Spirit (2)
Galatians 5:16-25

Today we continue our meditation on what it means to "walk in the Spirit." A fourth aspect is to walk in truth. (3 Jn. 4) All through Scripture the Word of God (both written and living) is "Truth." To walk in truth is to walk according to the written Word and to pattern our life after the living Word – Jesus. (1 Jn. 2:6)

To walk in the Spirit also means to walk in honesty. (Rom. 13:13) Practically, holiness is maintaining integrity in all our relationships. We may as well – there is no sense in trying to deceive the One Who sees and knows all!

To walk in wisdom is another Biblical aspect of walking in the Spirit. (Col. 4:5, Eph. 5:15) A great truth of Scripture is that wisdom has nothing to do with our intellectual abilities. Rather, it is the power and determination to apply God's Word (His wisdom) to my life. That means that every one of us can walk in wisdom. No one is exempt!

Finally, walking in the Spirit means to walk worthily of our vocation as Christians. (Eph. 4:1) We have taken on His Name – let's represent Him well! Paul prayed for the Colossians that they might "live a life worthy of the Lord, pleasing Him in every way" (and then he goes on to explain how, look it up in Col. 1:10-14).

Who ever said holiness wasn't practical? As we keep in step with the Spirit we will live worthy of His Name – walking in faith, the light, love, truth, honesty, and wisdom.

Dr. Bruce Moyer

The Secret Of Victory
Galatians 5:16-25

Early in my Christian walk I got the impression that entire sanctification was the mountaintop of spiritual attainment. The experience would eradicate the sin nature, that nature which was the source of overt acts of sin. Victory would more or less automatically follow, and I wanted that. I was also taught that this experience would stabilize me and I needed that. The experience would make me effective in Christian service. I longed for that.

I sought and claimed the experience and have no doubt about the life changing character of that event. I praise God for it. But, I still had problems. And I saw that other sanctified believers had problems too. As I searched the Scriptures and gained experience in Christian living, I learned that victory did not flow from a single crisis experience but from a daily walk in obedience to God. I learned that no experience of the past could keep me victorious now, but an Indwelling Person could. I discovered that the secret of victory is learning to walk in the Spirit.

The term "walk" in the Spirit occurs twice in Galatians 5:16-25. In verse 16 it suggests a continuous walk which is characterized by openness to the Spirit's leadership and surrender to His Lordship. The verse also contained a very strong negative statement, which in the AV reads, "Walk in the Spirit and ye shall not fulfill the lust of the flesh." Walking in the Spirit is the only guarantee we have that the ugly manifestations listed in verses 19-21 will not put in an appearance. No matter how radical and momentous the crisis experience of the past has been, it cannot keep me from sin today if I do not walk in the Spirit.

Why do conflicts, jealousies, and selfishness arise among sanctified people? It is due to a failure to walk in the Spirit. My prayer is that God will help me daily to "walk in the Spirit" and thus live out all that crisis experience of surrender and cleansing implies. Is that your prayer too?

Dr. Hollis Abbott

Keeping In Step
Galatians 5:16-25

The exhortation to "walk in the Spirit" occurs twice in Galatians. In v. 16 it is a walk that provided **POWER** to live victoriously. The word in v. 25 is a different word; it is a military term and literally means, "to keep in step." Here it suggests a **PATTERN** for daily living. Even as marching soldiers should keep in perfect step, so we who are Spirit-filled believers should keep in step with the Spirit. This requires concentration and sensitivity.

When in high school I played a trombone in the school band. This was a very enjoyable experience particularly when performing as a marching band. It did, however, take considerable concentration to keep in perfect step with each other while marching at a good pace and at the same time playing a difficult piece of music.

Keeping in step with the Spirit also requires concentration and sensitivity. We must be able to catch the Spirit's signals if we are getting out of step or falling behind. And having caught a signal there must be instant obedience.

As human beings we all have natural appetites and traits of personality. And satisfaction of these traits within certain boundaries is legitimate, but if pursued beyond those boundaries the result is spiritual breakdown. With each of these normal, God-given capacities there is a point beyond which we dare not go without grieving the Spirit. The Spirit is faithful to let us know when that point has been reached. And he who is walking in the Spirit will heed the Spirit's checks.

The secret of victorious living is keeping in step with the Spirit.

Dr. Hollis Abbott

Keeping A Clean Heart
Galatians 5:16-25

Commissioner Samuel Logan Brengle stated seven conditions for keeping the blessing of a clean heart. They are:

First, there must be continued joyful and perfect consecration. We have put all on the altar to get it. We must keep all on the altar to keep it. This consecration must keep pace with increasing light.

Second, there must be steadfast, childlike faith. It took faith unmixed with doubt to grasp the blessing. This same faith must be maintained in order to keep it. Peter said, "we are kept by the power of God, through faith."

Third, we must pray and commune with the Lord. We pray when we talk with God and ask Him for things. We commune with Him when we are still and listen, and let God talk to us and mold us, and show us His love and His will, and teach us in the way He would have us go.

Fourth, we must give diligent attention to the Bible. The soul needs the food of truth.

Fifth, we must confess it, be aggressive, and seek to get others into it. The man who withholds his testimony to this grace will lose it.

Sixth, we must constantly live in the spirit of self-denial. By yielding to fleshly desires, to selfish ambitions, to the spirit of the world, we may lose the labor of years in an instant.

Seventh, there must be no resting in present attainments. The Lord has clearer visions of Himself for us. We may be filled to the limit of our capacity today, but we should ever pray, "O Lord, enlarge the vessel," and this we should expect.

Rev. Gene Moyer

Doing What Comes Naturally
Galatians 5:19-21

"The Great Day" had arrived! I was taking my dog to the park in order to teach him to chase cats. That's right. He was a fast learner at "Come" and "Sit" and "Heel," so he would obviously be a fast learner at chasing cats.

Now, you know I just told you a story. It wasn't that way at all. When I got to the park for his daily romp, and my daily walk around the track, an unsuspecting cat crossed his path. The cat didn't wait around to see whether or not my dog was trained to chase cats. He had met other dogs. He knew their nature. He knew my dog would chase him as naturally as cats chase mice, or mice eat cheese.

Walking around the track I looked at the cat on the high post and at the dog at the bottom wagging his tail. "Yes," I thought, there is a lesson there, an illustration of a Bible truth about human nature. Human beings naturally "chase" each other, showing greed, jealousy, hatred, and pride. They lust, they fight, they cheat, they gossip, and they lie. And society thinks we teach each other to do it!

When will we learn? The only way to keep dogs from chasing cats is to change their dog nature. The only way to keep humans from tearing each other apart is by changing their nature. And only God can do that.

Rev. Ken Friesen

Real Joy
Gal. 5:22; Rom. 14:17

A religion without joy is a counterfeit. Christians have a responsibility to be joyful in order to radiate God's sunshine. God's joy is the oil that keeps human relationships harmonious. It is hard to quarrel with a joy-filled person.

A young farmer with vengeful spirit had a mean method of gratifying his spite. He put dead cats into his neighbor's well. One time he sought to do so, but when he threw the cat in, the force of the overflowing water washed it out. This was an artesian well.

One whose heart is filled with the joy of the Lord is like that. Satan may attempt to inject bitterness, resentment, and other uncleanness of spirit; but the overflowing joy will keep the heart pure. A joyless soul is a defeated soul. "The joy of the Lord is your strength." It is the means of victorious living.

We are not to be frivolous, flippant, or foolish; but the people with whom we live can well stand a great deal of wholesome, hearty laughter; of wise, illuminating good humor; of cheer and sunshine!

We are to join with others in proclaiming by word and attitude the "good tidings of great joy" to all people. It is good news that there is a remedy for man's sin and it has been provided through the blood of Jesus. We cannot lift the burden of sin from others, but we can be joyful samples of those who have experienced His redemption.

Praise, adoration, and gratitude put vitality into faith. Murmuring, complaining, and faultfinding kill it! Divine joy is good mental health – an inward abiding satisfaction issuing from the assurance of the approval of God. It is not a product or creation of our outward circumstances. It is a quality of spirit which minimizes difficulties through magnifying God.

Mrs. Clarice Moyer

Joy in the Spirit
Galatians 5:22-23; John 15:11

While serving in Burundi, Africa, one of our African schoolteachers was sanctified in a Sunday morning service. On Tuesday their baby died. Wondering how this would affect his spiritual life, I was thrilled to hear him testify in the Wednesday morning service, " I want you to know that I still have the peace and joy of the Lord in my heart!"

JOY! But in the midst of heartbreak? The world doesn't understand a statement like that. For most people, joy depends on favorable circumstances, the accumulation of things, finding acceptance in society – all of which focuses on self-interest. Many Christians even have difficulty at this point. They read what the Bible says about joy, upset when they can't have their way or get what they want. In fact, most of our church problems have their roots in selfishness.

Real joy is a fruit of the Spirit and springs from a sanctified heart. Sanctification cleanses out the carnal mind, which focuses on self-interest. Life becomes focused upon God and real joy comes from our relationship with Him. (1 Pet. 1:8) Jesus is clear; He wants us to have His joy. (Jn. 15:11) It's not just a thrill of emotion but also the steady current of blessing that flows from the throne of God through the depths of our souls and out to others. It's inward and doesn't depend upon the circumstances of life be they good or bad. (Hab. 3:17-18)

Just one word of caution. We do not seek His joy, we seek God Himself. The joy then comes as part of the fruit of the Spirit.

Rev. Nevin Williams

Self-Control
Galatians 5:22-25 (NASB)

Of all the fruit of the Spirit, Dayton, in the *Wesleyan Bible Commentary*, calls self-control "the crowning glory of life in the Spirit." I believe he is right, for this fruit of the Spirit offers us a freedom within our freedom. The sanctifying work of God's Spirit gives us the power to control what requires self-control instead of cleansing. His cleansing work deals with the uncontrollable.

With the fruit of self-control, we now have within us the power to govern our spirit through physical, emotional, or spiritual stress. We now have within us the power to control our natural feelings, natural reactions, and natural desires.

We now have within us the power to pause in the midst of panic. We now have within us the power to lay aside the satisfying of our wants that we might do that which furthers the kingdom of God. We are able to give up anything at anytime that will help the cause of God. We now have within us the power to keep on keeping on, even when others seek an escape. We can suffer need, we can suffer loss, we can suffer on, but turn right around and "consider it all joy."

We now have within us the power to wait before God when ambitions clamor for action. A man governed by self-control, is above all, honest with himself, concerning his true feelings, desires, and motives. Self-control will make a man sit down and calmly analyze his true feelings, and then seek and accept God's feelings. He is not compulsive in his spiritual walk.

There are all too many who are making claims to a Spirit-filled life who have never given any evidence of this fruit of self-control, and until this becomes prominent, it is highly unlikely that they really know what it means to live by the Spirit. This is why the Apostle Paul gives forth the call, "If we live by the Spirit, let us also walk by the Spirit." (v.25)

Dr. Hubert Harriman

Self-Control
Galatians 5:22-26

"The fruit of the Spirit is ... self control." Though the Spirit-filled life is a life of total abandonment to God, it is a life under control. Life which is lived under the influence of the rebellious sinful nature is life out of control and is characterized by hatred, discord, jealousy, fits of rage, dissensions, etc. (Gal. 5:19-21).

The Spirit-filled life is characterized by the absence of these traits, but it is much more than that. Spirit-given self-control is more than just the absence of "out-of-controlness." The Apostle Paul describes, in practical terms, what self-control is when he adds these two principles in 1 Cor. 10:23: "Everything is permissible for me – but not everything is beneficial (or, "constructive"). Everything is permissible for me – but I will not be mastered by anything. True self-control is not merely leaving behind a lifestyle which is really out-of-control, but it is evaluating all of our actions and decisions in the light of constructive benefits that they may produce. Something may not be "wrong" – but what will be the benefit of it? Will it have a positive impact on my spiritual well being? Will it prove "constructive" in the lives of others? Will it cause the Kingdom of God to move forward? The second positive principle of real self-control is that Jesus alone will master my life. Drugs, alcohol, tobacco, sexual drives, and habits of every kind – they all give way to His mastery in my life.

True self-control is the freedom to obey 1 Cor. 10:31, "So ... whatever you do, do it all for the glory of God."

Dr. Bruce Moyer

Chickens And Roosts
Galatians 6:6-10

Perhaps you've heard the old axiom: "Be sure, your chickens will come home to roost."

But what does it mean, and what does it have to do with life? And to what does it relate in Scripture?

Well, consider this: "Be not deceived, God is not mocked, for whatsoever a man sows, that shall he also reap. For he that soweth to his flesh shall of the flesh reap corruption ...." (Galatians 6:7-8) As surely as there is a just and righteous God who rules over us, evil people will meet the results of their years of sinful living in the great assize, the final and awful judgment.

What goes in will come out; what goes up will come down; what is concealed will be revealed. Yes, people's deeds, like chickens that roam will come back to confront them at the end of life, as surely as straying chickens return to the home roost at sundown.

<u>UNLESS!</u>
There is an exception! And it comes from the same passage in Galatians, which goes on to say, "But he that soweth to the Spirit shall of the Spirit reap life everlasting." (Galatians 6:8)

Well, praise God for this alternative! We may be born of the Spirit, filled with the Spirit, led by the Spirit and walk in the Spirit, and the end will be <u>life everlasting</u>.

And that is my choice! Continually! Eternally! Praise God forever! I hope it is your choice too.

Dr. Eldon Fuhrman

259

Always Know The Purpose
Ephesians 1:1-4

A basic challenge is to know the purpose of a piece of equipment before using it. As a child I had to learn that mom's kitchen tools were not for constructing roads in her flowerbeds for my toy cars.

Too many have no idea why they were created. Some are even in good fundamental churches, maybe even holiness congregations.

God's purpose is clearly defined by Paul: "He chose us in Him before the foundation of the world, that we should be holy and blameless before Him." (v. 4)

It is God's purpose. As our Creator, He chose what we are to be like. The architect must know the purpose of a building before he designs it. Is it to be a cathedral or stadium? God has designed us for His purpose.

It is an eternal purpose. We were chosen to be what God designed before the foundation of the world. Too many live today with only short-term purposes in mind. They are always inadequate, especially for the long haul of eternity.

God's purpose is practical. We have been chosen to be holy and blameless before Him. Holiness is life's most practical experience as we can chose to experience daily victory over sin. It practically is underscored by the mutation that we will be blameless before God. How freeing is this reality!!

When we know our purpose and experience it, we are free to be effective and contented in daily relationships. What a blessing.

Dr. John Sills

Do We Agree With God About Holiness?
Ephesians 1:1-4

Ephesians 1:4 never fails to jolt me. God's plan for me in Christ, from all eternity, is that I be holy. Not just seem holy, but to be holy. Not even just strive to be holy, but to BE holy.

The Word does not say that God's plan for us from all eternity was that we be handsome or beautiful, healthy or wealthy, or even necessarily happy, but holy.

This is God's "bottom line" will for all humanity. It is a purpose determined in the mind of God before a single star was hung in space or a single rose wafted its fragrance – a purpose from which He has never wavered or deviated a hair's breadth. And this is exactly His will for you and me today: that we be holy.

If this is true, then we are forced to draw a sobering inference: My attitude toward holiness is precisely the reflection of my attitude toward God. To reject holiness is to reject God. To belittle holiness is to belittle God. And so says the Scripture: "But God did not call us to uncleanness, but in holiness. Therefore he who rejects this does not reject man, but God, who has also given us His Holy Spirit." (1 Thess. 4:7-8, NKJV)

Dr. Richard S. Taylor

Christian Holiness, The Right Choice
Ephesians 1:1-12

Congratulations to the human race!

We have been called, elected, foreordained and <u>chosen</u> (in Christ) to "be holy and without blame before Him (God our Father) in love." Hallelujah! God has issued a decree- - that we should be holy (in our heart) and without blame (in motive) before Him (our all-wise and all-compassionate Father and Judge) in love (that is Christlike) for time and eternity.

And that choice is the <u>right</u> choice because (1) The Holy Spirit puts Christ at the center of our lives where once we lived for self, (2) it brings health to the heart that was once sin-infected, (3) it brings a regard for righteousness, where once we served the devil, and (4) it brings a song to the soul, that once languished in pessimism and gloom! Holiness of heart and life! It is a foretaste of glory to come! It is an intimation of eternity! It puts us at home in God! It is heaven's habitation in the heart! It is the best thing this side of heaven! May our God be praised and adored forever for such a high calling! Again, Hallelujah!

Holiness of heart and life <u>was</u> God's <u>creative</u> choice. Holiness of heart and life <u>is</u> God's <u>redemptive</u> choice. Holiness of heart and life <u>shall be</u> God's <u>determinative</u> choice. Yes, our attitude toward, acceptance of, and appreciation for holiness determine our final destiny. Let's wave our banner, sing our song, and herald our message – Holiness forevermore!

Dr. Eldon Fuhrman

The Holy Spirit (1)
Ephesians 1:11-14

One of the great illustrations in Scripture of the Holy Spirit and His ministry is that of the seal. Our text points this out as clearly as any. Several interesting comparisons can be made between the seal and the Holy Spirit.

The seal was used to make something secure. The Romans sealed the tomb of Christ in order to secure it. We lick and seal our envelopes before mailing them. In the same way the Holy Spirit is our security – He keeps us from falling, as long as we walk obediently.

The seal was also used to show ownership. An item belonged to the person whose seal was upon it. Ephesus was a trade center and it was common practice to place one's seal upon merchandise before shipping it (we still do that today). In the same way the indwelling Holy Spirit identifies us as belonging to Christ.

Another interesting comparison is that the seal was an identifying mark. The impression in the wax on a letter looked just like the signet ring of the owner. There was no mistaking its identity. The Holy Spirit's work is to make us look just like Christ – to think, and live and talk like Jesus. Is that true of my life today?

Finally (although there are many more), the seal also was used to indicate certain obligations. (Neh. 9:38) In our text we see that Christ has obligated Himself to give an everlasting inheritance to those who are sealed by the Spirit.

Dr. Bruce Moyer

The Holy Spirit (2)
Acts 2:1-4; Hebrews 12:29

Yesterday we saw how the seal could be used to symbolize the Holy Spirit's ministry in our lives. Today we turn our attention to fire. Again there are some interesting comparisons.

The Scriptures often refer to the purifying work of fire. The purifying work of the Holy Spirit is spoken of throughout the Bible, but one of the best illustrations is found in Isaiah 6. He is the active Agent of the Godhead not only in our initial cleansing at the moment of entire sanctification, but throughout the entire redemptive process.

Another picture of the Spirit's ministry is the way in which fire softens. Just hold a match near a candle and watch the wax soften. For hardened steel it takes a lot of fire, but eventually it will produce the same effect. Am I allowing the Spirit to soften me for the molding and shaping necessary for conforming to the image of Christ?

Then there's the way the fire engulfs and inflames that which it has taken hold of. Oh how necessary this is for every minister of the Gospel – yes, for every Christian! Paul wrote to the Thessalonians, "Do not put out the Spirit's fire!" (1 Thess. 5:19, NIV)

There's room here for just one more comparison – the illuminating effect of fire. One small candle in a large dark room dispels the darkness and reveals what was previously unseen. The Holy Spirit is the revealer of truth and the only One Who can properly show us the way to take in this sin-darkened world.

Dr. Bruce Moyer

The Holy Spirit (3)
John 7:37-39

Today we look at how water can be used to illustrate the work of the Holy Spirit.

The most important comparison to be made is that water is absolutely essential to life. Take away most water and you have a desert. Take it all away and you have death. Jesus said the same was true about the Holy Spirit and spiritual life. (John 3:5)

Water produces growth. Most plants will not grow without water. In the same way the Christian cannot progress in the Christian life without the Holy Spirit.

Throughout Scripture water is spoken of as a cleansing agent. For the Jews there were all kinds of "washings." For the Christian there is one washing – the cleansing work of God the Spirit.

Then there is the ability of water to refresh and revive. I recently was doing some work on our unfinished attic on a hot day. It didn't take long for me to break out in a good sweat and find myself drained of energy. However, a cool glass of water and a splash of water on my face refreshed and revived me for further work. Make the application yourself – and when you're drained and need refreshing, don't look for it in another seminar or book, seek the Refreshing One!

Along with this we could mention the ability of water to satisfy thirst. There is also its attribute of buoyancy, illustrating the Spirit's ability to lift and encourage us.

Jesus said, "*Whosoever drinketh of the water that I shall give him shall never thirst . . . .*" (John 4:14)

Dr. Bruce Moyer

Inheritance
Ephesians 1:11-18

One day my favorite aunt told me that she had included me in her will; I was to inherit her fur cape. Yes, I was to have it, but on one condition – the death of the donor. Upon her death this promised treasure became mine.

In the spiritual realm, also, an inheritance involves death. Because Christ died for us, "we have obtained an inheritance." (v. 11)

But there is another side to this truth of spiritual inheritance. Paul prays for the Ephesians that they may know "what [are] the riches of the glory of His inheritance in the saints." (v. 18)

What a mind-boggling truth – that the God of all creation should desire an inheritance in us! Scripture is clear that God desires fellowship with men and women; that He delights in those who love Him supremely.

Can the human heart, with its bent to self-centeredness, give delight to the Lord? How can He delight in us when our wills conflict with His highest will for us – that we should be holy as He is holy? (1 Peter 1:15-16)

The answer is death to self, not a popular idea in our day with its over-emphasis on our "right to ourselves" – on self-esteem, self-worth, and self-realization. Paul gives his testimony in Galatians 2:20: " I am crucified with Christ: nevertheless I live; yet not I, but Christ liveth in me: and the life which I now live in the flesh I live by the faith of the Son of God, who loved me and gave Himself for me." Is God realizing His inheritance in you?

Mrs. Susan (Schultz) Rose

That Is Just My Nature!
Ephesians 2:1-6; 2 Peter 1:1-8

"But that is just my nature! This is the way I am. I was born this way, and I can't help it." My heart rejoiced at her answer, for it opened wide the door for what I wanted to say to this really splendid young lady, a comparatively new Christian.

Her attitude was always enthusiastic, gung-ho, go-for-broke, get-the-job-done. But in her gung-ho process she hurt and wounded other believers, and her sharp tongue turned off many non-believers from hearing the gospel. She was beautifully saved, but the carnal heart and reactions were ruining her bright oral testimony. If there was a little fuss or difference going on in the church, she was right in the middle of it, adding fuel to the fire, rather than serving as a peacemaker.

Her response allowed me to say, "Exactly so. This is just what I have been trying to tell you." Our Lord, on Calvary, provided not only forgiveness for all our past sins, but also a cleansing of that old rebellious sin nature with which we are born. That cannot be forgiven, for it is not something we did. We cannot train, educate, or long suppress that horrible thing we were born with. But through the sanctifying grace of Christ's blood He will cleanse out that old rebellious nature, and make us to become "partakers of the DIVINE NATURE." I explained the terrific possibilities of "growth in grace" once we no longer have to spend more than half our strength fighting the old carnal traitor within. This experience with the young lady took place about 40 years ago. She sought and entered into a beautifully sanctified life, which continues growing and fruitful to this day. Thank God for the practical, continuing, blessed results of actual crucifixion with Christ. That is **Sanctification**!

Rev. John Kunkle

Purity – The Path To Maturity
Ephesians 4:11-16

In Ephesians 3:19 Paul's prayer for Christians is "that you may be filled to the full measure of all the <u>fullness of God</u>." In Ephesians 4:13 he makes his readers aware of the possibility of "attaining the whole measure of the <u>fullness of Christ</u>." Then, in 5:18 he includes the command, "Be <u>filled with the Spirit</u>." The goal of this teaching is so that "we will no longer be infants, tossed back and forth by the waves, and blown here and there by every wind of teaching." (Eph. 4:14) The same apostle explained to the Corinthian believers that they were still "mere infants in Christ" because they were yet carnal. (1 Cor. 3:1-3) We cannot help but notice the connection between purity and maturity, even though they are distinct. Real Christian maturity will never be attained apart from heart purity! Christian maturity depends on the "set of my soul," as we see is so eloquently expressed in the poem, "The Winds of Fate" (by Ella Wheeler Wilcox):

One ship drives east and another drives west
With the selfsame winds that blow.
'Tis the set of the sails
And not the gales
Which tells us the way to go.

Like the winds of the sea are the ways of fate
As we voyage along through life:
'Tis the set of a soul
That decided its goal,
And not the calm or the strife.

Dr. Bruce Moyer

Readjustment Necessary
Ephesians 4:23

All of life seems to move in cycles. There are both the crises and the continuous, the seasonal and the ceaseless. Life is not static, it is dynamic. One meal will not last forever; one prayer will not keep one indefinitely.

The Christian life is ushered in by the miracle of grace, but it is sustained by the Spirit's keeping power. Hence one must give frequent attention to his spiritual life and seek for seasons of spiritual blessing.

The Christian life is lived in an unfriendly world environment with the atmosphere charged by "the prince of the power of the air" to lull the believer to sleep, make him forget heaven, and to lead him into sin. Hence, periodically, there must be those periods of soul-searching adjustments and correction, and even of humiliation and confession before God. This is not meant to imply that one's spiritual life is one dreary round of sinning and repenting for there is glorious victory in the sanctified life. However, there is a toll of depleted reservoirs (physical, emotional, spiritual) which demands the replenishment of God's refreshing fountain.

If the present-day holiness movement lacks something of the vigor and ruggedness of the early Methodists, one reason may be the neglect of the vigorous, disciplined "going on in holiness." In any case, my friend, it is certain that we would do well to seek for constant growth in holiness and occasional renewing of the Holy Ghost in our personal lives such as that suggested by our Lord in 2 Chronicles 7:14!

Rev. Gene Moyer

Where Is The Point Of Victory?
Ephesians 4:25-32

One could put this question in another way – where is the point of compromise with evil? The answer to each question is clear and pointed.

The point of compromise with evil is any point this side of total destruction of the works of the Devil in the human heart. This point may be ever so close to total victory, but if it is this side of total victory it is still compromise. Any doctrine that allows the old man of the heart to live is a compromise. Anything that spares Agag is making a bargain with the Devil.

Why should the people of God, with a captain who has defeated completely the Devil, make any concessions to a defeated foe? Rather should the church boldly assert, "Give no place to the Devil."

When Moses was in Egypt preparing to lead the children of God out of bondage, Pharaoh offered several compromises. Moses put the line out at the point of total victory and said to Pharaoh, "not one hoof shall be left behind."

The dividing line in the holiness movement (and there is a line in the holiness movement) is drawn between those who give the doctrine lip service and those who have been crucified with Christ. There is one mark on the soul of those who have been crucified with Christ that sets them off from all other men. Those marks are the nail prints and the spear wound.

St. Paul spoke of bearing about in his body the marks of the Lord Jesus.

The point of victory is at the same place it has always been: Calvary! Anything short of Calvary for the believer is not victory. The old nature responds to one thing and one thing only – the death of the cross.

Rev. M. Max Morgan

Fill Me Now
Ephesians 5:14-21

People in many countries are experiencing hunger. Day after day they go to bed with an unsatisfied feeling. Some Christians are like those famine sufferers. The fourth beatitude promises, "Blessed are they that hunger and thirst after righteousness, for they shall be filled." The true believer has a hunger for holiness, Christ-likeness. Such hunger can only be satisfied when the Holy Spirit dwells in the fullness in our hearts. Jesus promised His disciples that His Father would give the Holy Spirit to all who ask for Him with sincerity and urgency. Paul urged the Ephesian Christians, "Be filled with the Spirit."

In His final teachings regarding the Holy Spirit, Jesus made it clear that all true believers do have the Holy Spirit. However, He makes a distinction between those who have the Holy Spirit dwelling with them and those who have the Holy Spirit "in them." The latter is a deeper and fuller experience. That is why Paul constantly urged the Christians to a full commitment, "Present your bodies a living sacrifice holy, acceptable to God." With the Holy Spirit inside the citadel of the heart, He can control the heart and mind and energize the will to be entirely submissive to God. Paul goes on to say, "And be not conformed to this world, but be ye transformed by the renewing of your mind, that ye may prove what is that good and acceptable and perfect will of God." The transforming power of the Holy Spirit is needed to reconcile our will to that of God. We must not only regard God's will as good, and accept it (without regret and sadness) but we must consider it as "perfect," the best possible for our good and God's glory.

If there is any reservation in our commitment, any room in our hearts not open to the Holy Spirit's entrance and supervision, then we are not filled with the Holy Spirit. Is the Holy Spirit only "with us" or "in us"? Have we obeyed the command, "Be filled with the Spirit"?

Rev. John Trachsel

Risk and Opportunity
Ephesians 5:15

A professor in a class I attended made the statement, "Life swings between risk and opportunity." We are made in such a way that we seem to automatically look for opportunities. The chance to purchase something on sale or sell an item to an eager buyer is claimed as a unique opportunity.

There are many opportunities that God offers to us and we must thank Him. The invitation to read His word, fellowship with the saints, enjoy His Spirit and escape from sin are all opportunities. These are privileges that everyone needs to take advantage of.

The text of today seems to be calling the Spirit-led life to some risks as well. The days are evil and the time is short. God's people must seek to reach out to those who are in need. The Christian must make an impact on the world and not just enjoy all of the blessings.

There is risk involved in reaching out to someone who is hurting because the hurt might touch me. There is risk in praying about the kingdom needs, for God may want me to help fill the need. There is risk in voicing concern for my neighbor's conversion, for God might demand my time in witness. How often after ministering to a certain need have we testified to the "opportunity?"

In the final analysis many of the unique opportunities that God opens for us are the result of a risk that we've taken. As we walk in the Spirit today let's be aware of some opportunity that may be hidden behind a risk.

Rev. Duane Erickson

Fulfilled With The Holy Spirit
Ephesians 5:15-20

Having been a missionary in Bolivia, I can recall a number of times when a slight mispronunciation of a Spanish word changed the entire meaning of what I was trying to communicate. Hopefully the Bolivians were able to catch my intent from the context of the message. Now, as a college professor, I sometimes get a chuckle from the way a foreign student pronounces a word or with the wording he or she may use in a sentence. One example of this was when a foreign student came in to discuss a paper she was writing. Instead of using the phrase "filled with the Spirit," she used the words "fulfilled with the Spirit." I silently chuckled at the moment, but after she left I found myself thinking about the profound truth she had accidentally stated. True fulfillment is found in a life fully surrendered to the Lordship of Jesus and carefully guided by the Holy Spirit!

Before one finds new life in Christ, temporary "fulfillment" may be found in a variety of ways – through people, possessions, activities, and the list goes on. For the Christian fulfillment comes through faithfully serving Christ. That fulfillment, however, is sometimes hindered by failures stemming from a carnal, selfish heart. (As long as our heart turns in on the self, lasting fulfillment is elusive.) Only when the heart is fully consecrated to God and carnality is utterly destroyed by the cleansing work of entire sanctification can we constantly be "fulfilled with the Spirit."

That foreign student spoke great truth. Life in the Spirit is fulfilling – emotionally, spiritually, physically – in every way. Quoting Ephesians 5:18 as "be fulfilled with the Spirit" is probably not bad theology after all!

Dr. Bruce Moyer

When God Speaks (1)
Ephesians 5:17; Matthew 7:21

Not long ago one of my close, Christian friends made a couple of remarks that disturbed me. The first remark went something like this, "I know you believe this is wrong, but can you show me a verse in the Bible that says, 'Thou shalt not ....'" (He obviously knew I couldn't.) The other remark was, "Well, God just hasn't spoken to me about that yet." I had heard those words so often that I determined to look again to God's Word for some answers. One of our texts for today tells us that God wants us to know what His will is. Surely God has ways of letting us know what is right and wrong, what is good and best.

How does God "speak" to us? How does He give us "light" and direction for decision-making? Hebrews 1:2 makes it clear that God has spoken to us through His Son, Jesus – the Living Word. His will has been revealed to us by what He said (as recorded in Scripture) as well as by the life He modeled before us. God also speaks to us through the written Word – the Bible. However, my friend's questions went beyond this. What about those areas of modern life to which Christ did not directly speak? What about questions that the Bible does not specifically address?

Let me suggest that God has a multitude of ways of "speaking" to us. Each is subordinate to the Word, Living and Written, but may be the medium through which I discern the will of God. God may use my pastor, a Sunday School teacher, or a close Christian friend. He may use a good Christian book. He might even speak to me through the guidelines and standards urged upon me by my church. He's not limited to any one method – but, He is always consistent with His inspired Word, the Bible.

Over the next several days consider with me some of the Biblical guidelines for making those tough decisions in life, especially in some of those areas where God doesn't seem to speak.

Dr. Bruce Moyer

When God Speaks (2)

Knowing that God wants to make His will known to us, now let us look at the principles He has given for making the tough decisions in life. A Scripture text will accompany each point.

(1) Psalm 119:4, 9-11. Does the Bible give any clear teaching about the decision I am trying to make? Here is where we must start. If God's Word is clear, I need not go any further! Here's where a clean heart comes into play. I must die to having my own way, or all my efforts to determine God's will shall prove fruitless. If I am not already walking in the light God has given me, why should He bother to give me more light in the details of my life? Obedience to God's Word is not legalism, but the true expression of our love for Him! (John 14:23-24) This is basic to all the other decisions of life

(2) 1 Corinthians 6:12; 10:23-24. Will the decision I'm about to make limit my Christian freedom? Or will its consequences enslave me and rob me of true Christian liberty? We have been told for a long time that freedom is the ability to do whatever we want, but God's Word tells us it is the power to do what we ought. Paul told the Corinthians that, even though some things might be "permissible," they might also become enslaving rather than an expression of real liberty. Other things might be "permissible," but not beneficial or constructive. There are times when we should not only ask, "Is it bad?" but "Is it good?"

(3) Luke 9:23. Here's a guideline we would rather ignore at times. Is the decision I'm about to make in harmony with Jesus' standard of self-denial? How many of my decisions are really made with this principle in mind? If all my decisions of the past week were placed on the scales – those made for self-gratification on one side, and those made out of self-denial in the other – which way would the scales tip? This is not to suggest we participate in some kind of self-abasing asceticism, but to remind us we live for Someone else!

Dr. Bruce Moyer

When God Speaks (3)

(4) 1 Corinthians 6:19. As I consider God's principles for making tough decisions in life, I must remember that my body is the "temple of the Holy Spirit." Will the choice I'm considering injure or mistreat this temple? That is the negative side of the question. The positive side is (based on Ephesians 5:10), will this decision enable me to please God with my body? Some decisions in life are made much simpler when we just consider the impact they might make on our physical frame.

(5) 2 Peter 3:18; Philippians 2:5. Will this decision enable me to become more and more like Christ? Isn't that our aim as Christians? Isn't that the purpose of holy living? My choices should be made in the light of whether or not I will be enabled to continue maturing spiritually.

(6) Matthew 6:33. This principle is closely related to the last. Will the choice I am about to make keep Christ <u>first</u> in my life? Will it affect the priorities I have established for holy living? Will it reflect that I love God above everything (and everyone) else in this life? Jesus said it this way to Peter, "Simon son of John, do you truly love me more than these?" (John 21:15) What do my decisions say about my greatest treasures and loves?

(7) 1 Thessalonians 5:22. Here's a Biblical principle that would save us a lot of grief and carry us to new horizons in holy living, if we would take it seriously! We are to avoid (or, abstain) from even the very appearance of evil. How would our decisions be affected if we began to see how much we could do for Christ, rather than subconsciously scraping by with the minimum requirements for entry into heaven? I'll never forget this quote from one of Dr. Richard S. Taylor's helpful books, "The minimum measure of grace acceptable, is an intense desire for the maximum measure of grace available." That ought to help us make tough decisions in life!

Dr. Bruce Moyer

When God Speaks (4)

(8) Romans 14:23. Another principle for guiding us through the tough decisions of life has to do with doubts. Paul was using the illustration of eating certain food as he wrote to the Christians at Rome, but the eternal principle found here is clear: Do I have doubts about the decision I am making? If I make a decision in which I am confident I have the clear leading of the Lord, and I later fall into trials and am tempted to despair, I can claim the promises of God for enablement, comfort, and anointing. However, if I deliberately choose a direction about which I have doubts, thus placing myself in temptation's way, can I really expect God to "bail me out?"

(9) Acts 1:8; Romans 14:21; 15:1; Titus 2:7; 1 Timothy 4:12. The Spirit-filled life is a life of witness both in proclamation and practice. Our witness is not only going on when we purposely speak or allow others to examine our lives, but all of the time. We never cease being a witness of some sort. As I make decisions in life, I must take into consideration how those decisions will affect my Christian witness. Will it make me a "stumbling block?" How will it affect my friends and others who are watching my life? As a minister, but more importantly, as a sanctified Christian, I deliberately choose not to do some things – not because they would be wrong for me, but because I believe they might influence others negatively. I would rather give them up than to cause someone else to stumble.

(10) 1 Peter 2:21. If you've never read Sheldon's great classic *In His Steps*, resolve to do so in the next month or so (it's not a theological textbook!). It tells the story of what happens in one community where God's people decide to live by this principle: "What would Jesus do?" As that becomes one of my abiding principles for making tough choices, the choices become fewer and easier to make. Am I willing to participate in things which I don't think Jesus would?

Dr. Bruce Moyer

When God Speaks (5)

(11) 1 John 2:28; Romans 14:12. We concluded yesterday with the question, "Would Jesus do it?" This verse prompts us to ask a similar question when we have decisions to make: "Would I like to be found doing it when Jesus returns?" Really the question causes us to take into consideration the fact that God really does see and know all that we do here and now. I wonder if sometimes we haven't forgotten that magnificent truth we learned as children. The children's chorus comes to mind which says, "Oh be careful little eyes what you see, ... Oh be careful little hands what you do, ... Oh be careful little feet where you go, ... For the Father up above is looking down in love." Are there some choices I've made that I would change if I really believed that Christ was by my side observing all that I do?

(12) 1 Corinthians 10:31. Some decisions would be more easily made if we simply asked, "Will it glorify God?" What is the ultimate purpose of the thing? What will its outcome be? We should not be afraid to move into positions or places where we receive greater recognition (or more money, or power, etc.) – if that is where God wants us. But we never dare allow that to be our motive for choosing a new direction in life.

(13) Ephesians 4:7-16. Here is one of Paul's passages about spiritual gifts. Every Christian is uniquely gifted by the Holy Spirit for serving and edifying the Church. Therefore, when I make decisions, I should consider whether or not those decisions would enable me to more fully develop. and use those gifts. That is not to say that God won't sometimes lead me to make decisions that will cause me to "stretch" in other areas in which I do not consider myself to be gifted. But generally my choices should point in the direction in which God has gifted me.

Dr. Bruce Moyer

When God Speaks (6)

(14) Colossians 3:15; Philippians 4:6-7. God's peace is another indicator that I am making the right choice. His peace is to rule (that is, to govern or umpire) in my heart. Uneasiness is often (though not always) an indication that I still have doubts or that the direction I am headed is wrong. I have personally found that a deep sense of God's peace always accompanies a good decision. This peace is much deeper than any human emotion based on circumstances or self-gratification.

(15) Hebrews 11:24-26. These verses speak about the principle Moses used for deciding between the "pleasures of Egypt" and the cause of Christ. The first were only temporary, the other was eternal. The first might have provided earthly pleasure, but the other was of "greater value." The statement has been made, "Never sacrifice the permanent on the altar of the immediate." That's the principle Moses lived by, and it ought to be for every Christian.

For six days we have been taking note of the principles found in God's Word, which will guide us in all the decisions of life. I have used these for making all kinds of choices. Some have been big, others small. But I have never come across a choice to which these principles did not apply. Put them to the test – see if you can think of any decisions in life that are not to be guided by at least one of these principles.

Holy living is a life of right choices. It is, in fact, following the whole will of God. We saw that God wants to make His will known to us, (Ephesians 5:17) and we saw that doing God's will is the requirement for entering Heaven. (Matthew 7:21) Let us simply "trust and obey, for there's no other way to be happy in Jesus!" He has given us every thing we need to know in order to discern and do His will.

Dr. Bruce Moyer

Under the Influence of the Holy Spirit (1)
Ephesians 5:18-20

For those of us in the holiness movement, the question is not whether or not we have accepted the doctrine of the Holy Spirit, but have we submitted to the influence of the Holy Spirit? It has become easy, and even acceptable, to say that we have been filled with the Holy Spirit, but the Apostle Paul's contention was that, "If we live in the Spirit, let us also walk in the Spirit." (Gal. 5:25) Or, as he says in our text, "And be not drunk with wine . . . but be filled with the Spirit." In other words, as some are given to the influence of wine, we should be under the constant influence of the Holy Spirit. Today and the next two days, we will see that this includes: the Spirit's management, the Spirit's mood, and the Spirit's moving.

The Spirit's Management

The Holy Spirit not only wants residency, He must have presidency in our hearts. The sign that hangs over every sanctified heart simply sates, "Under new management," which is to say, we are under a new influence. As the hymn writer put it, "He is with me everywhere, and He knows my every care. I'm as happy as a bird and just as free. For the Spirit has control, Jesus satisfies my soul, since the Comforter abides with me."

Dr. Hubert Harriman

Under the Influence of the Holy Spirit (2)
Ephesians 5:18-20

The Spirit's Mood

The Holy Spirit is not moody, with feelings that fluctuate and flip-flop on a whim, but He has moods, holy moods, by which sanctified hearts ought to be influenced.

We read that The Holy Spirit can be grieved, (Eph. 4:30) and we need to be sensitive to this mood, and be checked by it. How many have ended up in spiritual trouble simply because they were not mindful to this mood of the Spirit?

The Bible also speaks of joy in, and of, the Holy Ghost. We could do with more who are under this influence. Our text says, "... be filled with the Spirit; . . . singing and making melody in your heart to the Lord."

Christians should also be sensitive to the mood of the Spirit in certain settings, such as a worship service. Sometimes there may be a tremendous sense of settling down of deep reverence, quietness, and seriousness. How many times has a service been killed simply because someone was not subject to the mood of the Spirit and spoke inappropriately? The plague of our day is that we are trying to create moods by what we want expressed, rather than waiting to see what the Holy Spirit knows and wants to express.

Christians must also be sensitive to the Spirit's mood in prayer. Paul wrote that, "Likewise the Spirit helpeth our infirmities: for we know not what we should pray for as we ought: but the Spirit Himself maketh intercession for us with groanings which cannot be uttered." (Rom. 8:26) In Ephesians 6:18 he admonishes us to "pray always with all prayer and supplication in the Spirit..." Jude 20 also speaks of "praying in the Holy Ghost."

When in need of a clean heart, the Holy Spirit sobers us up. James wrote, "Cleanse your hands ye sinners; and purify your hearts ye double minded. Be afflicted, and mourn: let your laughter be turned into mourning, and your joy to heaviness." (James 4:8-9)

Dr. Hubert Harriman

Under the Influence of the Holy Spirit (3)
Ephesians 5:18-20

The Spirit's Moving

Throughout the Scripture one reads how great exploits were done as the Spirit of God moved upon men. These men were under the influence and control of God's Spirit. Just a few examples are:

- Judges 6:33-34, "Then all the Midianites and the Amalekites and the children of the east were gathered together...But the Spirit of the Lord came upon Gideon."
- Judges 14:6, of Samson, it says, "And the Spirit of the Lord came mightily upon him."
- 1 Samuel 10:10, "And the Spirit of God came upon him (Saul) and he prophesied." 1 Samuel 11:6, "The Spirit of God came upon Saul when he heard of the plight of Jabesh-gilead."
- 1 Samuel 16:13, "And the Spirit of the Lord came upon David from that day [of anointing] forward."
- Luke 2:25-28, "And the Holy Ghost was upon him (Simeon)...and he came by the Spirit into the temple and took Jesus in his arms and blessed God."
- Acts 2:4, "And they were all filled with the Holy Ghost and began to speak..."
- Peter spoke of "holy men of God who spake as they were moved by the Holy Ghost." (2 Peter 1:21)

Has God changed that He does not now move in men by His Spirit? No! A thousand times, No! He still moves, and He still moves through men, but He looks for men who will be under His control; under His influence; men who know that "it is not by might nor by power, but by His Spirit." Men who are not under this influence will make a front of religion because they don't know the fount of religion. A "Spirit-less" religion ends up being a farce rather than a force.

Dr. Hubert Harriman

Holiness In Our Homes
Ephesians 5:18-21

The church does not lack for an adequate doctrine or teaching on holiness and certainly the doctrine of the Holy Spirit is well represented in our hymnbooks. However I believe the real test of doctrine of the fullness of the Spirit is not in the theology, the hymnbooks or denominational statistics. It's found in a life and its most important area of influence -- the home.

The normal "house" today is not the same as the Biblical concept of "home." Households do not operate on the level of the Biblical concept of home. It is to be a place of self-surrender, which comes from a personal encounter with the Holy Spirit cleansing the believer's heart. To keep holiness active in the home, five habits must be practiced:

1. See the spiritual potential for each member (saved, sanctified, growing).
2. Base family relationships on the spiritual being the number one priority, and let your daily schedule reflect this.
3. Make a time commitment to each other.
4. From a pure heart, have a willingness to be open.
5. Practice the presence of Jesus.

A major function of the home must be that of providing a holy, loving atmosphere for each family member. It must be a place of safety. If relationships in the home are so fragile that only "some tension" is allowed or expressed, then the structure is faulty. The homes ought to be a place where family members may express themselves. Why? Because the family knows and understands each other in holy love (which only is accomplished through a surrendered and purified self). Family tensions overwhelm us when this is not evident or when the spiritual leader in the home is not leading.

Rev. Mark Purkey

What Kind of Church?
Ephesians 5:25-27

As we read the New Testament, the words purity, righteous, holy, without spot or blemish appear in connection with the church and God's people. The scripture is clear: the church is to be holy. It should be equally clear to us that we can only have a holy church when we are a holy people. The church has no life of her own independent of we who are members; therefore she can only be as holy as we are holy.

As we move into the third and fourth generation, we are in constant danger of "tipping our hats" to the doctrine of holiness because it's part of the articles of religion, forgetting holiness is a life to live. Unless the doctrine is written on our hearts and lives, it savors of fraud. There must be clear, definite holiness preaching from the pulpit as well as clear, definite testimonies in word and deed among God's people.

A second danger lies in concentrating on the standards of holy living until we begin to think the standards make us holy. Standards are the guardrails along the way; the blood of Christ sanctifies us wholly. Admittedly, this isn't much of a problem today. In trying to avoid "legalism," we've over-reacted against standards until worldliness is taking our people. Entire sanctification does produce certain outward standards of conduct affecting our entertainments, dress, speech, morals, and ethics. It's not a matter of legislating what we can and cannot do; it's a matter of what we want to be. Under the direction of the Spirit of God, there are some things we must do, others we will not be able to do.

God has given us a message of hope for today. Holiness works; holiness is necessary. God is building a holy church by transforming believers into holy people. Let's not be content with anything short of a holy church. And remember, the church will be holy, when and because WE are holy!

Rev. Nevin Williams

The Church
Ephesians 5:25-32

I have been thinking much about the church lately. Not the Friends Church, or the Free Methodist Church, or the Salvation Army – just the church. I have books that talk about successful churches, user-friendly churches, passive churches, dying churches, and churches that are on a plateau.

We talk about urban churches, inner-city churches, suburban churches, and rural churches. It's not hard to find something written on growing churches and great churches, but modern literature seems strangely silent about the destination that seems to have been the most important to Jesus – **the glorious church!**

Paul wrote to the Ephesians that "… Christ also loved the church and gave Himself up for her; that He might sanctify her, having cleansed her by the washing of water with the word, that He might present to Himself the church in all her glory, having no spot or wrinkle or any such thing; but that she should be holy and blameless." (Eph. 5:25-27, NASB)

The church that Jesus is going to present to Himself is "the church in all her glory" – the glorious church defined not in terms of finances, size, or program, but rather in terms of inner character and outer conduct. The glory of the church that Jesus is going to present to Himself is that she will be holy and blameless. We tend to get caught up in the images of the modern business world, but the image of the church that God would keep before us is the image of a bride. Could it be that the qualifications for marriage are even more important than strategies for marketing?

Whether urban or rural, small or large, I want to be a part of the only church that Jesus will present to Himself – a glorious church without spot or wrinkle!

Rev. Glen Boring

Heart Holiness And A Happy Home
Ephesians 5:25-33

For we who are Christians, heaven is our home! Hallelujah!

For we who are Christians, God has promised, through His Son Jesus, that we can have a bit of heaven in our home now! Again, hallelujah!

But for us to have heaven in our home we must have heaven in our hearts. Now! That means that He, Christ, the Holy One of God, must be hallowed in our hearts as sanctifying Lord, by the blessed Holy Spirit. Now! Again, I say, Hallelujah! Forever! Amen! So Christ is more than a heavenly guest; He is our heavenly host. Now! (1 Peter 3:15)

Now, heart holiness helps us have a happy home in several ways: first, it (He, the Holy Sanctifier) helps husband and wife to <u>love</u> as they should. No, holiness is not automatic; we are not spiritual automatons. But holiness of heart provides for spiritual health and growth and that contributes to a happy and harmonious relationship.

Second, this same holiness of heart helps us to <u>give</u> as we should. Give to each other as man and wife, as well as to God.

Third, it helps us to <u>forgive</u> as we should. Ours is not a perfect marriage because I am not a perfect husband. I am far from it. But, she, my precious wife, forgives my faults and blunders so freely. Bless her heart! She adorns this doctrine of heart holiness.

And what shall I more say about heart holiness and a happy home? It summarizes itself by saying we can <u>live</u> as God intended we should. By His grace and by the power of the sanctifying spirit! Glory to God!

Dr. Eldon Fuhrman

The Battle
Ephesians 6:10-18

While drawing plans for a church building, an architect needed to know what size windows the people wanted in the sanctuary. The people were evenly divided as to the size of the windows. Half wanted tall, narrow windows and half wanted short, wide windows. Neither side would budge so the architect jokingly suggested they put tall, narrow windows on one side and short, wide windows on the opposite side. In this way people could sit on the side with the windows they liked. The people like the idea and built the church in this way.

These people were struggling against flesh and blood and acted very childishly. We even see flesh and blood struggles in our own churches. Someone gets their feelings hurt because they aren't asked to sing often enough or aren't asked to teach a Sunday School class. Instead of waiting for the next opportunity to sing or teach, they find the music director or Sunday School Superintendent and go to doing battle with flesh and blood.

As long as carnality reigns in our mortal bodies, we will continue to struggle against flesh and blood. We will continue to find fault with the pastor, Sunday School teacher and/or a fellow Christian over things that don't make a bit of difference in eternity.

Carnality must be cleansed from the heart so that we might "take up the full armor of God." We need to quit worrying about how loud the pianist plays the piano or how many minutes the preacher preaches overtime or the size of the sanctuary windows. We need to take up our swords, (v. 17) get on our knees in prayer (v.18) and do battle with the "spiritual forces of wickedness" for the souls of men.

Brad Weinert

Attitudes of the Carnal Heart
Philippians 2:1-8

Some time ago I sat in a class under the leadership of Dr. Dennis Kinlaw. Leaving the main topic, he somewhat ended up "preaching" (rather than teaching) from the passage we read for today. In the midst of this portion of Scripture we see Christ as our pattern for holy living (vs. 5-11). What Dr. Kinlaw pointed out was that, on either side of these verses, four attitudes are revealed which dominate the unsanctified heart. I want to share these with you.

"WHAT'S IN IT FOR ME?" is a question the carnal person is continually asking himself, others, even God! Personal gain and selfishness (v. 3) are attitudes which control the conduct of those yet carnal.

"HOW WILL I LOOK?" is another question the carnal person uses to determine his obedience to the will of God. Paul describes this attitude in v. 3 as "vainglory." Conceit dominates the lives of too many Christians and renders then useless in the service of the King.

"I DESERVE BETTER THAN THIS!" Another attitude that characterizes and dominates the life of some Christians is that of grumbling and complaining (v. 4). They are never satisfied, because they have sought fulfillment in something or someone other than Christ.

"YES, BUT . . ." The carnal person can often be recognized by their constant arguing and disputing (v. 14) – a natural result of their grumbling and complaining.

Holiness is freedom from the tyranny of selfishness, conceit, grumbling and arguing.

Dr. Bruce Moyer

Holiness – Following Christ's Example
Philippians 2:5-11

One of the most beautiful things about the life of holiness is that it really is nothing more than patterning our attitudes and conduct after Christ. As the Apostle Paul testified, it is Christ living in me. (Gal. 2:20) In the passage we read for today there are three attitudes of Christ that ought to govern the life of every sanctified believer.

TOTAL CONSECRATION In verse 7 we read that "He emptied Himself" or that "He made Himself nothing." In order to save a lost human race, Jesus laid aside all the wealth, riches, honor, and glory that had been His in heaven. If we are ever to be sanctified and walk in holiness, we must follow His example. We must lay aside (in other places, "put off" or "die to") all that we are and have and become completely God's.

TOTAL CONDESCENSION In the first part of verse 8 we see that Jesus "humbled Himself." He became a man. He esteemed mankind as His equal. He did not exalt Himself above others, nor did He degrade Himself beyond the point of wholesome self-worth. He simply became what God wanted Him to be. Am I willing for God to make me all He wants me to be – even if it means a lower position, a lower salary, or less power?

TOTAL COMMITMENT The rest of verse 8 indicates that Jesus obeyed God the Father even to the point of death. What an example to follow! Impossible! Yes – if we try to obey in our own strength. But very possible (and even commanded – see verse 5 again) if we first allow God to cleanse from our hearts that inherited spirit of rebellion that we call carnality.

Dr. Bruce Moyer

What About Humility?
Philippians 2:1-8

In all my Christian life God has been "cutting me down to size." The sanctified life is full of refining, humbling experiences. Remember, no artist paints his masterpiece on a borrowed canvas. No complete remodeling is done on a rented building. "He must be Lord of all or He is not Lord at all."

One time in Taiwan, I decided to have my own project of visitation in a group of 100 military homes where no active work was being done. Every week I would ride out to this village and try to build bridges of friendship and evangelism to the Chinese. Nothing happened; homes did not open as no one was interested. God let me fail since I loved my own plans and ideas too much. I loved MY project more than getting God's plan of action.

Someone has suggested that "walking humbly with our God" is a conscience choice. The choice is to seek after God himself and then we will see how small we are (see Isaiah 6). Jesus told us to learn of Him because He is gentle and humble in heart. (Matthew 11:28-30)

Many of our humiliations are self-created. We worry about worldly status. But really our nearness and walk with our Lord is our status. "Kiss the cross" has been an inward comfort to me. If we are low enough we have not far to fall when we stub our toes and fall flat on our faces. Defensiveness is a plague in our lives; do we have to prove that we are right? That trait separates mates and friends because it is the opposite of humility.

"The sacrifice acceptable to God is a broken spirit; a broken and contrite heart, O God, Thou wilt not despise." (Psalm 51:17, RSV)

Mrs. Laura Trachel

The Mind Of Christ
Philippians 2:1-11; Isaiah 53

Did you read all the Scripture today? It really takes Isaiah 53 to see Phil. 2:5 demonstrated in the life of Jesus as He was despised and rejected by men, as He was smitten and afflicted and crushed with our iniquities and He opened not His mouth.

The mind of Christ is in direct opposition to the attitude of the world – what is in it for me? How can the church meet my needs? How can my mate better fulfill my needs? How can I have a secure future? What job will give me the fastest advancement?

In contrast, Christ's attitude was how I can meet the needs of others – my friends, my spouse, my church, my community? And even more important: how can I glorify the Father?

Not only is the mind of Christ revealed in service but in character. This is the test of whether our hearts are filled with His perfect love. To love when we are despised and rejected is Christlikeness at the very core. It is a supernatural attitude and supernatural work of the sanctifying Holy Spirit. God allows the difficult experiences in our lives to show forth the same humility and selflessness that Jesus did, we show to the world that He is life in all His beauty.

Let the beauty of Jesus be seen in me!

Mrs. Clarice Moyer

Humility
Philippians 2:1-13

Dr. James Bishop, now deceased, was the director of South India Bible Institute (World Gospel Mission) many years ago. One day one of the Indian students of the upper caste was assigned the task of cleaning the latrine. He came to Dr. Bishop and objected to being given this lowly chore and refused to do it. Dr. Bishop did not scold or lecture the student. Instead, he took off his jacket, rolled up his sleeves, and went out and did the work assigned to the student. This example of true humility broke the student's pride and he wept and prayed for deliverance.

Our Scripture lesson points out the Supreme Example of humility, our Lord Jesus Christ. He left all the glories of heaven and became Son of Man and humbled Himself even unto the death of the cross. How alone He was in His sufferings that not even His closest friends could stay awake and support Him in the garden!

We are enjoined in our lesson today to have the same mind or attitude as Christ has. Are there tasks we feel are beneath us? Can we truly enjoy the success of others? Do we have to be recognized and/or praised for our every effort? Can we live in less than ideal circumstances in order to do the will of God? Do we really desire to be shaped and molded by God's testings – or do we feel there's no need for this in our life? Can we take rejection and misunderstanding from others without bitterness or resentment? The list is endless. Only the destruction of carnal pride and the fullness of God's Spirit can enable us to fulfill this injunction for God's word.

Mrs. Clarice Moyer

A Call To Like-Mindedness
Philippians 2:1-21

While we usually think of holiness as an experience of the heart, the Bible also mentions the attitude of the mind. In this chapter there are three references to the mind and the call to like-mindedness.

Like-minded in love and unity is the emphasis of v. 2. This is in reference to our attitude toward our fellowmen. The problem of strife and vainglory as motivation for action is destructive to the church, and grieves the Holy Spirit. Our attitude toward others should be building their self-esteem and encouraging them in the Lord.

Like-minded in humility and dedication is the thought of v. 5. This is in our relation to the example of Christ, who emptied Himself, humbled Himself, and committed Himself to the cross for our redemption. The problem of pride and covetousness is devastating and defeating to spiritual life. God is calling us to follow the example of our Savior in our commitment to the work of the Kingdom.

Like-minded in our concern and consecration is the theme of v. 20. I think Paul wrote this verse and v. 21 with a breaking heart. There is no more tragic verse in the Bible. This is the problem of indifference and self-centeredness in Christian's lives. This is spoken in relation to the church. "All seek their own, not the things which are Jesus Christ's" is a tragic indictment of many people in the modern age, even in the church.

The Holy Spirit can cleanse the heart and fill the life, but the direction of our mind, and the motivation of our thoughts depends upon our will and volition. But God can help us. Rom. 12:2 says, "be ye transformed by the renewing of your mind." The experience of heart holiness not only cleanses and fills the heart, but also transforms and renews the mind. May this be so in all of our lives.

Rev. Roy Clark

The Ego And I
Philippians 2:5-8, Romans 12:3

I have noticed lately that many of the bestseller Christian books have centered on self-fulfillment, self-love, self-expression, and self-gratification. It occurred to me how different this is from Jesus' emphasis on self-denial, and self-surrender.

Perhaps this points up the problem. Self does not want to be denied; it does not want to die. Self wants to be coddled, to be gratified, and to be catered to in our lives. With many people it is not the sin problem but the self-problem that is the root of spiritual defeat. This is the age of self-expression but little self-control.

The paradox is that the gospel is basically self-exalting. Human worth is uplifted when Christ comes in and takes control. Self image is enhanced when I realize that Christ loved me enough to die for me. He thought I was worth saving.

But at the same time salvation demands the surrender of the self-nature. Christ must be on the throne, at the center of my life. There are several principles in Scripture that are relevant.

1. There is a self-centeredness that is the essence if sin. In Isaiah 14 there are five "I will's" that changed Lucifer from an archangel to a devil. In the parable of the rich fool in Luke 12, his life was centered in "my crops, my barns, my possessions, etc." and God said to him "thou fool."

2. There is a self-denial that leads to godliness. Matthew 16:24 lists the first principle of becoming a Christian – do something about the self-problem.

3. There is a self-surrender and self-crucifixion that leads to holiness. The testimony of Paul in Galatians 2:20 gives the secret of the sanctified life: Self on the cross, Christ on the throne. This is the secret of victory.

Rev. Roy Clark

October 17

What Is my Goal?
Philippians 3:10-17

I once heard one of the world's eminent guitarists being interviewed. He had played several outstanding pieces with a display of nimble fingers that practically left me gasping as I thought of my stiffening arthritic ones. Then the one interviewing him asked if he still had any goal left now that he had so excelled. I cannot forget the essence of his reply. Said he, "As a born again Christian, my goal has really never been to excel in my guitar playing. Rather my goal has been to give honor and glory to God; to know His will for me, and to do it."

That thought really struck home. It is really what the Apostle Paul was saying to the Philippian Church. "I do not want to remember the past; I want to know Him and press towards the goal of the prize of doing His will."

Any successes that one achieves are not the important thing in life in and of themselves. Call me doctor, call me general superintendent, call me president – those are not the real goals of life. The goal is always to know the Lord's will and to do it for His glory by the energizing of the Holy Spirit.

When it's all said and done – **HIS WILL**, that is what counts in life!

Dr. Arthur Climenhaga

God's Way And Our Desires Differ
Philippians 4:9-19

Many times the Lord doesn't supply what we think we need because He has something that is better for us and more for His glory. Our greatest need is to make a complete consecration to God and let Him cleanse our heart, crucify all of self-will and plans, and give us His Holy Spirit to direct our entire life.

When Gideon saw the multitude of the Midianites that were set against Israel he thought he would need a large army to face them. He sent out word to call men from various tribes, and 32,000 responded. God said there were too many for Him to give the victory. Read the story in Judges 6 and 7. God stripped him of all but three hundred, and with them, God gave the victory that was needed, and the glory went to the God of Israel to whom it was due.

When Daniel knew that the writing had been signed by the king and that he was destined for the lion's den, I feel sure that at the first prayer time, Daniel took his need to the Lord to deliver him from the lion's den, but God didn't do it. God had something better. God didn't deliver Daniel FROM the lions. But delivered him IN the lion's den, and God was glorified by the miracle.

When the three Hebrew children knew they were destined for the fiery furnace if they didn't worship the image that the king had set up, I feel sure they must have had an all-night prayer meeting presenting their need to be delivered from the hand of the king and from the furnace. They knew He could do it. But God didn't do it. He did something better than they had imagined. Instead of delivering them FROM the furnace, He did a greater miracle and delivered them IN the midst of the fire. God was glorified and His miracle of power was manifest to all.

God will do more than we ask or think if we will leave the choices with Him and wait for His time and way. Praise His name!

Rev. Marshal Cavit

Blue Ribbons And Holiness
Philippians 4:10-13

I enjoy the state fair. I'm too old to enjoy the rides anymore, but I still like the exhibits and all the other fair activities. One year at the fair I was especially interested in a rooster that had won a blue ribbon. He strutted about his cage as if to say to passers-by, "Hey, look here, I've won!" People weren't much different. There was a certain look on the faces of those who had won a blue ribbon for their antique car, their quilt, or their jam. What does all of this have to do with holiness? Take another look at Paul's words in Phil. 4:10-13.

Like me, you've read these verses a number of times, placing a great deal of emphasis on verse 13, "I can do everything through Him." That is the focus of this passage, but take a look at the context. Too often we see only the negative items Paul mentions. Like "whatever the circumstances," "I know what it is to be in need," "hungry," and "in want." Yes, even in those difficult circumstances, Paul says, we can be overcomers through Christ.

But notice that there are some positive images here as well. For instance, Paul also talks about knowing "what it is to have plenty," being "well fed," and "living in plenty." In other words, even the "blue ribbon" times of life must be lived out by the power of Christ.

It is one thing to humbly state that, yes, through Christ's power I can endure the hard times – I can handle the defeats. But am I also able to say that I can handle the successes with grace? Or do I find myself "strutting" a bit like that blue ribbon rooster? In a world that says, "if you're ahead, get further ahead; when you've won, take a bow," may God give us as much holy ability to succeed gracefully, as He does to help us endure difficulty and defeat.

Dr. Bruce Moyer

Getting People Sanctified Wholly
Colossians 1:21-29

J.C. McPheeters, at over 90 years of age, was preaching in our college chapel. Every new year, he said, he would ask God what special ministry God wanted him to work at during that year. This year God has said, "I want you to work to get people sanctified wholly." McPheeters answers the Lord, "I preach holiness, Lord." "I want you to work to get people sanctified wholly." Finally, he gets the message. God wants him to pray and work to get specific people sanctified wholly, not just people in general.

Isn't this what Paul is saying in Colossians 1:28-29? He wants to present <u>everyone</u> perfect in Christ, not leaving out any. He works on specific individuals. He proclaims Jesus as the perfect Sanctifier from inbred sin; he warns this one and that one not to fall short of the grace God has to sanctify wholly; he instructs each one about what it means to be holy, how to die to sin and self, and how to lay hold on the promises for entire sanctification.

Paul thinks long and hard on how to better teach holiness of heart, because he knows that carnality clouds the issues in the believer's mind and Satan tries to sidetrack everyone from definite seeking and finding.

In this definite and determined effort to see each person sanctified wholly, Paul and Christ are a team, Paul laboring and struggling, Christ providing His powerful energy, all of the energy of the Godhead. O that I, too, would be Christ's constant partner in struggling to get specific people, and all people, to experience the grace of entire sanctification.

Rev. Ken Friesen

The Commandments And Doctrines Of Men
Colossians 2: 20-23 (NKJV)

Most of our holiness denominations have in our disciplines some statement acknowledging the Holy Scriptures as "alone containing the will of God as far as it is necessary for us to know for our salvation." Yet we too continue in the time-honored tradition of men in trying to improve upon God's plan by adding to His word "the commandments and doctrines of men." In fact we often prescribe piety and righteousness with religious rules and regulations which God's word simply does not substantiate! In so doing we create unnecessary barriers to the Gospel. We also dilute the strength of those commandments and doctrines that are of God. And we often supply the very "stuff of strife" as we hotly contest our own adopted set of religious rules and regulations against those of other functions. But these are not the gravest perils of man-made religion.

The New King James Version translation of Colossians 2:23 reveals the greatest peril of the commandments and doctrines of men: "These things indeed have an appearance of wisdom in self-imposed religion, false humility, and neglect of the body, but are of no value against the indulgence of the flesh." Codes of external religious conduct and standards simply cannot prevail in the battle against carnality! How embarrassing are the frequent indulgences of hatred, contentions, jealousies, outbursts of wrath, selfish ambitions, dissentions and envy among those who rely on the commandments and doctrines of men for righteousness. How unlike Christ is maliciousness, deceit, backbiting, pride, boasting and unloving, unforgiving, unmerciful spirit so often manifest among those who place great emphasis upon rules and regulations.

The commandments and doctrines of men fail miserably as a substitute for the sanctifying grace of God in the battle against the indulgence of the flesh!

Rev. Chris Neilson

Living The Risen Life (1)
Colossians 3:1-4

Jesus commanded us to go into all the world, to all nations, proclaiming the good news. But before that can happen, we must leave this world. We must be delivered from "this present evil age," (Gal. 1:4) and become a part of Christ's kingdom, "which is not of this world," (John 18:36) and to sit together in heavenly places in Christ Jesus. (Eph. 2:6) Our citizenship is in heaven. (Phil. 3:20) Here we have no lasting city, "but we are seeking the city which is to come." (Heb. 13:14) It is only when we rise above the world that we can begin to unfold the power of heavenly living on earth.

First of all, Paul gives us <u>a Reminder</u> when he says, "If [or since] then you were raised with Christ." We must always remember that as those who have believed in Christ, we have been co-raised with Him. We have begun to walk in newness of life. (Romans 6:4) We have received eternal life, which is not just endless existence, but a heavenly quality of life brought to us by the indwelling Lord. We have become alive in Christ. We have been given "all things that pertain to life and godliness, through Him who called us by glory and virtue." (2 Peter 1:3)

To remember that we have been raised with Christ is the path to holiness. We have been raised to live on another plane of life than the world lives. We do not have to be victims of sin. We can now live in the realm of the Spirit.

Paul wants us never to forget what we received in Christ.

Rev. John Moyer

Living The Risen Life (2)
Colossians 3:1-4

Paul not only gives us a reminder of what we have in Christ, but he shows us a <u>Responsibility</u> we have in maintaining that risen life.

We are to have a preoccupation with the eternal realities that are ours in Christ. We are to do as Jesus said, "Seek first His kingdom and righteousness ...." This preoccupation with heaven, and the One who reigns from there will govern our earthly responses to the many circumstances in which we will find ourselves. To be preoccupied with heavenly things will keep our view of things, people and events of this world in eternal perspective through His eyes.

The "things above" refers us to the spiritual values that are a part of heaven, like tenderness, kindness, meekness, patience, wisdom, forgiveness, strength, purity, and love.

When we live in the heavenlies and commit ourselves to seeking the things above, then we will live out the heavenly values in this world to the glory of God. To seek things above is to strive for things that are centered in Christ, with our attitudes, ambitions, and our whole outlook on life.

How do we seek the things above? By setting our mind on things above. (v. 2) Don't just seek heaven, think heaven, "where Christ is." (v. 1) Heavenly values dominating the mind will bring forth godly behavior. The Christian life is not only having been delivered from something, but to something. We're not only to quit doing things that are wrong and sinful, but we are to start thinking and working out a consistent new life. The Christian life is not only to seek heaven, but also to think heaven. Even things harmless in themselves become harmful if permitted to take the place that should be reserved for things above.

Rev. John Moyer

Living The Risen Life (3)
Colossians 3:1-4

In verse 1 we can see we have a Resource to live the risen life. He is the risen and glorified Christ, who is seated at the right hand of God, the place of honor and majesty. He is the fountain of blessing for His people. And "all the promises of God in Him are yes, and in Him Amen, to the glory of God through us." (2 Cor. 1:20) When we seek things above and set our affections on them, we have the Resource of Christ's promises to flow through us to the glory of God.

Paul goes on to give a Reason for living in the heavenlies. We have died and our life is hidden with Christ in God. (v. 3) Having died refers to the believer's reaction to the world here and now. Instead of being dead in sin, we have died to sin. And we are now hidden in Christ, which means it is not knowable to those who do not come to Christ, because it has been veiled to those who are perishing having been blinded by the god of this age. (2 Cor. 4:3-6)

Paul goes on to say that to those living the risen life, there is a Revelation. The world doesn't recognize those whose lives are hidden with Christ in God. But we will be revealed to them with Christ at His second coming, when He who is Faithful and True enters on His white horse, with eyes flaming with fire, His head crowned with many crowns, His robe having been dipped in blood, and the sharp sword coming from His mouth. Those who are with Him will be the armies of Heaven, who are clothed in fine linen and following Him on white horses. (Revelation 19:11-16) Those who really belong to the Lord will be revealed to the world that day.

The key to living the risen life is to have a life centered on Christ.

Rev. John Moyer

God's Will – Your Sanctification (1)
1 Thessalonians 4:1-8

As Paul admonishes the Thessalonians in v. 1, so we should desire to walk and please God and actively look for ways in which we might excel still more. This is particularly true when receiving a commandment from the Lord Jesus as Paul notes in v. 2. The command is striking in its power, clarity, and simplicity. We are to be sanctified, v. 3a. This means set apart from sin and set apart to God, cleansed by the Spirit, and surrendered to God's control. But here Paul chooses to define sanctification in a very specific, concrete way, vv. 3b-8, that centers around our sexual conduct. Sometimes, as believers in sanctification/holiness, we have concentrated on the theological definitions and neglected the practical implications. As in Paul's day, so in ours, sanctification/holiness is to be characterized by sexual purity.

The first area of sexual purity as a definition of sanctification addresses out will. We are to abstain from sexual immorality, v. 3. For the single person this means no sexual relationships/intercourse, period. For the married person, this means no sexual relationships with anyone other than our spouse – fidelity, period. The major reason for such a strong and absolute standard is because sexual sin affects not only the physical but spiritual nature of man and woman (see 1 Cor. 6:15-20). In addition, God has chosen the faithful relationship between a husband and wife as the primary illustration of His relationship with His people. When we are sexually immoral, we shatter that beautiful picture, and we break the covenant. This should not be. It is not God's will. We are called to say willfully, "No, to sexual immorality."

God help you and me to reflect faithfully in our lives a commitment to say no to sexual immorality. God desires such obedience; the world seeks such a witness.

Dr. William Vermillion

God's Will – Your Sanctification (2)
1 Thessalonians 4:1-8

The second area of sexual purity as a definition of sanctification/holiness addresses our mind. We are to <u>know</u> how to possess our own vessel in sanctification and honor. Vessel may be understood as our own body and/or as our own spouse. First, let us focus on our own body. Paul is vitally concerned that we be aware of what tempts us, what causes us to give in to our bodies so that we commit sexual immorality. We must observe that what tempts one may not tempt another. We are responsible for knowing our own vulnerabilities. We are also responsible for knowing what causes our bodies to be holy and to bring honor to God.

Second, if vessel also refers to spouses, we are to know how to keep our spouse holy and in honor. I believe this involves three important areas: respect, faithfulness, and prayer. God grant us a new sense of respect for our partners. When we lose respect for our partners, love slackens, and the adversary has an entrance. We must be faithful in thought and in actions, in showing our spouse that he or she is the only one for us. We must pray for our spouse, for in doing so we knit more closely to them and God is honored.

In knowing and doing these things, we demonstrate that we know God. We are not like the pagans who know only lustful passions. (v. 5) Brothers and sisters, God is seeking for couples who will model sexual purity, couples who know how to keep their vessels in sanctification and honor.

God gives us the power to say no to sin and the ability to know ourselves. May we be willing to use the power and exercise the knowledge.

Dr. William Vermillion

God's Will – Your Sanctification (3)
1 Thessalonians 4:1-8

The third area of sexual purity as a definition of sanctification/holiness addresses our <u>sense of ethics</u>. Anyone who is involved in sexual immorality transgresses (sins against) and defrauds (deceives and cheats) his brother, v. 6, and I would add sister as well. In context, Paul is talking to the believers. He is concerned that sexual immorality could take place right in the church. In addition, he suggests that sexual sin has a ripple effect. It is not a one or two person sin, but it affects the other spouse, children, family, friends, the community, and even the nation. Such an act of sexual immorality is sin and deception, the breaking of the covenant. Consequently, the Lord Himself is the avenger. There will be very real consequences for such sin. Little wonder Paul calls this a solemn warning. After all, who wishes to face the Lord's vengeance?

We have been called by God, not for impurity but in sanctification. God wants a people who are pure. To reject this is to reject God who has given the Holy Spirit to us. (vs. 7-8) After all, we are the temple of the Spirit and sexual immorality not only violates the temple, but is gross disobedience of God's clear will. His will for us is to abstain from sexual immorality, know how to keep our vessel in sanctification and honor, and not to transgress or defraud our brother or sister. May we obey His will with our will, mind, and ethic. God wants such a witness; the world needs such a witness.

May we also remember that as devastating and crippling as sexual immorality is that it is not the unforgivable sin. In John 7:53-8:11, Jesus clearly forgives the woman taken in adultery. May we be quick to forgive the repentant and uphold God' standard of sexual purity.

Dr. William Vermillion

Happified Are The Sanctified!
1 Thessalonians 5:16-18

John Wesley struck a New Testament chord not always sounded in our modern teaching. To be entirely sanctified, he says, is to "experience a total death to sin, and an entire renewal in the love and image of God, so as to rejoice evermore, pray without ceasing, and in everything to give thanks." This depiction of Christian holiness found everywhere in his writings is drawn for Paul's admonition in our reading for today. It is the very design of the gospel that, being saved from guilt, we should be happy in the love of Christ!

Holiness and happiness are two aspects of one experience. The holy life is one of uninterrupted happiness in God. (Eph. 5:18-20, NIV) Christian perfection is exuberance in the Spirit. **It is not** rigid, sterile orthodoxy. **It is not** self-righteousness, censorious legalism. **It is not** asceticism or a straightjacket of rules. "For the kingdom of God is not meat and drink; but righteousness, and peace, and joy in the Holy Ghost." (Romans 14:17)

So, what is the "happiness" of the sanctified?

1) It is the happiness of sins forgiven - forgiveness through the shed blood of Jesus in the foundation of all holiness and happiness. "Pardoning lives is the root of it all." Every moment of my existence I am justified, not by the merit of my works but by the merits of Him who loved me and gave Himself for me. And from the depths of my soul I sing, "Oh, the joy of sins forgiven! Oh, the bliss the Blood-washed know!"

2) It is the happiness of inward harmony and peace, the fruit of a heart made pure and right.

3) It is, supremely, the happiness of a childlike trust that **every moment** receives the Holy Spirit from the Father (Luke 11:11-13, NIV).

Rev. Gene Moyer

The "Allness" of Holiness
1 Thess. 5:23-24; Mark 12:28-30

"… and the very God of peace sanctify you <u>wholly</u> (entirely, fully, completely) …."

Heart holiness is all-inclusive in its work on the individual person. It refers to the "whole spirit and soul and body" – all there is of us in our present existence.

To God's all-inclusive <u>demand</u> we are to make an all-inclusive <u>dedication</u>. To our all-inclusive dedication, when offered up in faith, the Holy Spirit affects an all-inclusive <u>deliverance</u> from sin as an inherited tendency. The result of this all-inclusive deliverance is an all-inclusive <u>devotion</u>. We are enabled to love God with all our heart, soul, mind, and strength. (Mk. 12:28-34)

Consider just one effect of this "allness" as it relates to the mind. It means I must <u>regulate my reading</u> to things that enrich. Amen! It means I must <u>monitor my memory</u> to think on things that I need to retain for future use. It means I must <u>control my curiosity</u>, lest a natural desire to know becomes an illicit desire for forbidden fruit. It means that I <u>harness my humor</u>, so that I don't tell jokes with double meaning.

This truth has many more applications when you think about the heart, soul, and strength. A few examples include: I must <u>master my moods</u>, <u>treasure my time</u>, <u>adjust my attitudes</u>, and <u>enlarge my education</u>. To all these all-inclusive demands comes God's all-sufficient grace – holiness of heart and life! Hallelujah!

Dr. Eldon Fuhrman

How Can We Be Made Holy?
2 Thess. 2:13-15

If God wants me to be holy, then how is my holiness to be brought about? In myself I am not holy but sinful. Attempting to make myself holy by my own efforts is futile. Rather, according to this passage, we are made holy by the sanctifying power of the Holy Spirit.

Now this means that our being made holy is not a work of grit but a work of grace. As a work of grace it is a supernatural change of nature, by which we are changed from the feebleness and depravity of inbred sin to the strength and purity of a cleansed heart.

This change, which we call sanctification, begins in the New Birth. This is called initial sanctification. At the very least this includes a desire to be holy and a commitment to live a holy life.

But this new desire struggles with the old nature that wants to continue on as before, doing my own thing. Sooner or later there will have to be a showdown, a veritable "knock-down, drag-out" battle, when we allow the Holy Spirit to dethrone the "old man" of an unsanctified ego once and for all.

This will require a CRISIS of self-searching, self-discovery, self-loathing, and self-surrender, that is so total and radical that the Holy Spirit will be able to do His purging work and the very nature of holiness will be imprinted on our hearts.

Dr. Richard S. Taylor

One Reason Why
2 Thess. 2:13-17; 1 Thess. 5:23-24

One reason, among many important ones, why Christians should be <u>entirely</u> sanctified is that this grace is the best safeguard against backsliding, this side of heaven. Persuaded as we Wesleyan Arminians are that there is no such thing as an "unconditional" eternal security until we are "secure in eternity," let us remember that in entire sanctification God has provided the best protection against backsliding that an all-wise, all-good, all-powerful God could devise, and yet at the same time preserve in His people freedom of choice.

While full sanctification does not destroy the <u>possibility</u> of sinning again, it certainly destroys the <u>necessity</u> for it and greatly reduces the <u>probability</u> of it.

In other words, entire sanctification is no guarantee against forfeiture of saving grace; but it is God's greatest fortification against forfeit that He has for us this side of glorification. In this gracious experience God re-enforces the soul by imparting an inward righteousness, which strengthens the innermost self with an energy that is Divine.

As one has suggested, the sanctifying baptism with the Holy Spirit is God's way of making spiritual millionaires out of His children. He thereby supplies them with abundant working capital with which to "run the business" of holy living. Such spiritual resources are ours when Christ truly becomes our total Sanctifier.

Dr. Delbert Rose

A Man's Potential (1)
1 Timothy 1:12-17

As a pastor sometimes I think I don't like to admit how foolish I can be at times. I recently had an experience that taught me several great and valuable lessons.

I was very frustrated with a member of my church and I let the frustration get the best of me. I went to this person and told them I was through with them, that God would never use them, and literally that they were basically done spiritually. To be honest, I felt this was something I was supposed to do.

The results of my actions soon came back to haunt me. The person who I talked to was angry, people in the church who knew of it lost confidence in me, and I felt crummy. I kept trying to tell myself, "Well no matter what anyone else thinks or says, you just did what God wanted you to do." I didn't want to admit I was wrong.

God kept talking to me, I was getting under a cloud, I was losing my joy, and I was getting grouchy at my wife. Thank the Lord for His longsuffering and grace! When I came to my senses I sought forgiveness of God, and forgiveness from the person I had talked to, (this is making a long story short), and I received the forgiveness I desperately needed.

Well, from this episode I learned many lessons. One was to be very careful in trusting my feelings. Another was to remember what Dr. Richard Taylor told me when I was ordained, "Be patient with your people." And another was that I don't know the potential that this person has in Christ.

When we criticize, or speak unwisely, or in my case become judge, jury, and executioner, I am not taking into account what God can do with that soul, and I'm not taking into account what God did for my own soul.

Rev. Rodger Moyer

A Man's Potential (2)
1 Timothy 1:12-17

Yes, it is an amazing thing that we can forget what God did in our lives. I was ready to cast aside a soul even though God had such mercy on my soul.

I can't imagine where I would be today if my parents would have given up on me. I mean with the drugs, the smoking, the drinking, they had every right to give up on me. NO they didn't, God saved them too!

Here was the apostle Paul: a blasphemer, a persecutor, mean, hating Christians, the chief of sinners, and God made him one of the greatest Christian men of all time. Yes, a man's potential in the hands of God is a great thing. Let us pray, let us be patient, let us not give up for who knows what God might do.

Another lesson I learned is that not everyone has the privileges that I had. I was raised in a good godly holiness home. Christianity was taught daily and I never got involved in sin that I didn't know was sin. When I was saved I attended every service, tithed my money, made restitution, followed God's call on my life, all because I was taught.

I'm in the minority; most people didn't have that privilege. I don't know how hard it can be, and I wonder if I was raised like others if I would even be in my church trying to do my best. No wonder Dr. Taylor told me to be patient. I have to be, for who knows what kind of obstacles some people are battling.

I ask that God would help us all to be kind and tenderhearted, forgiving even as God for Christ's sake has forgiven us. I ask that God would give us all patience for He was more than patient with us, He was long-suffering. I would ask that God would help us to love others even as He loved and gave Himself for us.

Rev. Rodger Moyer

Godliness Is Gain
1 Timothy 6:3-10

Paul is dealing with his young pastor, Timothy, about some false teachers who were going around showing how godly they were because they had gained material wealth. To them, gain meant godliness. Paul wants to squash that idea. Growth in grace and godliness does not guarantee material gain. Wealth is not necessarily a sign of God's blessing, or else organized crime, pornographers, drug dealers are godly.

Paul understood that godliness with contentment is great gain. That doesn't mean that all our wants are put in proper perspective. The real gain of godliness is godliness itself. And with godliness comes contentment.

Paul goes on to say that we need to keep material wealth in proper perspective (v. 7) when he reminds us that we brought nothing into this world and we'll carry nothing out of the world.

Accumulating and multiplying wealth is a curse rather than a blessing. It removes us from the place of dependence on God; the more wealth, the more time it takes to manage; it leads to temptation (lure), then into lusts, and finally to loss. (v. 9)

Money is not the problem; it's the love of it. We think it will bring contentment, security and take away anxiety, but in reality it only brings the opposite – discontent, insecurity (have to put security fences around our wealth), and brings untold anxieties.

Paul uses the words "snare" (v. 9) and "piercing" (v. 10) to describe what happens to those who will be rich and love money. Those words describe the ancient method of hunting, where a man would dig a pit, fill it with spikes, cover the pit and wait for an animal or enemy to fall into it and be pierced by several of the spikes. That's the warning Paul gives concerning the pursuit of riches and the love of money.

Real contentment comes by godliness. The cure for greed is to be content with God.

Rev. John Moyer

The Gain Of Godliness
1 Timothy 6:6-11

It seems that regarding almost any proposal; somebody is bound to ask, "What's the bottom line?" Usually this is thought of in monetary terms with the interest being in profit or loss. It is remarkable, however, how often the "bottom line" turns out not to be the bottom line after all. A temporary loss may be instrumental in bringing about a long-term profit, and likewise, the immediate profit may spell disaster in the long run.

In 1 Timothy 6:5, Paul warns concerning those "who suppose that godliness is a means of gain." Our world is filled with those who are eager to make a fortune off of the religious inclinations of the masses. They may look like winners now, but ultimately they are losers. "For what does it profit a man to gain the whole world, and forfeit his soul?" (Mark 8:36)

Paul is quick to point out to Timothy, though, that the real bottom line of godliness is gain when it is accompanied by contentment. Actually, godliness provides both short and long-term profit—"godliness is profitable for all things, since it holds promise for the present life and also for the life to come."
(1 Timothy 4:8)

When we seek first His kingdom and His righteousness, His promise is to provide for our needs. God rescues the godly from temptations, sets apart the godly man for Himself, and gathers His godly ones to Himself. Truly, great is the gain in godliness with contentment!

Rev. Glen Boring

You Owe Your Community
1 Timothy 6: 11-19

Members of a holiness church owe its community a warm, Spirit-led kind of worship service. We have enough church buildings containing cold, dead, formal public worship – with no hint of God's presence, no testimony of His great grace! A genuine, Spirit-empowered time of worship will honor the Lord, allow for the flow of the Holy Spirit in touching and transforming lives, and will proclaim the message of heart holiness. The Spirit-empowered worship service will attract the earnest seeker of truth.

Members of a holiness church owe its community the reality of godly living in the every day life of an individual Christian. More than rhetoric, the Christian religion must be demonstrated in the Christlikeness of daily private and public life of all believers. Praise God – the experience of entire sanctification makes this possible!

Members of a holiness church owe its community a commitment to fight sin and the devil, continually strive to upgrade the moral standards of the community, and lead in the fight for what is good – for what is holy – for what will preserve our God-given freedoms! We can never be a people who sit back and allow our community to drift further from God and go to the devil, without apparent concern on our part.

Members of a holiness church owe its community a church that is more than just "an ark of refuge!" We are, and must continue to be, a great battleship – aggressively fighting against the enemy of the soul!

Dear reader, are you a member of a holiness church? Never forget, God has given Himself! Jesus Christ is our Counselor, our Guide, our Mighty Fortress, our Deliverer, Our Full Armour, and He is our Victory! You owe your community and, by God's grace, you cannot fail her!

Rev. William Kren

The Sanity of Saintliness
2 Timothy 1:7

"God hath not given to us the spirit of fear, but of power and of love and of a sound mind." What a great spiritual concept is embodied in this verse!

We should recognize first of all that these three things are inseparable. To possess one without the other two attributes is a distortion. Power without love and sound mind makes one a religious tyrant. History records that terrible things have been done in the name of religion. To have love without a sound mind makes one a religious fanatic. Blind mysticism is a spiritual tragedy. To have intellect without power and love is deadening and paralyzing, and makes one a cynic.

In power the attitude of life is positive and active. With love the emotions of the soul are sensitive and compassionate. With a sound mind, the thinking of the intellect is objective and rational. These three combine to make a victorious joyful Christian.

Three things are necessary for a sound mind – according to William Barclay. The Greek word is *sophronismos* and is almost untranslatable in English. It involves a holy character, and life completely yielded to God, a cleansed heart filled with the Holy Spirit. It demands a disciplined life. A servant of Christ must be a master of himself, with self-restraint over his body and mind. It implies a sensitive mind, and intellect that is God-directed. It involves a sensible and sensitive understanding and attitude toward others.

Here is God's antidote for fear and anxiety, God's secret of victory in the Christian life -- the religion of power, love and a sound mind.

Rev. Roy Clark

The Common Denominator
2 Timothy 2:14-21

In grade school I was taught the way to multiply and divide fractions was to find the lowest common denominator.

The Bible says something about "rightly dividing the word of truth." (2 Tim. 2:15) We are forbidden to add or subtract from the Word, but Paul tells Timothy plainly we should actually study how to divide it. Of course, we all know he is not talking about looking for ways to cause division, but to study laws of hermeneutics that will give us the true meaning of the Word.

With all of the shades of meaning and interpretations of holiness offered by modern man, we must return to basics. The one basic tenet from which we cannot swerve is simply this: Sanctification is a second definite work of grace wrought instantaneously in the heart by the Holy Spirit who at once cleanses the heart from inbred sin and fills it with His love. This is our lowest common denominator, which rightly divides all else.

The devil delights to dupe us into either over defining or under defining; to either expect unobtainable perfection, a goal that invariably throws the seeker into a rut of depression; or not to expect any kind of perfection or cleansing.

Just what is inbred sin or carnality? The Israelites, who were freed from the bondage of slavery but wandered in the desert, give us a clue. They were freed from the outward bondage of Egypt but not from the inward tendency of their hearts. After crossing into Canaan, God not only removed this "longing for Egypt" but He supplanted it with something much better. Their hearts were now inclined toward the milk and honey of Canaan. Carnality, then, is a bent in our hearts to want to have our cake and eat it too. God not only removes that bent but also gives us something much better. The attraction for the world "grows strangely dim in the light of His glory and grace."

Rev. Harold Harriman

Walking In Holiness
2 Timothy 2:22

2 Timothy 2:22 is the advice of a man who has long walked on the highway of holiness speaking to those who still have a long way to walk. *"Flee also youthful lusts: but follow righteousness, faith, charity, peace, with them that call on the Lord out of a pure heart."* The walk of holiness involves **fleeing, following,** and **fellowship**.

"Flee also youthful lusts." Youthful lusts are no worse than those that are shown in old age, but Paul was writing to Timothy, a man much younger than himself. If he had been writing to someone else he might have worded it differently. "Flee also the lusts of middle age," or "the lusts of later life." At every point in this holy way there are things with which we must not trifle nor tarry. Instead we must get away from them as quickly as possible. **Flee** for your life.

*"**Follow** righteousness, faith, charity, peace."* Holiness without righteousness is a fake. Holiness without faith is false. Holiness without charity or love is a farce. Holiness without peace is not holiness at all. Neither can today's walk be on yesterday's path of righteousness, faith, love or peace. We must follow and find fresh things of the Lord each day.

This **Fleeing** and this **Following** is to be in **Fellowship** *"with them that call on the Lord out of a pure heart."* Proverbs 13:20 declares, *"He who walks with wise men will be wise, But the companion of fools will be destroyed."* Form holy friendships if you would walk the way of holiness. Join with God's praying, purified children, and on to heaven go.

Flee from all sin. Follow all that is sacred. Fellowship with the saints of God. This is the way of holiness that gives us glory now and guarantees glory for eternity.

Dr. Wilfred Fisher

The Penalty For Excess Baggage
Hebrews 2:1-2

Life is a race! Most would agree. Life wasted is usually thrown away in little pieces and it is in the framework of time. Time is made up of a series of events that added together make up history. The writer to the Hebrews had just finished listing those who were in God's "hall of fame." No doubt others have been added since. How did they make it? Were they exceptional people? I think not, but they were a committed people.

We have to ask ourselves if we are committed. The next question would be, "To whom are we committed?"

As I view it, many will not make it because of "excessive baggage." Tragedy lies in people coming down to the end of their time and wondering what their part really was. They were not really committed or they had "excess baggage" – they were too wrapped up with the "cares of life." To the man or woman of God, the commandments of God are no more grievous to be borne than wings are to a bird.

I just returned from a trip by air and they very carefully checked my baggage and my person. Since I triggered the surveillance equipment, I was taken alongside and carefully searched. Actually they were looking for the "wrong" kind of baggage. By showing my implant card, I was able to continue on, but they were interested in security as I was returning back to our country after a week away.

God is not at this point especially concerned about security, but He knows that anything less than purity will not get us through. There were some things Jesus "endured" for the joy that was set before Him.

Let us "look to Jesus" to discover if any items that we are clutching too tightly might be "excessive baggage" not really needed for the trip.

Rev. Delmer Ransdell

Drifting Is Too Easy, Too Dangerous
Hebrews 2:1-4

At the end of the old Oregon Trail, in Oregon City, Oregon, is beautiful Willamette Falls. The first electrical transmission in the U.S. was from this spot. The Willamette River goes over the falls. About one mile upstream the Tualatin River enters the Willamette. Because there is sort of a natural dam at the falls, a rather large quiet pool of water backs up toward the Tualatin. It is a place for fishing and water skiing.

Occasionally boaters anchor their boats to fish or just enjoy the solitude. More than once a boat has drifted in this quiet eddy and suddenly gone over the falls. Usually the process begins with an innocent catnap. There is no thought of physical harm.

The writer to the Hebrews is concerned with spiritual drifting. It is a process that begins when we quietly let down our guard and spiritual intensity. We do not pay close attention to spiritual priorities, as we should. No matter how quick we intend the catnap to be, the end result is always the same – great spiritual devastation.

Hebrews does not promote unconditional eternal security in any way. There is spiritual security to be sure, but it is conditioned on our ongoing spiritual posture. This first warning flag here is more urgent. We are to beware lest we drift <u>away from</u> what we have heard. We do this by paying close attention to our basic commitment and daily walk. May it be a joyous posture.

Dr. John Sills

Keeping Up To Date
Hebrews 3:13-14

Having walked with the Lord over fifty-five years, I cannot dwell in an experience of the past. I must keep my relationship with Christ up to date. Past victories are not enough for today. I must obey Him and walk in the way that He leads now.

Everyday I ask Him to keep me filled with the Holy Spirit and to keep my experience fresh. The Disciples, after the initial filling on the day of Pentecost, were filled again, and again. Throughout the Book of Acts they met new crises and new situations in the power of the Holy Spirit. We too, need to be filled to meet the demands of life, and to carry out our part in the "Great Commission."

I also ask to be filled with Divine Love according to Romans 5:5. Love is to be dispensed and passed on. The supply is replenished as I give it away. If I try to keep it to myself, it grows cold.

When I was a boy, my parents lived in a house with a galvanized, metal roof. Rainwater running off it was clear and tasted good. Water caught in a barrel was fresh at first, but soon it became stale and full of wiggle-tales (mosquito larvae). Green scum formed over it.

An out of date Christian experience can become stale, and even lost until repentance and restoration takes place.

May we: "Encourage one another daily, as long as it is called today, so that none of you may be hardened by sin's deceitfulness." (Hebrews 3:13, NIV)

Rev. Ivan Olson

Dealing With Disappointments
Hebrews: 4:12-16

As human beings living in an imperfect sin-tarnished world, we are subject to disappointments in our daily lives. It was through one such disappointment that I learned a valuable spiritual truth.

In finding it hard to sleep one night due to a difficult situation, I sought comfort reading my Bible and praying. I asked the Lord to help me deal with the disappointment in a way that would be honoring to Him. As I opened my Bible, the Holy Spirit reminded me of many scriptures relating disappointments Jesus suffered during His earthly ministry. He suffered during the rejection of His people the Jews, (Matt. 23:37) the unbelief of His earthly family, (John 7:1-5) and the forsaking of His closest companions in the garden of Gethsemane. (Matt. 26:46-56) This same Jesus is my High Priest, making intercession for me before the Father's throne.

This realization helped me see that I needed to take my disappointments to Him. To harbor such feelings would give root to sins of resentment and bitterness. To feel hurt and disappointment was not sin, but how was I going to deal with those feelings would determine the condition of my soul. In committing it all to the Lord, He took away the sense of disappointment and left in its place a deep peace and a greater trust in Him.

Times of disappointment will come even to the sanctified heart – not a spirit of touchiness and easily hurt feelings, but times of true disappointment. In those times we can remember that Our Heavenly Father cares about every need in our lives and can abundantly meet each one.

Mrs. Brad Weinert

Rare, Medium, Or Well Done? (1)
Hebrews 10:22-27; James 4:17

I dropped into Hamburger Heaven one day for lunch. After taking my order for a sandwich with everything on it, the young lady asked me if I wanted it rare, medium, or well done. "Medium," I replied, and soon I was munching on a delicious, juicy, hamburger, trying to keep my necktie out of the danger zone, and wishing I had three sets of hands in order to keep up with the drips, drops, and disappearing napkins. While I was eating, the words "rare, medium, and well done," came back to mind in relationship to our spiritual lives.

God has for each of us the plan for a well ordered life, with everything in it and on it that His holy will knows will be best for us. But He leaves the choice with us. God's orders have never included anything "rare" or even "medium." With God, and in the center of His will it is "well done" all the way!

Do you know any of these so-called Christians, who are rare? Frankly they don't even make good Sunday morning bench warmers. They are rarely in Sunday School, rarely in church, rarely make a real offering, rarely read their Bibles, rarely pray, and rarely witness in any way. I think it will be even rarer for any of them to hear the Master say, "Well done; enter thou into the joy of the Lord."

A simple couplet, learned as a boy, comes to mind, but I cannot remember to whom the credit belongs, perhaps to a McGuffy Reader.

"What thy hands find to do, do with thy might;
Things done by halves are never done right."

For the real origin of this, see Eccl. 9:10.

Rev. John Kunkle

Rare, Medium, Or Well Done? (2)
The "Medium" Christian
Rev. 3:14-22; Luke 9:57-62

"Medium Christians" are fence straddlers. They remind me of Ephraim, in the Old Testament, who was referred to as half- baked, or a "cake not turned." He was like a pancake, burned black on one side, but a sticky, raw mess on the other. A yucky, mucky mess, totally worthless, and headed for the garbage. Ephraim, claiming to be a part of God's people, was so mixed up with the godless heathen around them, that they had lost all identity as a part of God's people.

The New Testament refers to these "medium" folks as "luke warm" -- neither hot, nor cold. In a figure of speech they make God Himself sick to His stomach, so that He finally spews them out of His mouth to utter and eternal loss. These Medium Christians put their hands to the plow, and then do a lot of looking back. I remember from my farming days that in working with an old fashioned "walking plow," I had to fix my eyes on a goal ahead, and keep them fixed there. If I started looking back, I wound up with a mighty crooked furrow, and sometimes got out of the furrow altogether. Jesus said that such persons were not fit for the "Kingdom of God." That sounds mighty serious to me. I certainly don't want to fool around as a "Medium Christian."

A missionary on furlough once said to me, "So many seem really interested in missionary work, but so few are willing to make any real commitment any more." That total commitment that only comes with entire sanctification is the desperate need of the whole church of our Lord and Savior Jesus Christ today.

Rev. John Kunkle

Rare, Medium, Or Well Done? (3)
The "Well Done" Christian
Philippians 3:13-15

Paul puts it so beautifully! Here we find no cocky self-righteousness, but no silly wallowing in sins, weaknesses, and bad habits of the past either, as though these are to be the expected norm of daily Christian living for the rest of life. It was heads up, eyes front, and a joyful, zestful eager reaching out for the prize ahead. The symbolism is that of a racer really pressing it out, straining every nerve and muscle to reach the goal. Paul brings us, you and me, into the picture in verse 15 where he says, "Let us, therefore, as many as be perfect, be thus minded. And if in anything ye be otherwise minded, God shall reveal even this unto you." Even in our own churches these days, when we refer to Christian perfection, folks will snarl and sneer, "Well, nobody is perfect," or "After all I am just human!" As though, forevermore, these were to be the perfect and God given excuses for all sorts of willful sinning, evil habits, and failures in their supposed to be Christian lives.

Paul claims no resurrection, heavenly, angelic, nor even human perfection. But as a "Well Done" Christian, he did claim a perfection of heart purity, submission, consecration, and commitment, that made it possible for him never to "look back" once he had put his hand to the plow. He never again purposely, habitually, lived in sin. He could have, but he didn't have to do so, and he did not. The provision Christ made for us on the cross fully covered justification, sanctification, and glorification, which is still to come. The merits of Calvary make it possible for us to have the same reality of "Well Done" Christian living that Paul enjoyed. That in turn, will make it possible to hear our Lord say, some day soon, "Well Done, good and faithful servant, enter thou into the joy of the Lord!"

Rev. John Kunkle

Receive The Promise!
Hebrews 10:32-39

In our Scripture reading today we have this marvelous promise "that when you have done the will of God (see 1 Thess. 4:3), you will receive what He has promised." The promise spoken of here was not unknown to the believers of the first century. They had it in the writings of the Old Testament prophets. Some of them may have read it in Isaiah (44:3), "I will pour out my Spirit on your offspring." Others may have understood it as recorded by Ezekiel (36:27), "And I will put my Spirit in you." Still others may have learned of the promise by reading Joel 2:28-29, "... I will pour out my Spirit in those days." It may be that some of these early Christians had heard of the promise through John the Baptist who declared (Matt. 3:11), "He will baptize you with the Holy Spirit and with fire." Perhaps some had been there when Jesus promised, "streams of living water [by this He meant the Spirit] will flow from within." (Jn. 7:38-39) Others may have heard the promise of One who would come to comfort, guide, instruct, and teach (Jn. 14:26; 15:26; 16:13) as the disciples went about preaching what Jesus had promised in His last sermon. The words of the promise had even been on Jesus' lips as He ascended into heaven. (Luke 24:49; Acts 1:4-5)

The promise was clear – and it remains for us today! Will we receive it by faith? In Num. 23:19 the question is asked, "Does He promise and not fulfill?" The answer is clearly stated in Psalm 145:13, "The Lord is faithful to all His promises."

HAVE YOU RECEIVED THE PROMISE?

Dr. Bruce Moyer

Holiness An Adventure
Hebrews 11:8

Webster defines "adventure" as "a venture; a risk". To attempt an adventure means attempting a feat even though you know danger may be involved and even though you do not know what will happen. It involves the excitement of the unknown.

Holiness is an adventure because it means going through life with God. It means living under God's direction, belonging only to God, being guided by the Holy Spirit, and learning from Him who made us. It is all too common for us to think of holiness as following and never breaking any of the written rules. To think thus is to invite certain defeat. Instead, I invite you to think of holiness as a personal walk through life with a personal God – following our living Lord, by His grace and help.

This does not mean there are no written rules, such as the Ten Commandments, etc., but in following God personally we go far beyond written rules. Rules are primarily negative. Holiness is positive guidance (see the Sermon on the Mount). As stated, the true nature of holiness is that it is an adventure. It is walking moment-by-moment by the Spirit's guidance. And while we do not know the way ahead, nor what we will have to face, or when we will have to face it, we do know the Guide Who will go with us every step of the way! But, then we are happy to go anywhere, anytime, and anyhow so long as He will go with us! The God Who commands us to be holy in following His way by submitting to learn and do His will is the God Who will empower us to do so.

My friend, our love for God makes the life of holiness a life of joyous adventure. Following Him is not hard – it is the most pleasant and rewarding life we can imagine! There is nothing less we would choose to do; nothing else we want to do! And, in our love for Him, we resist every temptation that may come to forsake His way! The love for God makes all of life a thrilling adventure – the adventure of holiness! Will you join me in the adventure?

Rev. Gene Moyer

Holy Spirit -- Unclutterer
Hebrews 12:1

One day, while I was treasurer of Kentucky Prayer Bands (now called Prayer Ministries), I needed to check a pledge card for one of the bands. I kept all of my prayer band materials – monthly reports, letters, receipt books, coin holders, addresses – in a large box on a shelf. Each month, the contents of the box increased.

To find the pledge card, I had to rummage through an array of papers – papers that were at one time essential and useful; but now they had become clutter.

That afternoon I filled three wastebaskets with these once useful – not unessential – papers, reports, and letters. And what a feeling of release it brought! I felt exhilarated, free. Was I blessed or just relieved? I'm not sure, but it was a good feeling.

It occurred to me that perhaps my spiritual life, like this box, could be <u>cluttered</u> – not with sinful things, but with good things, once needful but now obscuring God's best. Was there <u>clutter</u> in my praying? Were things I had committed to God still taking my prayer time? Were daily activities, good in themselves, crowding out Christ's priorities? Was anything impairing my vision of Christ Himself and His interests in people? Was my witness to entire sanctification as clear as it used to be?

I invited Christ to unclutter everything in my life that interfered with His kingdom purposes. And I found that this is an ongoing process. Last week's newspaper may be this week's <u>clutter</u>. And last month's meditation, if dwelt upon too long, may keep us from receiving today's fresh truth.

The Holy Spirit is indeed our Friend, Comforter, Guide, Keeper, and Anointer. He is also our skilled <u>Unclutterer</u>.

Mrs. Alice Fisher

Excess Baggage
Hebrews 12:1-3

In his book, <u>Blind Courage</u>, author Bill Irwin describes hiking the Appalachian Trail from Georgia to Maine – a distance of over 2,000 miles. Not bad for a blind person! Of course he did have a seeing-eye dog that was a great help. Since he was an inexperienced hiker, he loaded "everything" into the pack that he might need – "excess baggage." Significantly, after trudging the first lap of the journey, he began discarding whatever was not necessary and tended to make his hiking more difficult – if not impossible. He found this to be a common practice of "thru-hikers" to discard the "excess baggage" along the trail.

It was right then I thought about our pilgrimage as believers, headed for the "celestial city." I thought of Pilgrim in Bunyan's *Pilgrim's Progress*. I thought of his near escape in Vanity Fair, the city of bright lights and easy living, where he almost gave up the journey.

I thought of "excess baggage" I needed to lay aside – "every weight and the sin." I needed to get on with the journey. I determined, by the help of God, to not let the vanity fairs of this life slow me up or dim my vision of what I was here for.

We pilgrims are often cautioned today, to not get too "heavenly minded" that we forget some of the "legitimate" claims of this world – the "gadgets" we so desperately must have. But, it's amazing that so many of these "things" become totally irrelevant and meaningless the nearer we come to the end – excess baggage.

And <u>now</u> abideth "faith, hope, and love, these three." Beyond most of the rest is excess weight that in one way or another tends to blur the image of the finish line, and to drag us down. So, fellow traveler, let's run with perseverance the race set before us looking unto Jesus the author and finisher of our pilgrimage. Get rid of your excess baggage, and press on!

Dr. Gerald Dillon

Weighted Struggles
Hebrews 12:1-11

Two students planned a day of fishing. With gear and food in hand they rented a rowboat and started off for the other side of the lake. As they neared their destination, they noticed that heavy dark clouds were forming in the west, the direction from which they had come. Not to be denied their plans, they let down the anchor, baited their hooks, and began to fish.

It became darker and the wind began to blow. Realizing this was not just a threat but a real storm, they pulled in their lines and started to row back to the boat landing. It seemed they were not only fighting the storm but that the boat itself was fighting them. Two hours later they finally reached the dock. As they secured the boat, they realized that they had forgotten to pull up the anchor. The drag of the anchor had made their trip and labors even greater, and had almost cost them their lives.

How many Christians are like these two young men? They have definite desires to do God's will. They are involved. They are walking with the Lord. But in the storms of life they find that they are not just fighting the difficulties and temptations of life, but they are struggling with themselves. They find something inside that is dragging against what they know God wants them to do.

The writer to the Hebrews saw this in the lives of those to whom he was writing and admonished them to "lay aside every weight, and the sin which he so easily besets us, and let us run with patience the race that is set before us, looking into Jesus…."

What a shame when a child of God will not look unto Jesus and cut loose from the drag of sin. They struggle, labor, and almost go under and maybe do because of the pull of sin in their hearts. Someone sees their struggles and encourages them to cut loose from the drag of sin, but due to pride or ignorance they struggle on. Jesus came to "destroy the works of the devil." (1 John 3:8) Praise God, that includes the weight of inbred sin!

Rev. David Kushman

329

Do Not Despise The Chastening Of The Lord
Hebrews 12:5-13

The woodshed has become a veritable symbol of parental discipline and childhood "chastenings." Responsible, loving fathers have been taking their children to the "woodshed" for generations, not because they hate them but because they love them too much to permit them to persist in harmful conduct.

The child of God will have "trips to the woodshed" because he has a responsible, loving Heavenly Father who "deals with you as with sons." God cares for us too much to permit us to persist in harmful conduct. "For whom the Lord loves He chastens, and scourges every son whom He receives."

How is the Christian to respond when God has to take him to the woodshed? Our text has some very important answers to this question. 1) Don't forget that it will happen. (v. 5) 2) Don't despise it when it does happen. (v. 5) 3) Don't be discouraged when it happens. (v. 5) 4) Endure it. (v. 7) 5) Expect it. (v. 8) 6) Submit to God in it. (v. 9) 7) Recognize God's purpose in it. (v. 10) 8) Look forward to its passing and the peace which will follow. (v. 11) 9) Get a grip on yourself and take it like a man. (v. 12) 10) Whatever was wrong make it right. (v. 13)

Frequently the devil meets the Christian on the path back from the woodshed and whispers accusations in his ear. "Aha! So you thought you were sanctified during the revival meeting! Well, if you had a clean heart God would have never had to deal with you the way he has!" How must we respond to such accusations?

1) Recall that all God's sons experience His chastening. (v. 8) 2) Just deal with the "lameness" God has pointed out. (v. 13) 3) Resist the temptation to begin doubting what God has done for you in days gone by. 4) Thank God for loving you and caring enough about you to take you to the "woodshed."

Rev. Chris Neilson

Discipline
Hebrews 12:11

"I'll never make my children do that!" As a boy growing up I was forced to eat a few peas when they were served at a meal. Peas! Why would my parents be making me eat peas? Everyone knows that the peas are a result of the fall. Why would they be "forcing" me to eat something that was a result of Adam's sin? "I'll never make my children do that, they can decide for themselves."

Not only was I taught to eat a little of everything that was served (thank goodness Mom didn't like spinach), but I was also taught to respect my elders and those in authority over me, to be kind to my brothers and sisters, to tithe, to obey my parents, etc. But my children were going to be allowed to decide for themselves. This was my inward response to my childhood training because the writer of Hebrews is right when he said, "no chastening seems to be joyful for the present, but painful." I remember some times it was quite painful.

Today, thirty years later, I have three children of my own. Do I let them decide for themselves? NO! Absolutely not! In fact, one day my wife served peas and I made my children eat some. (Yes, I ate some too). Why did I do it? Why did I do what my parents did to me? Why did I not let my children decide for themselves? Because even though discipline is painful at the time "afterward it yields the peaceable fruit of righteousness" or as the New American Standard puts it "it leads to salvation."

There is no question in mind that the reason I and my five brothers and sisters are serving God today is because we were taught obedience (quick and immediate) to our parents (many times through pain) and to God.

I thank God daily for the lessons I learned as a child from my parents so I can better teach my children. Thank you, Dad. Thank you, Mom.

Brad Weinert

From Bitterness To Christlikeness (1)
Hebrews 12:12-17

Bitterness. What is it? An adverbial form of bitter and, according to one dictionary, it is "piercingly harsh or cruel; stinging; caustic; acrimonious." So it isn't any wonder that the Scriptures identify an unrighteous person as one "whose mouth is full of cursing and bitterness." (Romans 3:14) Thus St. Paul instructs us to "Let all bitterness, and wrath, and anger, and clamor, and evil speaking, be put away from you, with all malice." (Ephesians 4:31) Moreover, the call to "follow holiness" is followed by a warning to "look diligently lest ... any root of bitterness springing up trouble you, and thereby many be defiled...." (Hebrews 12:14-15)

Bitterness begins in a root. This is one way of describing a carnal human heart, which could easily lead to a self-pitying attitude.

Bitterness, if unchecked, goes on to develop a shoot. It springs up. It brings trouble. It is contagious and others are likely to be defiled. (Hebrews 12:15)

And bitterness can go one step further. It produces a fruit -- the fruit of anger, dissension, and strife -- not to mention personal problems from the same source. From such, O Lord deliver us. And he will -- by the purifying baptism with the Holy Spirit. (Acts 15: 8-9) Amen!

Dr. Eldon Fuhrman

From Bitterness To Christlikeness (2)
2 Peter 1: 1-4

If bitterness is to be abhorred, Christlikeness is to be pursued. To be Christian is impossible without Christ. And to have Christ in us as the hope of glory (Colossians 1:27) means that we become new creatures (2 Corinthians 5:17), that we become partakers of the divine nature (2 Peter 1:4), that we have the Spirit of Christ (Philippians 2:5), that we put on Christ (Galatians 3:27), and that the seed of Christ dwells in us (1 John 3:9).

Thus we happily say that Christlikeness begins in a grace that is bestowed. For like begets like and, in disposition and deportment, Christlikeness begins in the grace of the new birth. But it is only a beginning.

To be Christlike continues as a goal to be pursued. Peter tells us that Christ left us an example that ye (we) should follow his steps (1 Peter 2:21) and we have a long, long way to go. We agree humbly and heartily with Paul that we have not attained, that we are not perfect, that we press on, that we look continually to Christ as our model, our goal. (Philippians 3:12-15) So we must grow and go on!

Finally the call to Christlikeness is a glory to be gained. In the resurrection morning "we shall be like Him, for we shall see Him as He is." (1 John 3:2) We shall see Jesus face to face (Revelation 22:4) and that will be glory forever! Hallelujah!

Dr. Eldon Fuhrman

Keep The Tongue Clean!
James 3: 1-10

A health tip suggests that an effective method of keeping one's breath fresh is to brush the tongue! According to medical authorities, cleaning the tongue not only will help reduce build up of dental plaque, but it will also sweeten the breath for hours!

This pursuit for fresh breath should not end with a toothbrush in hand! Our mouths must also be spiritually clean! This means that we have a tongue that does not gossip, engage in negative criticism, speak abusive or unloving words, break confidences, or engage in foolish babblings. Cleaning our tongues spiritually, however, requires a bit more than standing in front of the vanity with a tube of Crest.

James writes: "The tongue is a little member, and boasteth great things... the tongue is a fire, a world of iniquity: so is the tongue among our members, that it defileth the whole body, and setteth on fire the course of nature: and it is set on fire of hell... no man can tame it; it is an unruly evil; full of deadly poison."

In reading God's Word, have you discovered that YOU need a spiritual tongue cleaning? Do you find yourself speaking words and later regretting you've said them? Do you enjoy engaging in "idle chit-chat" that somehow, always evolves into "galloping gossip?" If you need a clean and healthy tongue – there is a cure!

In Proverbs 16:23, we are told, "the heart of the wise teacheth (or "maketh wise") his mouth, and addeth learning to his lips." It's clear that the key to having a clean tongue is related to the condition of our heart. The cleansing of the heart has an immediate effect in delivering the believer from his unruly tongue. A clean heart is the answer in our search for that "spiritual brushing" of the tongue. How is it with your tongue today?

Rev. William Kren

Grace or Glory?
James 4:1-10

Some years ago an older couple began attending our church. Converted at an early age, married over fifty years, their membership was in the nearby local church of their youth. Their frustration was deep. It involved the spiritual perspective and practice of their current pastor.

Their pastor was a proud man. He had a "scholarly" divinity degree. He was intellectual. He was serving one of the "in" churches of the community. He enjoyed his position and prestige. He had glory.

Neither of the two particular individuals that this pastor ministered to has graduated from high school. The husband had been a dairy farmer for many years. His last working years were spent as a postal clerk. Both were humble. Both manifested the grace of God.

As this couple eventually became part of our congregation, their prayers enriched us all. Their faithfulness to the things of God blessed us often. The wisdom of the husband provided me with Spirit-anointed guidance many times. What a contrast!

Their pastor sought glory, received it, but manifested little of God's grace. This humble couple had long sought God. They knew Him in full surrender. They daily manifested God's grace in a powerful way. Surely, their testimony of God's grace, in contrast to the obtainment of glory, is what most people remember.

Dr. John Sills

"Draw Nigh To God"
James 4:8a

This little phrase is one of the most glorious thoughts in the entire world. We are born into this world sinful, having gone on and committed acts of sin, and yet we are invited to "draw nigh" to a Holy God; but even more than that He says, "And I will draw nigh to you." Friends, that's love at the highest degree!

But drawing nigh unto God means some things. It means that as I draw nigh to Him I am willing to leave this world behind. It means that I have forsaken sin It means the sinful nature has come to an end, and that I have come into the place of total submission to the will of God by faith. It means that, as a sinner, I cleanse my hands, asking forgiveness for my outward acts of sins, and that I have my heart purified from the inward presence of sin by God's sanctifying grace.

But what does it mean for God to draw nigh to me? It means the greatest blessings in all the world. It means all my needs supplied, spiritual and temporal! It means all my sins are forgiven, and my carnality cleansed away It means the anointing of the Holy Spirit and His abiding presence in my heart It means grace sufficient in every time of temptation It means victory over the world and the devil It means joy and peace in my soul that passeth all understanding!

Yes, praise His name, all is mine, when I draw nigh unto God. And friend, all is yours if you will draw nigh unto Him as well.

Rev. Rodger Moyer

Patience
James 5:7-11

The crisis of sanctification can never do for us what only the maturing process will do. Patience is not given in a big package delivered straight from Heaven. Romans 5:3 says, "We glory in tribulations also; knowing that tribulation worketh patience." James 1:3 says, "Knowing this, that the trying of your faith worketh patience."

Delays at the checkout counter, delays at the doctor's, or delays by the slowness of others can give us an opportunity to grow some patience. In a plane transfer at Hong Kong, several passengers lost their luggage. They were angry and denounced the airline. One woman even declared she would never travel by that line again. We thanked God for His calmness engulfing us in the storm of protest. Later we received the luggage in Java after its trip to Tokyo and back! Unselfishness and kindness are wrapped up in patience over delays. I am sure we learned a new lesson in God's school those days.

Disappointments are another nurturing ground for patience. Plans and high expectations are thwarted, children disappoint us, doors of service do not open. Bitterness can creep in and we feel God is cruel to us. Such thoughts are to be immediately killed. David was rejected for years by Saul and double-crossed by Absalom. Yet, we all turn to Psalms written by David to find comfort. Let us substitute the letter, "D" in disappointment with "H" and read it thus, "His appointment." In accepting all from His dear hand we find peace and rest.

Mrs. Laura Trachsel

The Heart That Dances
1 Peter 1:1-9 (vs. 6, 8)

There is an intriguing line in a little-known hymn by Charles Wesley that says, "**And my heart doth dance** at the sound of His name." How expressive of the joy and gladness of the Christian life! Charles' brother John added, "True religion cannot be without cheerfulness."

There are many religious folk who do not live up to this standard. There are even some holiness people who give evidence of being sour, austere, unsociable, and unfriendly. But to the extent to which they lack the joy of the Lord or are sour and unfriendly, to that extent they betray the cause they profess to represent!

Joy, as the Bible uses the term, and as the Wesley's understood it, does not mean hilarity or effervescence of spirit. It is real in spite of heavy burdens, sorrow, testing and trial. Peter found no contradiction between "Heaviness through manifold temptations" and "joy unspeakable and full of glory." This is because, as one has said, "joy is the echo of God's life within us." It is a quality of heart and soul, and carries us through hardship and pain. It does not come from physical well-being or favorable circumstances, and cannot be destroyed for lack of them. Joy is the reflection of spiritual health in the soul. It is a deep presence of the Heavenly Guest who Jesus called "the Comforter."

Perhaps, my friends, what we need most in our tense and troubled times is to better give expression outwardly to the "dancing heart" within! Where there is more winsomeness and radiance about us, there would be fewer in family or community who identify salvation with a long face and holiness with gloom!

Will you join me in allowing the indwelling Holy Spirit to make yours and mine a "dancing heart?"

Rev. Gene Moyer

Is Holiness Required? (1)
1 Peter 1:13-21; Leviticus 19:2

Shopping malls and super shopping center grocery stores emphasize a new phenomenon since WWII: Multiple choices. Gone are the days when all phones were black, all bathtubs white and checkbook covers green.

While we are blessed by many positive choices to make, we must be careful to avoid transferring this dynamic to the basics of our walk with God. I may choose a style of worship service. It may be good to be able to choose between prayer meeting at church or Home Bible Study. But we dare not choose between the basic standards of God as found in His Word.

Our text, "be holy," (1 Peter 1:16) quotes the central message of Leviticus. The challenge to holiness of heart and life is God's requirement, not that of a movement, a particular seminary or even family of denominations.

God's requirement of holiness stems from His holiness. Those whom He created to worship and praise Him are to be holy in character (not stature) as He is holy. He created us so we operate at our human best when we function within the framework of holiness. And holiness is the only lasting remedy to the evil bent that causes us to rebel and fall short of God's glory.

Occasionally when a doctor prescribes a procedure, a patient will ask, "do I have to take this?" Or, "do I have to undergo this surgery?" The answer? "No, only if you want to get better." So it is with God.

Dr. John Sills

Is Holiness Attainable? (2)
Luke 1:68-74; 1 Thess. 5:23-24

It is one thing to agree that holiness is God's requirement and we dare not ignore it. It is something else to believe it can happen to me or to you.

The father of John the Baptist believed the reign of Messiah meant holiness could be more then ceremonial. Holiness of heart and life would be experiential. He saw that humans could serve the Lord "... in holiness and righteousness before Him all the days of our lives."

Paul believed God could do it now, that is, sanctify His people for holiness in this life. Paul's belief was based on God's ability, His faithfulness to keep His word.

While we know God is not mocked, (Gal. 6:7-8) we must also remember He does not mock us. He neither requires that which is unobtainable, nor says He will do something for us in this life He cannot accomplish.

If we believe He is our Creator, and Redeemer from the guilt of sin, it is not illogical to see Him as the One with the power who can also provide for Holiness of heart and life.

If there is a limitation toward your experiencing holiness, don't lay the blame on God. Pray you will have the necessary faith to accept His requirement and respond to His gracious offer to make it happen in your life.

The question is not, "is it attainable?" It is, "do I believe He will do what He says?"

Dr. John Sills

Being Normal
1 Peter 2:21-22

I once heard a preacher ask, "Are you average, or are you normal?" This thought has really stuck with me and has added a new dimension to my life and to my thinking.

Being a normal Christian is to be like Christ. Too often we tend to look at one another or to judge ourselves by how good or bad others may be. In the church many people look at each other and say, "Well I'm pretty much like them, I believe what they believe, I act like they act, I talk like they talk," and they conclude that they are normal Christians. That fact is that they have only figured out that they are average, but not necessarily normal.

Husbands and wives can do this as well. They may look at each other and say, "Well my husband or wife is doing this, my husband or wife is watching that on TV, my husband or wife isn't really sold out to God, and my husband or wife doesn't want to be in all the services, or give the tithes, so it's OK."

The fact of the matter is we need a standard to judge ourselves other than ourselves. The Bible says it is unwise to judge ourselves by ourselves, so why do so many do it?

It is because looking at Jesus, at His "example," to "follow in His steps" really reveals to us whether we are living right or not. If we would just keep our eyes on Jesus, how holy we would be! How in love with God we would be! How we would hunger to do the will of God because it would be our meat and drink!

Let us look at Jesus, "who did not sin." Let us not shrink back from the challenge, let us be normal Christians, sanctified and living holy!

Rev. Rodger Moyer

Holiness Works!
1 Peter 3:14-17

During a recent routine treadmill test, the doctor said, "Everything is working well under stress!" On the way home, I began thinking about the spiritual application of that statement. My mind went back to a particularly difficult meeting in Africa where a lot of accusations, lies, and just plain unkind comments were directed at the mission and me in general. The only other missionary in the meeting said afterwards, "How could you sit there and take that?" I simply said, "Holiness works!"

In our own strength we can't keep that spiritual composure, but the Spirit of Christ in us can. That's why He must cleanse and take His place at the center of our lives. That's why the mark of a holy heart is love for God and love for man – including our enemies.

God really does expect us to maintain our spiritual life and testimony under stress. How do you react when there are false accusations, misread motives, and unkind remarks directed at you? Can you keep a sweet spirit when you're voted off the board, your idea isn't accepted, or someone else is asked to sing on that special day? What about your co-worker whose unethical maneuvering results in him receiving the promotion you should have been given? This is when holiness moves from theory to practical reality. To maintain a Christlike spirit under adverse circumstances will bear a strong witness to the church and the world.

Prayer: Father, when the hard places of life come my way, may You be able to say of me, "Everything is working well under stress!"

Rev. Nevin Williams

God First
1 Peter 3:15

As people who have had our hearts sanctified wholly, this commandment is reality – God truly is first in our hearts and lives. However, this reality is tested every day of our lives in the choices we make.

If he is really first, seeking audience with Him early in the day will be a first priority. It is His direction we need in our lives – not a blessing to prosper our own plans and purposes.

When the times of worship and Bible study come, there will be no question where we will be. When the church doors are open, we are there to edify our souls and learn more of Him and to worship Him with others.

When the Holy Spirit prompts us to witness to someone, to phone a word of encouragement or to write a letter of Christian love, that becomes a top priority. When he calls us to prayer, everything else becomes secondary.

The principle of "God first" needs to be instilled in our children and young people. God comes before homework, school, TV programs, and social activities. He comes before family and friends. Whenever this is practiced in actuality in the home, the family will not suffer and the children will benefit by learning the most important rule of spiritual life. God honors those who honor Him first.

Mrs. Clarice Moyer

Above All, Love Each Other Deeply
1 Peter 4:8

Holiness people have always maintained that a cleansed heart expresses itself by, first, loving God fully and, second, by loving others as we love ourselves. (Matt. 22:37-40) In our text for today Peter repeats (see 1 Peter 1:22) the command that above everything else we ought to love each other deeply (earnestly, eagerly, fervently). Meditating on that thought, I realized that there are several Scriptural reasons for such a mandate. They are made clear by John, the Apostle of Love.

First, if we don't love others, we cannot claim to love God. Not only can we not claim to love God, it is impossible for us to love God. (1 John 4:19-21) This is not because loving God must be preceded by loving others, but because when we do love God, that relationship naturally produces love for others. Previous to this John has even gone so far as to say that, if we do not love others, we cannot even claim to know God. So we must love others – it is a natural product of our knowing and loving God.

Second, in 1 John 4:18 the Apostle tells us that a heart not full of love is open to the influences of carnal, slavish fear. When we allow our hearts to be cleansed and then filled with perfect love, our ministry and service are motivated by a new source. Things and situations that once brought a hindering fear to our service for Christ are overcome by divinely produced love.

Third, if we do not love one another, we are simply breaking the clear command of God. (John 15:12, 17)

Finally, if we do not love one another deeply, we destroy our witness to the world. (John 13:34-35)

Dr. Bruce Moyer

The Testing of Perfect Love
1 Peter 4:12-19

"Beloved, think it not strange concerning the fiery trial which is to try (prove) you, as though some strange thing happened unto you: but rejoice, insomuch as ye are partakers of Christ's sufferings; that, when His glory shall be revealed, ye may be glad also with exceeding joy." (1 Peter 4:12-13)

Holiness of heart enables us to love God with all out heart, soul and strength and our neighbor as ourselves. When all things are going well with us and men praise us and appreciate us, it is very easy to love in return. But the real test of whether our hearts are filled with perfect love comes when we are ill-treated and misunderstood, when we are betrayed by those we trusted, and when we experience some of the reverses in life. When we have these things happening to us, we are told by Peter to rejoice. This is the proving of the grace of God bestowed upon us. Jesus tells us in Matthew 5:46, "For if ye love them which love you, what reward have ye?" Instead, when we pray for those who persecute us and hate us and despitefully use us, we show that God has, indeed, perfected love in our hearts. If we do not experience these reversals of life, how can we manifest to the world that perfect love abounds in our hearts?

This kind of love cannot be worked up by gritting our teeth and exclaiming, "I'll love him if it kills me!" No, only the love of God spread abroad in our hearts by the Holy Ghost can bring about a flowing forth of that love to others.

So let us thank God for the opportunities that come for us to show forth His perfect love knowing we are being conformed more fully to the image of His own Son.

Mrs. Clarice Moyer

It's The Little Things That Matter
1 Peter 5:5-10

I'm far from being the world's greatest husband but, after several years of married life, I've learned that it's the little things that matter. Things like ... a wink ... an unexpected hug ... a little squeeze of the hand ... an arm around the shoulder ... flowers or a card for no special reason ... an evening just to sit (or walk) and talk. All of these far outweigh the big anniversary party, birthday gifts, etc. when it comes to keeping our marriage fresh and alive.

The same is true in many other areas of life as well. A speck of dust can hardly be seen, but don't dust your house for several weeks and then look again. Or just forget about greasing the car or changing the engine oil for a few years. It's just a little thing ... but eventually it will matter.

The little things are important for holy living too. That daily quiet time when just you and the Lord talk with each other is vital. Or maybe it's church attendance ... or participating in Sunday School ... or regular involvement in the midweek prayer service ... or becoming actively involved in some ministry of my local church. It's so easy to dismiss them all as just "little things." But these are the things that keep us fresh and alive. They dare not be neglected. At first the impact of their neglect may not be noticed, but eventually a price will be paid. Take time today to pay attention to the "little things." They really do matter!

"The most dangerous thing is that the soul, by the neglect of little things, becomes accustomed to unfaithfulness."
(Francois Fenelon in *Christian Perfection*)

Dr. Bruce Moyer

The Trading Post
1 Peter 5:7

To my wife, trying to operate our household on a meager budget, trading stamps were a boon. More than once some item she really needed was obtained by exchanging trading stamps which all of us helped collect.

It was, however, something of a bondage to have to make purchases where they gave stamps. It was not easy to remember to put them in the designated drawer in the dining room – the result being a sticky mass in my pocket. And there were those times when it was her turn to plan our weekly "family time" activity, that we spent a time of togetherness licking those stamps and putting them in appropriate books. Surely a chocolate-flavored glue for those stamps would have enjoyed a great sale!

But one day something remarkable happened! Sue asked me to go downtown with her. At her direction I parked in front of a building bearing the sign, "Redemption Center." We walked in, laid on the counter a lot of those trading stamp books I was sure no one would ever want, and she got in exchange a beautiful household item. I decided then and there a redemption center is a great place to visit.

Then, of course, I remembered another great event when I visited THE Redemption Center. I took what had long controlled my life, the carnal nature, and "traded" it for a clean heart. What an amazing transaction! Phillip Dodderidge wrote of it in his great, untitled hymn: "I'll drop my burdens at His feet, and bear a song away."

I don't know that any hymn has ever been written which focuses upon THE Redemption Center. But there should be one, for it is a good thing to keep in mind that time and place when God took what we no longer wanted and in its place gave that which we never wish to exchange.

Dr. Merne Harris

The Devil Is Out To Get You
1 Peter 5:8

No doubt about it, we have an adversary the devil. His handiwork is all around us. Murder, divorce, abortion, and many other evils show us that he is alive and well.

We in the church world take the devil too lightly. We look at all the work he is doing in the world and we forget that his real work is in the soul. He comes as an angel of light, and his ministers transform themselves into ministers of righteousness.

They are very gifted, very spiritual, very positive. They preach about healing, about getting rich, about gifts and tongues, and power. But they skip right over repentance, right over genuine salvation, right over leaving sin behind, right over sanctifying grace.

But in it all the devil has but one major goal, to take your soul and to keep it from full surrender to God and His sanctifying grace. He will always try to get us to hold back from our cross of crucifixion.

He did it to Jesus, he did it to Eve, and he is at it like a roaring lion today. Like Peter said to Ananias and Sapphira, "Satan hath filled your heart to keep part back."

Yes, the devil will say go to church, join the church, be active in the church, pay your tithes, but just keep some back, let Christ rule in everything.

My greatest concern on this world is that we never lose sight of the need to discern the devil's work, that we never lose sight of our need to be sanctified wholly. So don't forget, the devil's out to get you! How? By getting you to keep a part back, of yourself, of your heart. Don't let it happen, give your all to God.

Rev. Rodger Moyer

The Provision For Godliness
2 Peter 1:1-4

There is absolutely no doubt about the fact that God's requirements are great. He told Abraham to "walk before Me and be blameless." Jesus said, "You are to be perfect." Both the Old and New Testaments declare, "You shall be holy, for I am holy."

When we look at God's requirements alongside our resources, discouragement is not only possible – it is inevitable. We ought to thank God, however, that there is always a relationship between the requirements of God and the gifts of God! When Jesus told the disciples to feed the multitude, He kept giving to them until they were able to feed everyone and have food left over.

That God requires godliness in our lives should come as no surprise to any student of God's Word, but we also need to realize that "His divine power has granted to us everything pertaining to life and godliness." If God has granted to us everything pertaining to life and godliness, we have no need to turn elsewhere. Indeed, it is foolish to turn elsewhere! We can no more live a godly life in our own strength than the disciples could have fed the multitude through their own bread-breaking skills.

Knowing that God expects godliness in my life today, the only reasonable thing that I can do is to put no confidence in my resources, but come in faith and obedience to the One who supplies everything pertaining to life and godliness.

Rev. Glen Boring

December 11

The Disciplines Of Holy Living
2 Peter 1:3-11

In *A Plain Account of Christian Perfection,* John Wesley summarizes the Biblical teaching in eleven important points. Point number eight is, "It is improvable." He further explains, "One perfected in love may grow in grace far swifter than he did before." In other words, there is advancement in the holy life.

In today's Scripture, Peter says the same thing: now that you're in, here are the steps for growing and moving ahead, and ... if you follow these steps it will result in productivity (v. 8), perspective (v. 9), perseverance (v. 10), and a promotion (v. 11). He lists seven disciplines that need to be added to our faith (vs. 5-7). Space only permits us to consider one of these: self control.

Self-control literally means to "hold oneself in," to keep the senses under proper restraint. As I have studied Scripture, I have come to realize that self-control is not simply a Christian controlling his/her conduct by adhering to strict self-discipline. It rather means that the "self" – all that I am (body, soul, and spirit) has come under Christ's control. I have become an individual, not self controlled, but controlled by God. I have placed every aspect of my life under His authority. As odd as it seems, Biblical self-control is not self-rule, it is almost the opposite. It is turning myself completely over to God ... placing mind, will and emotions under His command ... allowing Him to govern my appetites, drives and desires. I am His with out reservation. It sounds like slavery, and it is – but it's also the only way to freedom!

Dr. Bruce Moyer

Balaam: the Double-minded Man
2 Peter 2:12-17

Some people are so refreshing that each time we meet them we are the better for it. Of some the opposite is true. Such a man was Balaam. The New Testament writers had nothing good to say about him. Peter refers to Balaam as one "who loved gain from wrongdoing." (2 Peter 2:15) Jude speaks of Balaam's "error," (Jude 11), and John wrote of Balaam as one "who taught Balak to put a stumbling block before the sons of Israel." (Rev. 2:14)

When we first see Balaam he looks good. He says to Balak, "I can do only what God permits me to do; I can say only what God gives me to say." These are his convictions and it sounds impressive. But, as Mathew Henry points out, there was a struggle between Balaam's convictions and his corruptions. He knew he could not curse Israel publicly but he wanted the reward the king offered. So he worked out a plan whereby he spoke to the king privately giving counsel that led to Israel's downfall.

Balaam's problem was he knew what he OUGHT to do; he also knew what he WANTED to do. And the ought and the want led in different directions -- a classic case of double-mindedness. He had divided loyalties.

This kind of internal civil war ends only in a full, unconditional, no-strings-attached surrender to the Lordship of Jesus Christ. This is the heart of holiness. No one can make it as a Christian without this kind of commitment.

Balaam got what he wanted, that is, the reward offered by the king. But one thing he wanted he did not get. In Numbers 23:10 he says, "Let me die the death of the righteous, and may my end be like theirs." Instead he was killed along with the enemies of God. (31:8) He not only brought shame and loss to himself, but his bad counsel brought judgment on others.

Double-mindedness always leads to ultimate tragedy. Full surrender leads to victory and blessing.

Dr. Hollis Abbott

What Manner Of Person Ought Ye To Be?
2 Peter 3:1-15

When you think about it, the Bible is the only source that gives us reasonable answers to these important questions:
-Where did we come from?
-Why are we here? And ...
-Where are we going? This is a passage that answers all three of these questions.

First, "Where did we come from?" Verse 5 says, "By the word of God the heavens were of old, and the earth standing out of the water and in the water." It was the power of God's word that created all things that we see. How much time and money would be saved if scientists believed this verse?

Second, "Why are we here?" Verse 11 says, "Seeing then that all these things shall be dissolved," referring to the day of the Lord when the earth and works will be burned up, "What manner of person ought ye to be?" "You ought to live holy and godly lives," NIV. How? By each one of us genuinely experiencing the New Birth (forgiveness of sins) and cleansing of carnality (entire sanctification).

Third, "Where are we going?" This question is wholly dependant upon the second! Our refusal to live holy and godly lives determines our place with the Devil and his angels. Our choosing by faith to live holy and godly lives now, gains us heaven with Christ and the redeemed forever.

The conclusion? Verse 13 and 14 states, "Nevertheless we, according to his promise, look for new heavens and a new earth, wherein dwelleth righteousness. Wherefore, beloved, seeing that ye look for such things, be diligent that ye may be found of Him in peace, without spot, and blameless." AMEN!

Rev. Stephen Burkhart

Bumper Stickers And Holy Living
2 Peter 3:8-18

Not long ago as I was driving along our city streets, the bumper sticker on an old battered and rusted car caught my attention. It simply read, "Destination Unknown!" I chuckled at first, thinking it must refer to the battered old car. I was sure that its final destination would be determined sooner, rather than later – but would it be to a metal recycling plant, or to the used auto parts yard, or simply to a quiet out-of-the-way place in the back yard? Then it came to me that the bumper sticker might be referring to the driver himself. Perhaps he was just out for a "Sunday drive" – headed in no particular direction. The way some people drive, that would be no surprise! Finally my thoughts shifted to a more serious note, and I began to wonder if the simple bumper sticker might have some reference to eternal matters. It is quite possible that the driver really didn't know where he would be spending eternity. At the same moment I wondered how many other drivers around me, if asked about eternity, would simply respond, "Destination Unknown!"

In the text we read for today Peter speaks about the confidence Christians have with regard to eternity. He connects those words of comfort with the admonition that, in the light of eternity, "You ought to live holy and godly lives." (v. 11) The apostle John affirms the same in his first epistle where he again and again says, "we know . . .." Paul states, "I know whom I have believed, and am convinced that He is able to guard what I have entrusted to Him for that day." (2 Tim. 1:12) What a joy it is to be among those who are walking in holiness! We know our destination!

Dr. Bruce Moyer

Rhubarb And You
2 Peter 3:18

In our vegetable garden we have a rhubarb plant. Last year we planted two of them. Both grew for a time, promising the sweet-sour succulence of pie and sauce; but growth was slow. At harvest time, one was dead and the other was stunted.

This Spring the remaining rhubarb poked up its head. I cultivated and dusted it. All summer it had rain and sunshine. Yet today, it has only one stalk, three inches long. Its future is predictable. It will grow or die.

Grow or die! This is the law of life in Christ. Adam Clarke, the Methodist commentator and preacher, wrote, "There are many who boast of the grace of their conversion; persons who were never more than babes, and have long since lost even that grace, because they did not grow in it. Let him that readeth understand." This could be said, too, of some of the sanctified. They did not grow in it, so they lost it.

I am sure many of you gardeners would tell me that my slow growing, dying rhubarb plant is my fault. I suppose it is, since a plant can't will itself to grow. But what about us? We have the Holy Spirit. We can confess our little growth. We can repent. We can ask our heavenly gardener to stir our soil and to pour heavenly showers upon us. If asked, He will dust us with strong, spiritual powder for bugs or blight that threaten our growth.

If you don't grow, you will die. Why don't you choose to grow and live!

Rev. Ken Friesen

Traitor of the Heart
1 John 1:5-10

One day, while leafing through the morning paper, the following headline caught my eye: BULLETS KILL EX-HUSBAND 26 YEARS LATER. Needless to say, with a headline like this the article deserved closer scrutiny.

The story was told of a man whose former wife shot him twice in the stomach during a domestic dispute – 26 YEARS AGO! He died as a direct result of the old gunshot wounds when they became infected and the infection proved to be fatal!

Dear reader – all men are born with a depraved and sinful nature. The psalmist declares: "Behold, I was shapen in iniquity; and in SIN did my mother conceive me." Original sin (carnality) left unchecked in the heart is a crippling, deadly infection that ALWAYS proves fatal! There is only one provision in dealing with this sinful nature and that is cleansing.

In our scripture reading, the Apostle John has given us the "prescription" needed to destroy this terrible infection: "...the blood of Jesus Christ his Son cleanseth us from ALL SIN."

If you have not experienced that second work of God's grace in your life, why not ask for the cure today? Faith in the blood of Jesus Christ to cleanse the heart from carnality will result in the outpouring of the Holy Spirit and COMPLETE healing of your heart.

"And behold, I send the promise of My Father upon you." (Luke 24:49) "And when the day of Pentecost was fully come...they were all filled with the Holy Ghost." (Acts 2:1,4) "God...put no difference between us and them, purifying their hearts by faith." (Acts 15:8-9) "Be filled with the Spirit." (Ephesians 5:18)

Rev. William Kren

Overcoming Setbacks (1)
1 John 2:1

The grace of God provides for full and lasting spiritual victory. As we live in Jesus' fullness, sin shall not be our master. (Rom. 6:14) However, as recorded in man's first historical encounter with God (Gen. 3), God continues to give us the responsibility to choose. Our text today highlights this humanizing element of our spiritual walk. We must choose, and in so doing we <u>can</u> choose consistent victory. Several items related to our text must be kept in mind.

1. We don't have to sin. As G. Campbell Morgan wrote, it is not that we are <u>not able</u> to sin, but <u>able not</u> to sin. Being able to thus choose, we are humanized. Sanctification does not make us robots.

2. Noting the possibility of sin does not mean we have to or will sin. We can choose not to, thus again indicating we are humans. We need not sin daily!

3. The Word of God is a primary resource against sinning as we note Psalm 119:9-11 and John 17:17.

4. If we do suffer a relapse it is not the end. We have as our advocate with the Father, Jesus Christ the righteous. Here is positive provision for our need.

The point of our text is not to major on the possibility of defeat and resulting insecurity. We need not <u>continue</u> in sin. But, if we do lapse <u>momentarily,</u> victory is renewable and thus we can sense great ongoing security in the love and grace of God. Let us rejoice, then, that God maintains our humanity and grants us the responsibility to choose the path of spiritual victory daily.

Dr. John Sills

Overcoming Setbacks (2)
Joshua 7:1-13

Israel had God's instructions regarding the conquering if Jericho. (Joshua 6:3-5) God granted full victory. (6:20) This victory at Jericho followed Israel's earlier entrance into Canaan. (3:17) Crossing the Jordan into Canaan marked the end of the self-life, the beginning of Christ-centered, Spirit-filled living. They were no longer carnal or men of flesh, but spiritual. (1 Cor. 3:1-3)

Following Israel's sudden defeat at Ai, Joshua and the elders went to prayer. (Joshua 7:6) They discovered that Israel had sinned. (7:11) Howcould this have occurred? Can a similar experience happen to us? What can we learn and apply?

1. Israel had quickly become self-confident. (7:3) The victory at Jericho was not theirs. It was God's. Though Ai was small, they forgot they still needed God's help.
2. Israel forsook the place of prayer. Before Jericho, Israel spent time at Gilgal, renouncing (Joshua 5:3) and remembering. (5:10) Essentially it was a time of spiritual renewal after crossing the Jordan and before they went up to Jericho. But, before Ai they did not return to Gilgal, to pray. If they had, I believe God would have revealed Achan's sin.
3. So Israel disobeyed God. (Joshua 7:1) Yesterday we reminded ourselves that God's Word was written that we might not sin, but we may choose to do so. (1 John 2:1) Today's text illustrates how this tragedy occurs. May we guard our hearts by taking careful note of those things that tripped up Joshua and his people. We don't have to suffer spiritual defeat.

Dr. John Sills

Overcoming Setbacks (3)
Joshua 7:13; John 2:1

Following Israel's defeat at Ai, Joshua and the Elders went to prayer. (Joshua 7:6-9) If we fall short (which is not necessary), we must immediately seek our advocate through prayer.

The requirement of God was for a re-consecration. It was to be done in the light of what had gone wrong. Israel had become self-confident, prayerless, and thus disobedient to the Lord. There had to be introspection followed by re-consecration.

There also needed to be repentance and re-consecration. A good model here is David's prayer. (Psalm 51:1-13) We must ask for a clean heart, for a <u>renewing</u> of God's steadfast spirit within us. (Psalm 51:10)

We must then by faith believe God for His forgiveness and a renewing of the cleansing presence of the Holy Spirit.

However, God does not mean for us to walk in spiritual defeat. Israel did not have to be defeated at Ai. But they were. We <u>may</u> suffer defeat too. But thank God for His full provision for our need at that moment: "…I am writing these things to you that you may not sin. And if anyone sins, we have an advocate (helper) with the Father, Jesus Christ the righteous."

With all this in mind, may we daily choose the consistent path of victory in Christ.

Dr. John Sills

Overcoming Setbacks (4)
1 John 2:1; Romans 6:1-2; 2 Peter 3:17-18

As we conclude this mini-series of devotionals, the emphasis is on sinless Christian living, on victory, not defeat. We don't have to sin after entire sanctification. But, because we are not robots, but human, we may. If we do, our advocate stands ready to restore us.

As a lad, I lived near a state fairground. The circus came to town often. Especially as a middle teen, I was able to go often by working my way into the circus. I really enjoyed the trapeze artists. I still do. From them I learned a spiritual truth that applies here.

They never train without a safety net. They do not have a net so they can fall. They do not plan on falling. But the net is there just in case. And the net allows them to major on perfecting their artistic skills. Without a net they would likely think a lot more about falling – and probably fall more than they do. Instead, they focus on flying through the air in freedom and poise. They become masters of their art.

God wants us to maintain the victory of sanctification (which was not gained by training but dying to carnality and selfish self-centeredness). He wants us to concentrate on flying spiritually, as it were. The safety net of 1 John 2:1 is not meant to indulge us. Never!! It is meant to release us to grow on "… in the grace and knowledge of our Lord and Saviour, Jesus Christ." May this be our aim.

Dr. John Sills

Sin And The Sanctified Christian
1 John 2:1-2

Though we, the holiness people, have often been accused of teaching "sinless perfection," this has never really been the case. Even John Wesley stated (in *A Plain Account of Christian Perfection*), "We do not find any general state described in Scripture from which a man cannot draw back to sin." We believe that God can give us grace not to sin (i.e., willfully transgress the known laws of God), but that we never reach a place in this life where we cannot sin. The question is, if a sanctified Christian can sin, and does, what does he/she do then?

One danger is that the person committing the transgression will simply throw up their hands in despair and give up. The devil would like us to think that all is lost, we may as well not even try to change things. This response always leads to further defeat and complete backsliding.

Another response is to rationalize away the guilt ... to make excuses ... to pretend that nothing is wrong. This is too often the case, and again we are deceived by the enemy and fail to find any victory.

The Biblical response to sin is to immediately stop it, confess it, repent, and ask for the Father's forgiveness. We have an "Advocate" (a defense lawyer) Who has paid for all our sins. The Scriptures are clear – God does not make allowance for sin in the life of the Christian, but He has made provision for it. We need not fall, and the standard is that we do not fall – but, if we do, we may rise again, probably sadder but wiser.

Dr. Bruce Moyer

Secure In The Savior
1 John 2:1-6

As I was traveling through Ohio, I passed under a bridge. This area of Ohio is somewhat hilly and this particular bridge was old, with large steel girders. It spanned across the lanes, 30 or 40 feet in the air. I noticed, as I sped underneath this impressive structure, that repair crews were busy working on the bridge. Two trucks were parked on the overpass and two "cherry pickers" were extended out and over the sides so that each crew could work on the steel facing. It was a precarious position for a worker! Forty feet below – speeding autos, trucks and unforgiving concrete! Not much chance for survival, should an accident occur and a man fall! However, each worker was safely inside a steel basket. Each wore a hardhat and protective clothing. And, if that wasn't enough, stretching underneath the bridge and a few feet beneath the underside, was a SAFETY NET!

Living the sanctified life is NOT to say we are eternally secure and cannot fall. Through our own negligence, we can lean out over a ledge, disregard the checks of the Holy Spirit, and plunge to what could be our SPIRITUAL DEATH! Certain spiritual death, except, God has made a provision for our safety. He has provided a safety net!

The net is found in 1 John 2:1: "My little children, these things write I unto you, that ye sin not. And if any man sin, we have an advocate with the Father, Jesus Christ the righteous."

John penned this message to THE CHRISTIAN! The Spirit-filled believer does NOT plan to sin, and will do everything in his or her power to avoid sin and temptation, and live a life that is holy and pleasing to the Lord. They make no provision for sinning, but God has made such a provision! Our Heavenly Father has provided a safety net that "if any man sin, we have an advocate with the Father, Jesus Christ the righteous."

Rev. William Kren

Confident At His Coming?
1 John 2:28; 3:3

A pair of twin boys lived on our mission station in China. One day when their parents were in prayer meeting they went to the kitchen to gleefully crack and drop eggs on the floor. The frantic Chinese cook had a lot to show their mother. She found them way back under the double bed. When confronted they innocently said, "You never told us to not break eggs." She was quick to reply, "Then why did you run and hide under the bed?" They were NOT confident and unashamed at the coming of their mother.

How can we be "confident and unashamed" at His coming?

We will need to call on all the resources of grace God has provided for us. In verse 3 it says we must purify ourselves, as He is pure. Another similar verse is 2 Cor. 7:1, "Having therefore these promises, dearly beloved, let us cleanse ourselves, from all filthiness of the flesh, and spirit, perfecting holiness in the fear of God."

If we want to be like Him when He appears then we need to be like Him now in this pilgrim world of ours. The crisis of cleansing sets us on the highway of holiness but there is a long process of laying aside weights that hinder. New lessons of faith must be learned and fears must be cast out. Perfecting holiness in the fear of the Lord comes in a lifelong commitment to walk always in the light of God's Word and will. With "nothing between our souls and the Savior" we can be confident in that day of His appearing.

Mrs. Laura Trachsel

Givers Or Takers!
John 3:16

This is the season where the theme "giving" is certainly appropriate. We give gifts to friends and to relatives. We give to needy families, etc. At least some of us get a sense of gratification out of giving.

God was clearly the originator of this activity. He gave us the world and everything that's in it <u>and</u> "For God so loved the world that He <u>gave</u> His only begotten Son . . .." But it didn't stop there! Salvation is given through Christ's blessings, which are given to each one of us through our life. Surely God gave and gives and continues to give!

That is not the characteristic of our lives before we came to Christ. In fact, it is just the opposite. "Get what you can, while you can," is a popular theme of today's life style. Taking and getting are what makes us happy!

God's will and desire is that of changing our themes from a "taker" to a "giver." Saving and sanctifying grace are His operations on the heart that makes this change possible. With our sins forgiven and our hearts purified, verses like, "Give and it shall be given unto you," (Luke 6:38) and "It is more blessed to give than to receive" (Acts 20:35) are not sources of conviction but cheerful opportunities!

Thank the Lord, He can change our hearts so we don't need a "season" for the reason to give but makes us a "giver" all seasons by His glorious grace! Amen!

Rev. Stephen Burkhart

Angels' Robes
2 Peter 3:10-14

A lot of work was going into the annual Christmas program. The Sunday School Superintendent had planned with the staff, people were rehearsing their lines, and props were being gathered. That's when a Sunday morning announcement got my attention.

In both the Sunday School opening and the Morning Worship period, this was announced: "We need some white sheets for the angels' costumes. Please make sure they don't have any holes or stains." In other words, no self-respecting church actor was going on stage wearing a robe unless it met the standard for one of God's holy creatures, spotless and hole-less.

If we feel this way about our representing angels in a Christmas program, how do we feel about representing ourselves as sons and daughters of a holy God? Besides, He Himself has made the announcement: "Be ye holy, for I am holy."

Peter has caught this, and says, make whatever sacrifices it takes to make sure that, when you appear on stage before God, you are in garments of white, without spot, worthy of the new heavens and the new earth.

Rev. Ken Friesen

Proclamation vs. Demonstration
1 John 3:14-24

The evangelist H. Gilbert Williams, under whom we were saved asked this question in the morning Bible studies of that meeting: "Which is worse: to aim at a tiger and hit a man or to aim at a man and hit a tiger?" The question was intended to show the spiritual significance of having our motive life purified.

In this same line of thought, we can ask the question, "Which is better: to profess perfect love but exhibit bitterness, resentment, hostility, prejudices, and indifference, or to **not** profess perfect love but show forth compassion, consideration, kindness, and sacrificial service?"

In verse 18 of our lesson John says, "Let us not love in word, neither in tongue; but in deed and in truth." Rev. Robert Geyer, former WGM missionary to Bolivia, said one time that "what the world needs even more than a proclamation of perfect love is a demonstration of it!" That is another way of saying "actions speak louder than words."

We can **say** we love everyone but we need to demonstrate that this is, indeed, a reality in our attitudes and in our actions. Are our relationships with others clear? We can **say** that we love God with **all** our heart, soul, mind and strength, but is it manifested in the daily choices we make? Is pleasing Him truly the governing motive of our lives?

The crisis experience of entire sanctification is the only means provided in God's grace to enable us to demonstrate this love "in deed and in truth." May every believer avail himself of this marvelous provision!

Mrs. Clarice Moyer

To Please God
1 John 3:20-22; 1 Thess. 4:1; Hebrews 13:20-21

One of the beautiful realizations in the walk of holiness is that through the cleansing work of salvation and sanctification we are made acceptable in God's sight. Not only does this walk bring stability and increased spiritual growth as a blessing to our own lives, but it also enables us to be pleasing in His sight.

The definition of "to please" is "to give pleasure or satisfaction; to delight." To think that a common, ordinary Christian can bring pleasure and delight to the heart of an infinite, eternal God is almost beyond belief. Not just any Christian can measure up to this wonderful attainment. Romans 8:8 says that those who are in the flesh cannot please God. Those who are yet carnal cannot affect the heart of God in the same way. Only after the "blood of the everlasting covenant" cleanses from all sin can He complete His will in us and make us well pleasing in His sight. Not of our own merit can we please God. Only through Jesus Christ can we satisfy and bring pleasure to our Lord.

To live a life pleasing to God, is not only possible, it is what He desires. He does the empowering as we walk in obedience.

Mrs. Kristy Weinert

Love
1 John 4:7-21

The Epistle of 1 John was written to the Church with the desire to build up in the faith those whom God had rescued from a life of sin. Few writings of such short duration will ever match this letter in the volume of truth revealed or the dynamic presentation of the way of holiness.

Among the many subjects that are dealt with in this Epistle is the important issue of love. An interesting exercise would be to spend a few minutes and mark in your Bible every reference to love that can be found in 1 John. Indeed, in the Scripture passage for today there are nearly thirty references to love. In a society that talks so much about love, yet is so obviously hungry for caring fellowship, that is a relevant message.

In the fast moving world we live in, and amidst the pressure of business decisions, we who call ourselves Christians must be careful to let the love of God touch others. It is so easy to let every day be "business as usual" without seeing where we can be an encouragement by a word or deed of love. God wants us to be a holy people, and that spirit of holiness can best be reflected in the marketplace by words of concern and deeds of kindness that spring from a heart overflowing with divine love.

One of the important aspects of love that John mentions several times is the unique relationship among the brethren. Sometimes the most difficult places to show love, but certainly one of the most needed arenas for love, is the church. Love that accepts, forgives, builds confidence and conquers fear comes only from God. This type of love must replace the self-love that by nature is self-seeking and self-serving. As the world looks at us today, do they marvel at our love?

Rev. Duane Erickson

The Holy Man – A Glimpse Of God
1 John 4:7-21

The human race has always had a "built-in" longing for God. And whether or not one admits it, there is within the human spirit a desire to see God. The harsh fact of Scripture, however, is that, "no one has ever seen God." (v. 12) For that reason, most people draw their own mental "picture" of God, or they set up their own "god" (which could be about anything!) to satisfy their heart's desire. How, then, is the world to truly see the One for whom their heart craves?

In 1 John 4:12 we have the answer: "But if we love one another, God lives in us." The only real look at Jesus that most people will ever have, comes when they see Him at work through us! Charles Wesley described Jesus as One who "empties Himself of all but love." Isn't that what God does for us when He cleanses our heart? Isn't the sanctified heart one that is emptied of all but love? And when we allow God to accomplish that cleansing work in us, then others will truly begin to catch a glimpse of what He is like – because He is free to live in us.

What are your friends and neighbors seeing these days? Are they getting a clear look at the Savior as they watch your life? Are they seeing a clear demonstration of Godly love? The holy man is truly one through whom God is making Himself known to this world!

Dr. Bruce Moyer

God's Messenger Center
Jude 17-25

"And a highway shall be there, and a way, and it shall be called The Way of Holiness; the unclean shall not pass over it; but it shall be for those: the wayfaring men, though fools, shall not err therein." (Isaiah 35:8)

On the instrument panel of our family auto is the "Messenger Center." The purpose of the "Messenger Center" is to provide the driver with a graphic indication of conditions in the automobile. A number of gauges are used to disseminate this information, one, of which is the LOW FUEL gauge.

When the fuel level is near empty the words: LOW FUEL will light up along with a picture of a gas pump. This warning will remain on until fuel is added. Should the driver elect to ignore the gauge, the result would be a forced walk to the nearest gas station!

The Spirit-filled Christian life is a journey upon the highway of holiness. We have surrendered our all to God, are constantly trusting Him for guidance and strength, and depend on the Holy Spirit (our "Messenger Center") to help us retain the blessing of a clean heart!

God's promise is that He is "able to keep you from falling" so that we may finish the journey. So when confronted with a temptation that would lead to our spiritual downfall, the Holy Spirit is faithful to check us! Like the warning light of the LOW FUEL gauge, the Spirit quickens the heart with a caution: "Don't do that.... don't say that... stay out of there... do this instead!" Our obedience to the checks of the Holy Spirit will keep us traveling on God's highway of holiness!

The believer who is sanctified wholly and filled with God's Spirit has the ability to sin and lose the blessing. But, praise God, if we listen to and obey the checks of the Spirit, we need never fall!

Rev. William Kren

The Deceptiveness Of The Gradual
Revelation 2:4

No one becomes overweight overnight. No one shows noticeable aging within an hour's time. A man does not suddenly become disenchanted with his wife and family to the point he leaves. A good leader doesn't "go bad" all in a day's time.

It must have been shocking, and indeed devastating to the saints in the church at Ephesus to learn that God was displeased with them. They thought they were doing just fine. Their publicity release was impressive – hard workers, sound doctrine, and a productive church. How could anything possibly be wrong?

Well, God said there was – He told them through the messenger that He was displeased because they no longer loved Him with the same intensity they had once shown.

Oh, the tragedy of doing "spiritual business as usual!" It is the deceptiveness of the gradual. Not many saints would fall from a head-on collision with Satan. But many of them collapse under the steady drip, drip, drip of years, becoming marred by diminished fervor. It goes undetected like a lurking cancer, yet constantly growing deep inside.

It can happen to all of us! We get wrapped up in events as we see them today – not from an eternal perspective. And Satan, who could never have access to our lives in any other way, begins his insidious assault into our souls through the deceptiveness of the gradual.

It is a serious matter to allow our "first love" of God to diminish. "But I still attend church! I still teach my S. S. class, I still give to the church and missions!" Thank God for all of that. But do you love Him? That is the question! Do you love God with all your heart and soul and mind and body? It is the only standard of love that He will ever accept from you. Anything less permits the deceptiveness of the gradual to erode your soul and break the heart of God.

Rev. Gene Moyer

CONTRIBUTORS AND INDEX